PRESENTED BY

KEI MURAYAMA

A Centaur's Life

17

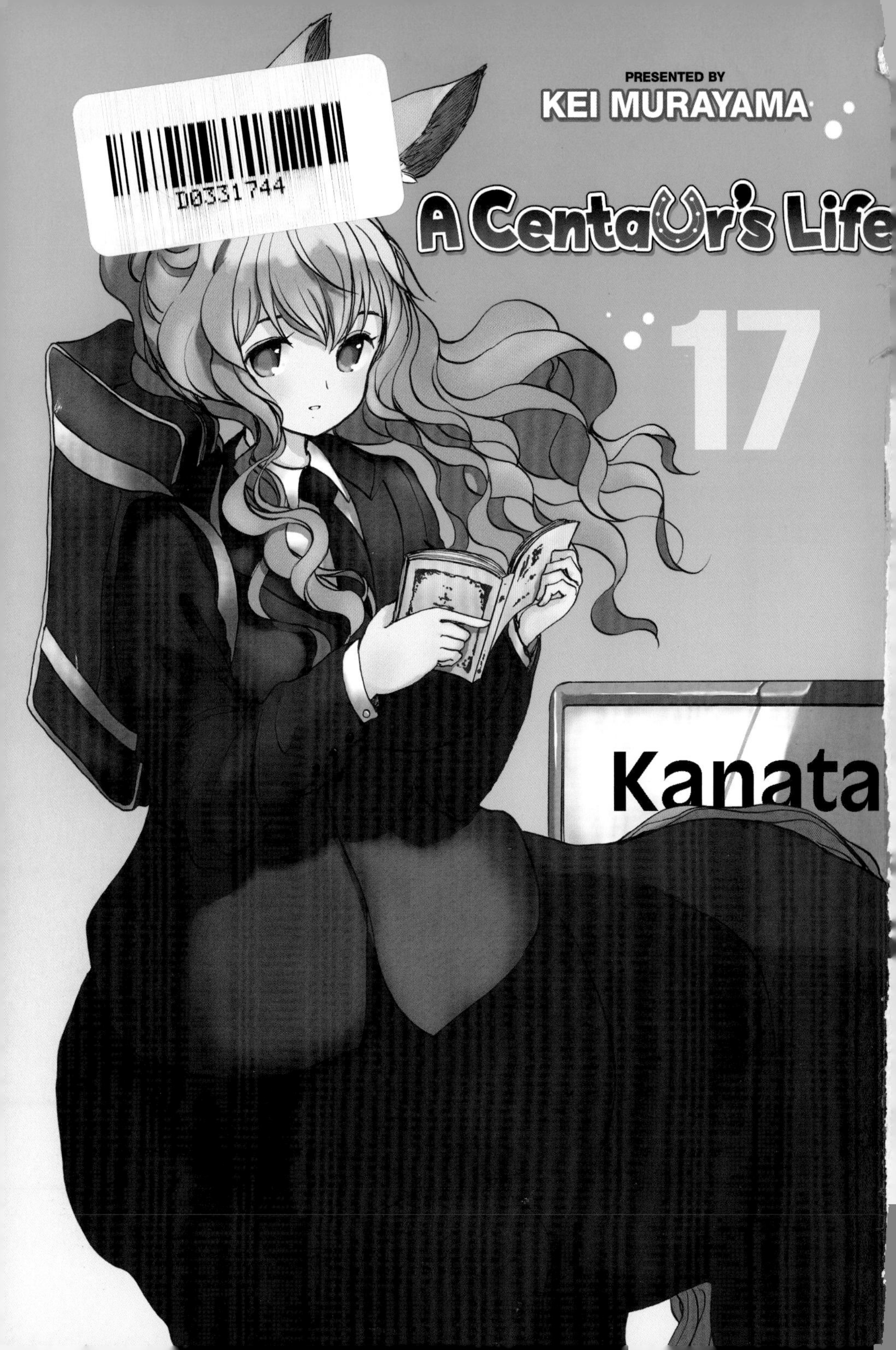
Kanata

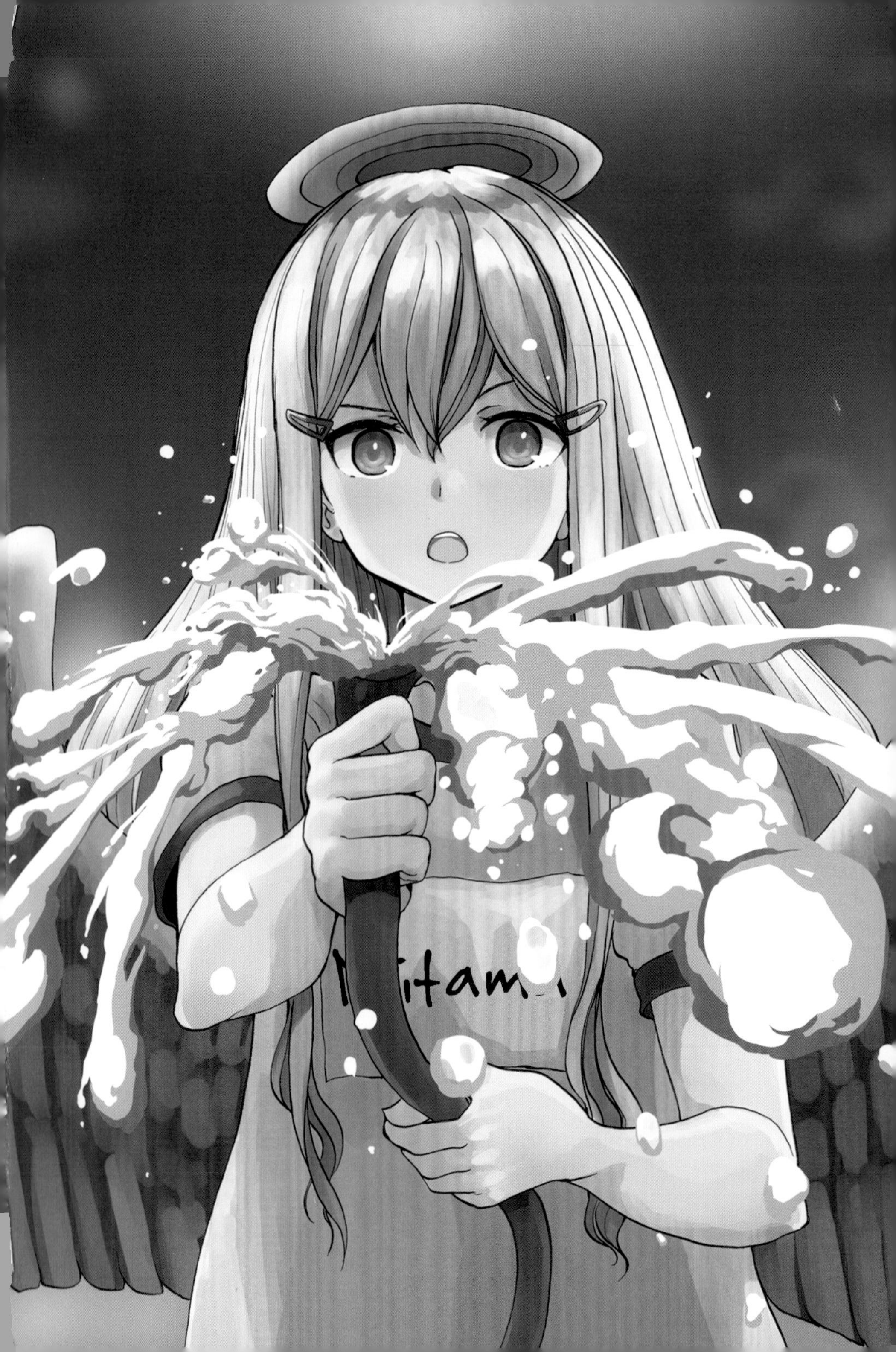

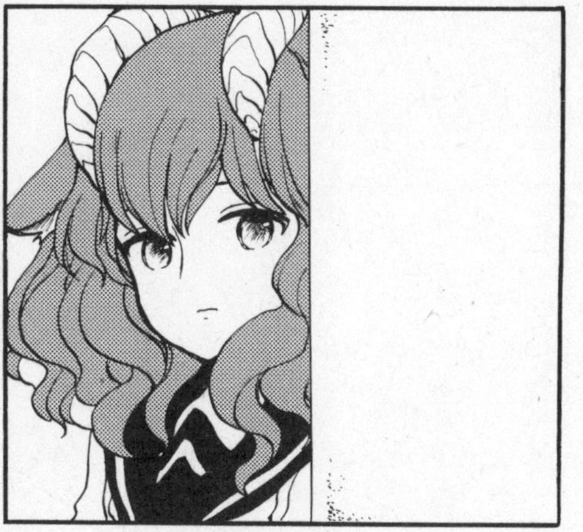

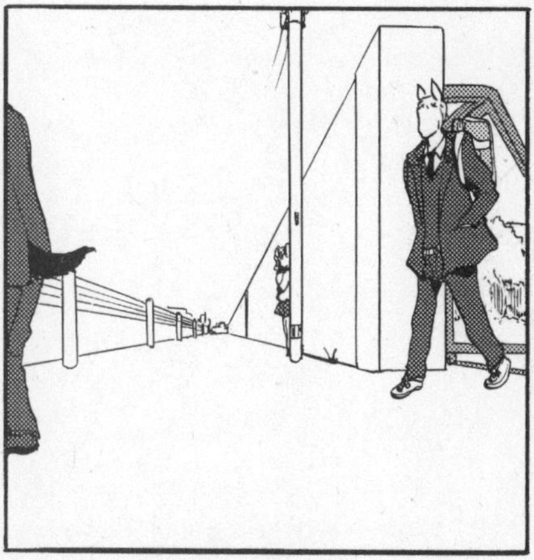

CHAPTER 128

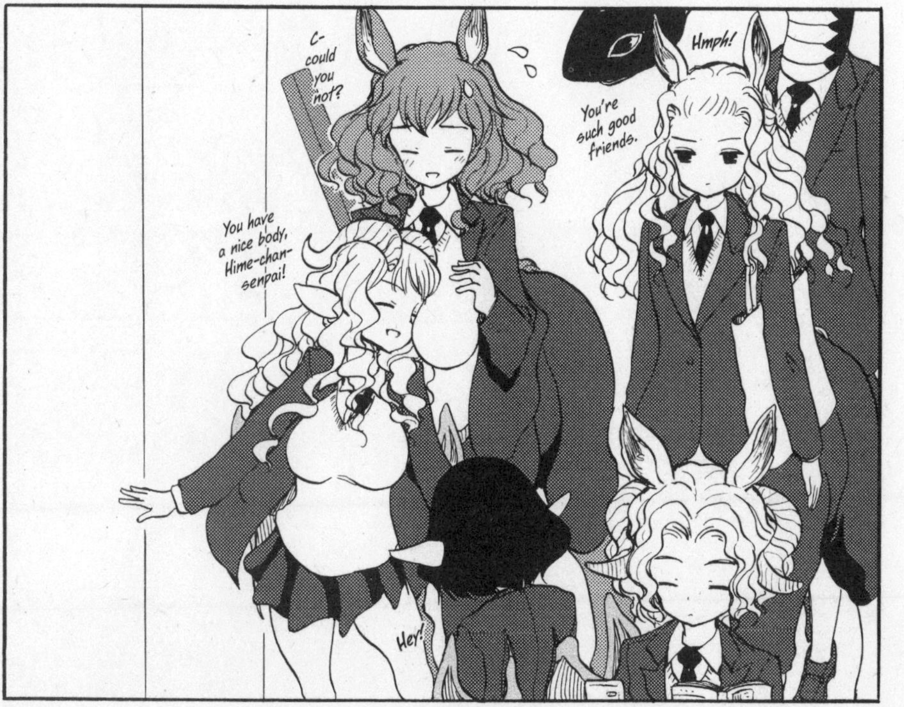
Hmph!
You're such good friends.
C-could you not?
You have a nice body, Hime-chan-senpai!
Hey!

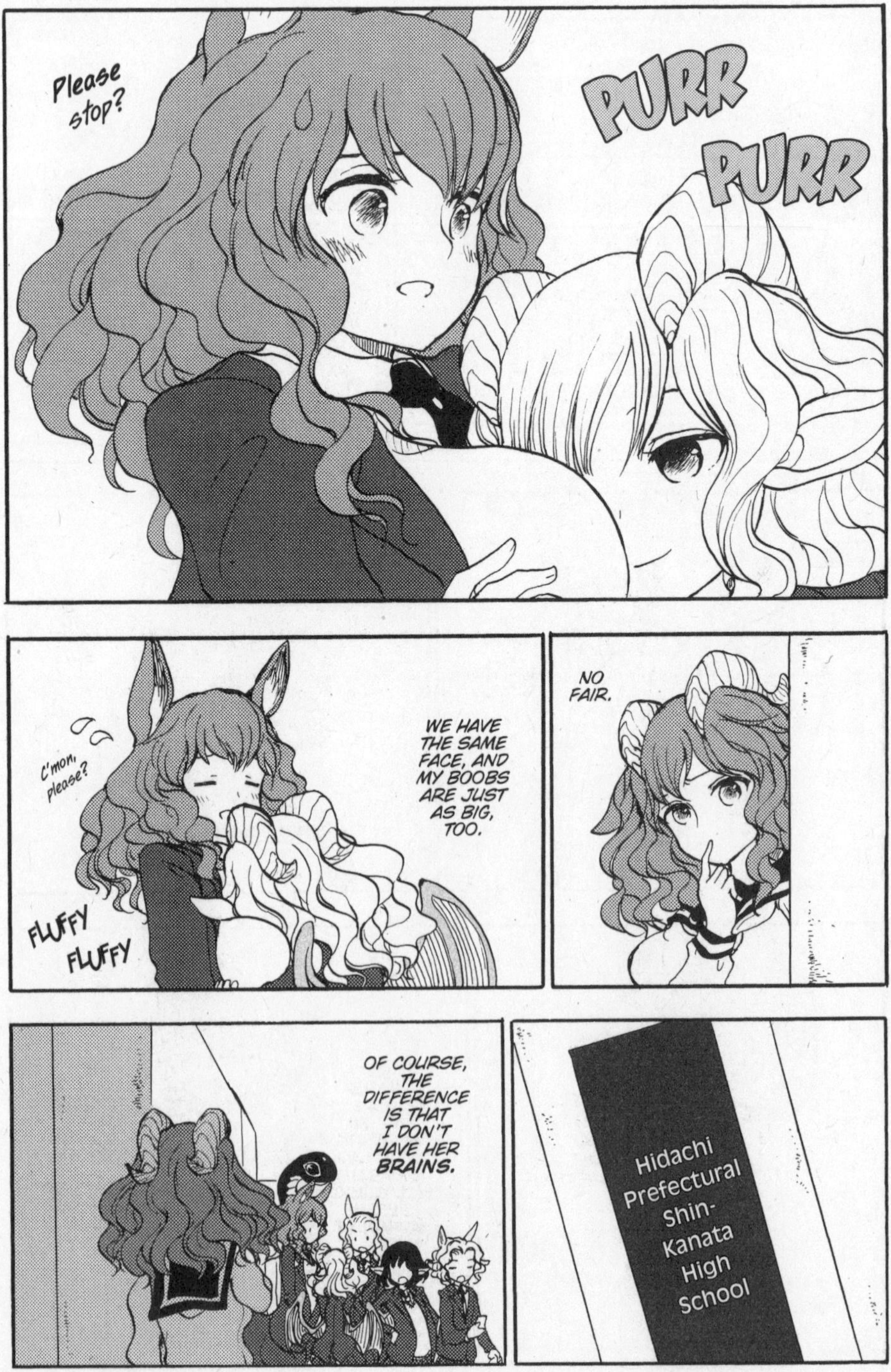
PURR PURR
Please stop?
NO FAIR.
WE HAVE THE SAME FACE, AND MY BOOBS ARE JUST AS BIG, TOO.
C'mon, please?
FLUFFY FLUFFY
Hidachi Prefectural Shin-Kanata High School
OF COURSE, THE DIFFERENCE IS THAT I DON'T HAVE HER BRAINS.

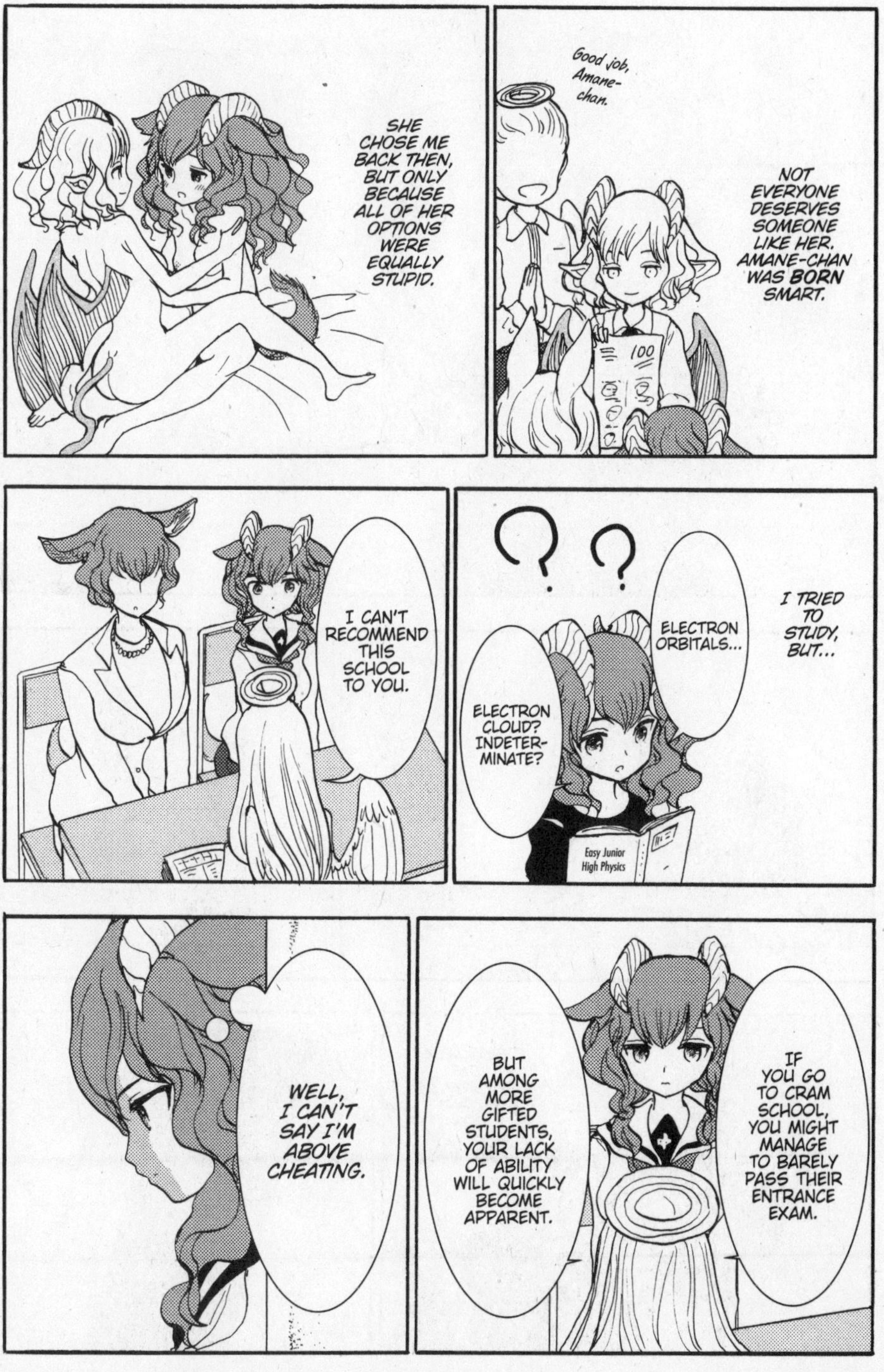

Good job, Amane-chan.
NOT EVERYONE DESERVES SOMEONE LIKE HER. AMANE-CHAN WAS **BORN** SMART.
SHE CHOSE ME BACK THEN, BUT ONLY BECAUSE ALL OF HER OPTIONS WERE EQUALLY STUPID.
I TRIED TO STUDY, BUT...
ELECTRON ORBITALS...
ELECTRON CLOUD? INDETERMINATE?
Easy Junior High Physics
I CAN'T RECOMMEND THIS SCHOOL TO YOU.
IF YOU GO TO CRAM SCHOOL, YOU MIGHT MANAGE TO BARELY PASS THEIR ENTRANCE EXAM.
BUT AMONG MORE GIFTED STUDENTS, YOUR LACK OF ABILITY WILL QUICKLY BECOME APPARENT.
WELL, I CAN'T SAY I'M ABOVE CHEATING.

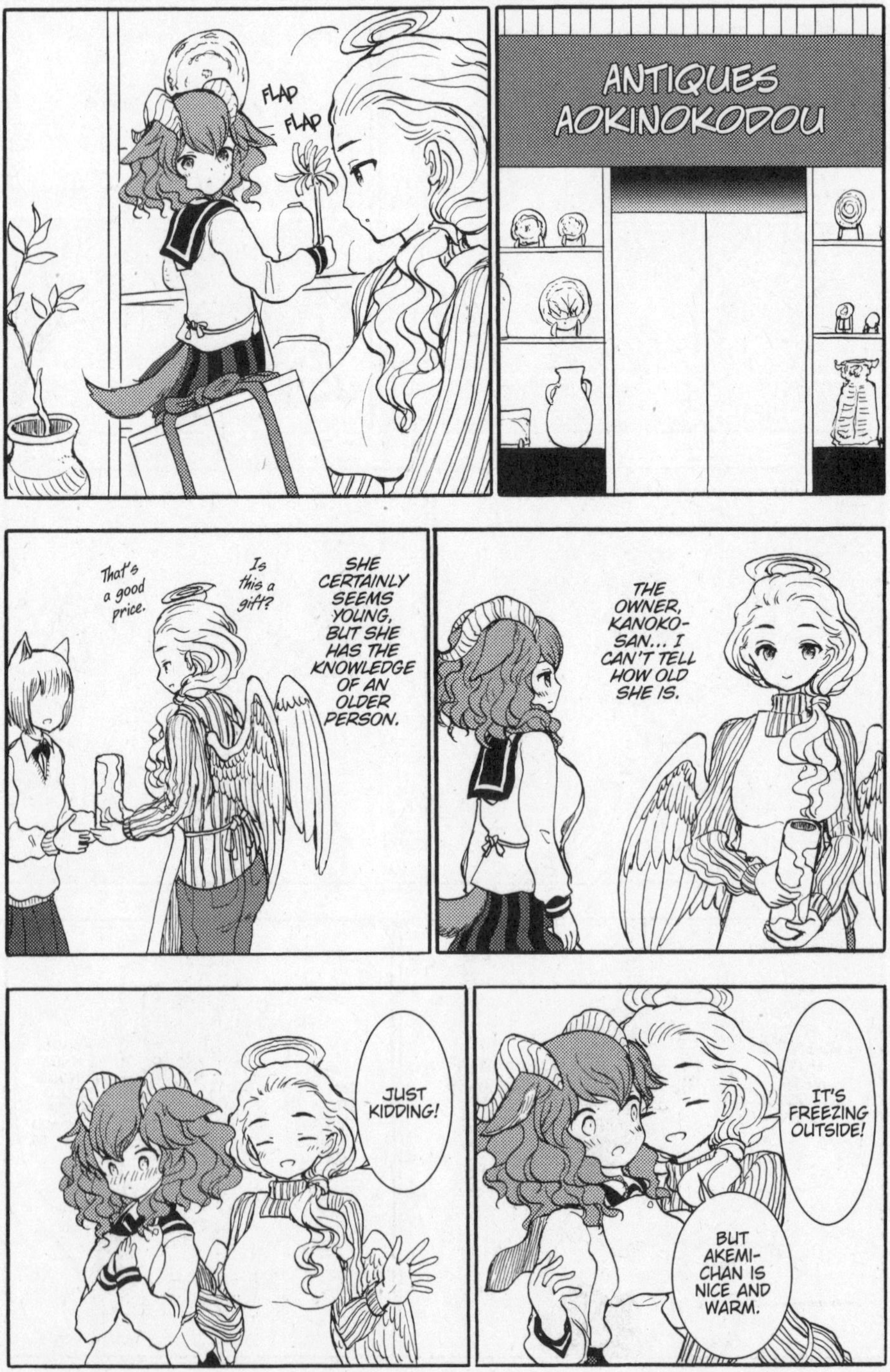
ANTIQUES AOKINOKODOU
FLAP
FLAP
THE OWNER, KANOKO-SAN... I CAN'T TELL HOW OLD SHE IS.
SHE CERTAINLY SEEMS YOUNG, BUT SHE HAS THE KNOWLEDGE OF AN OLDER PERSON.
Is this a gift?
That's a good price.
IT'S FREEZING OUTSIDE!
BUT AKEMI-CHAN IS NICE AND WARM.
JUST KIDDING!

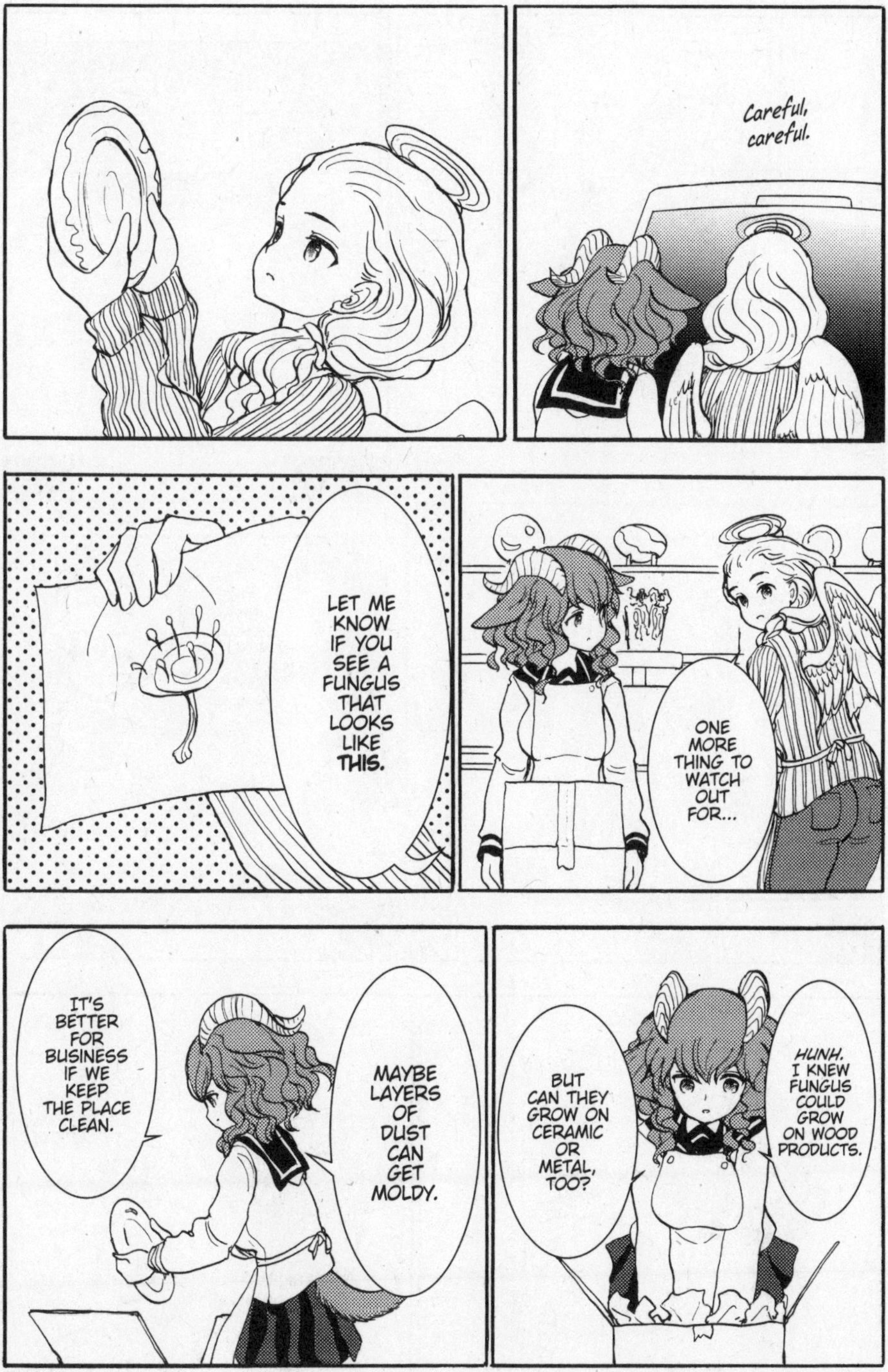
Careful, careful.
ONE MORE THING TO WATCH OUT FOR...
LET ME KNOW IF YOU SEE A FUNGUS THAT LOOKS LIKE **THIS.**
HUNH. I KNEW FUNGUS COULD GROW ON WOOD PRODUCTS.
BUT CAN THEY GROW ON CERAMIC OR METAL, TOO?
MAYBE LAYERS OF DUST CAN GET MOLDY.
IT'S BETTER FOR BUSINESS IF WE KEEP THE PLACE CLEAN.

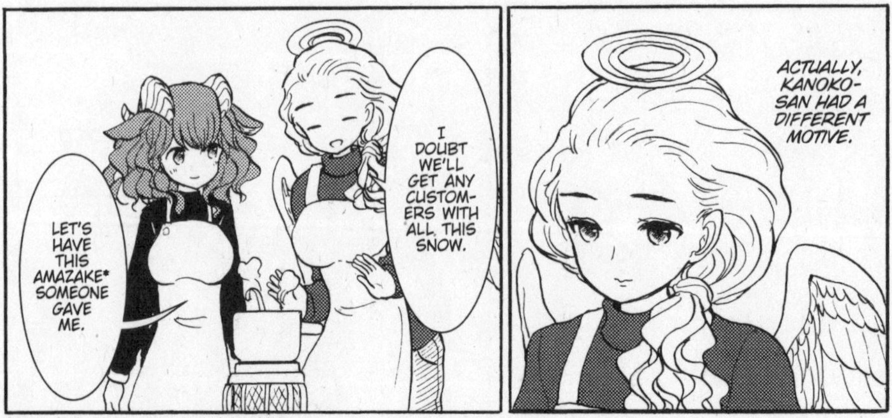
ACTUALLY, KANOKO-SAN HAD A DIFFERENT MOTIVE.
I DOUBT WE'LL GET ANY CUSTOMERS WITH ALL THIS SNOW.
LET'S HAVE THIS AMAZAKE* SOMEONE GAVE ME.

*Amazake is a sweet, low-alcohol rice drink.

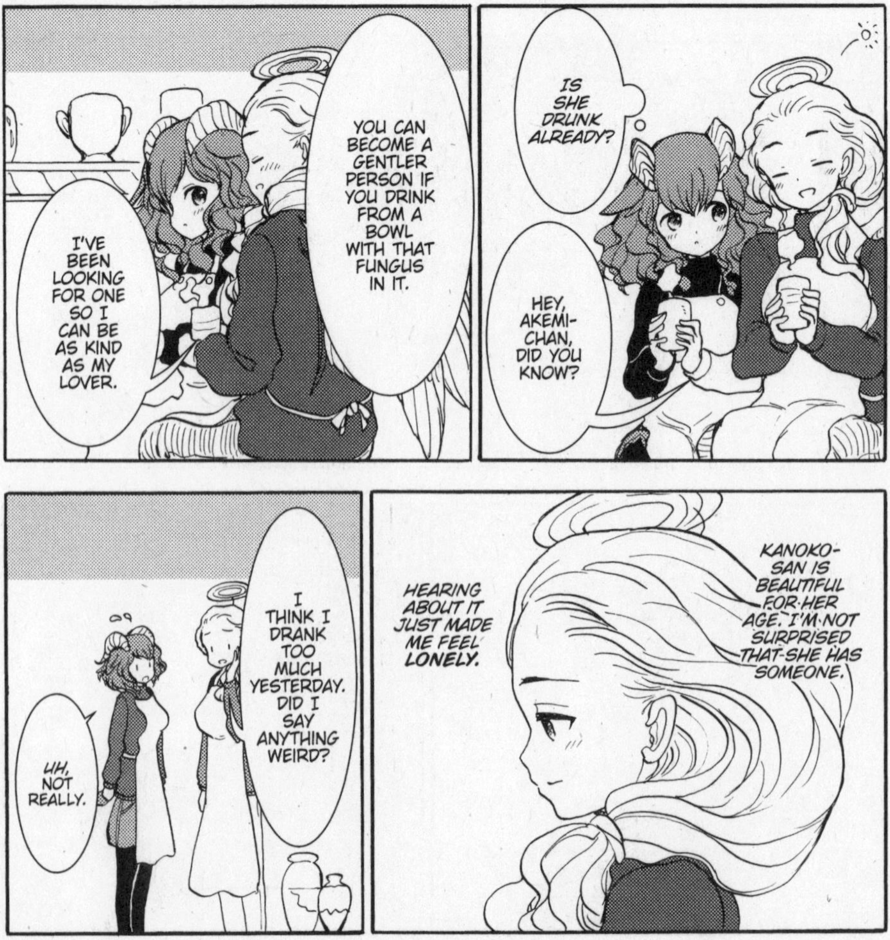
IS SHE DRUNK ALREADY?
HEY, AKEMI-CHAN, DID YOU KNOW?
YOU CAN BECOME A GENTLER PERSON IF YOU DRINK FROM A BOWL WITH THAT FUNGUS IN IT.
I'VE BEEN LOOKING FOR ONE SO I CAN BE AS KIND AS MY LOVER.
KANOKO-SAN IS BEAUTIFUL FOR HER AGE. I'M NOT SURPRISED THAT SHE HAS SOMEONE.
HEARING ABOUT IT JUST MADE ME FEEL **LONELY.**
I THINK I DRANK TOO MUCH YESTERDAY. DID I SAY ANYTHING WEIRD?
UH, NOT REALLY.

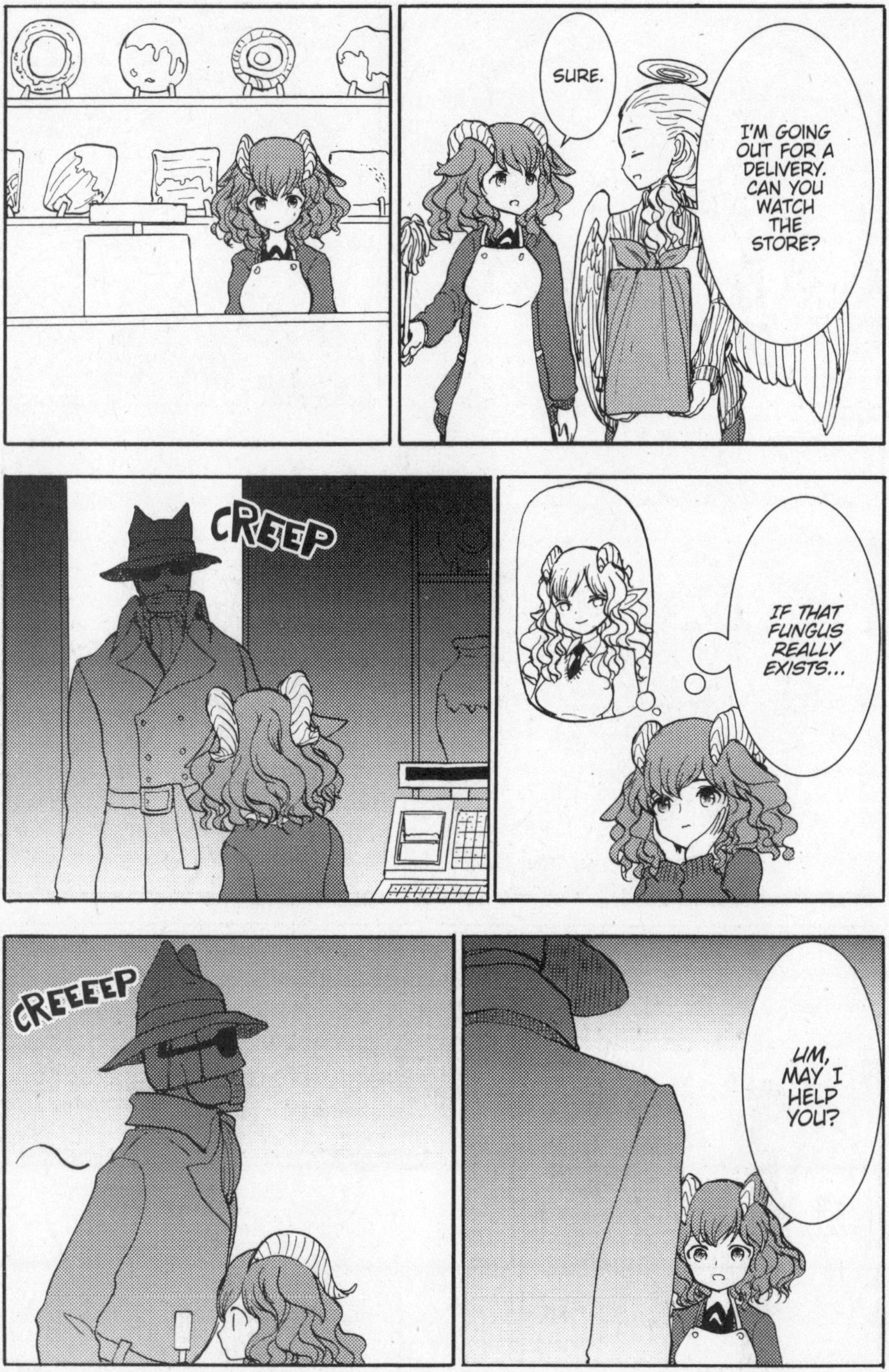
I'M GOING OUT FOR A DELIVERY. CAN YOU WATCH THE STORE?
SURE.
IF THAT FUNGUS REALLY EXISTS...
CREEP
UM, MAY I HELP YOU?
CREEEEP

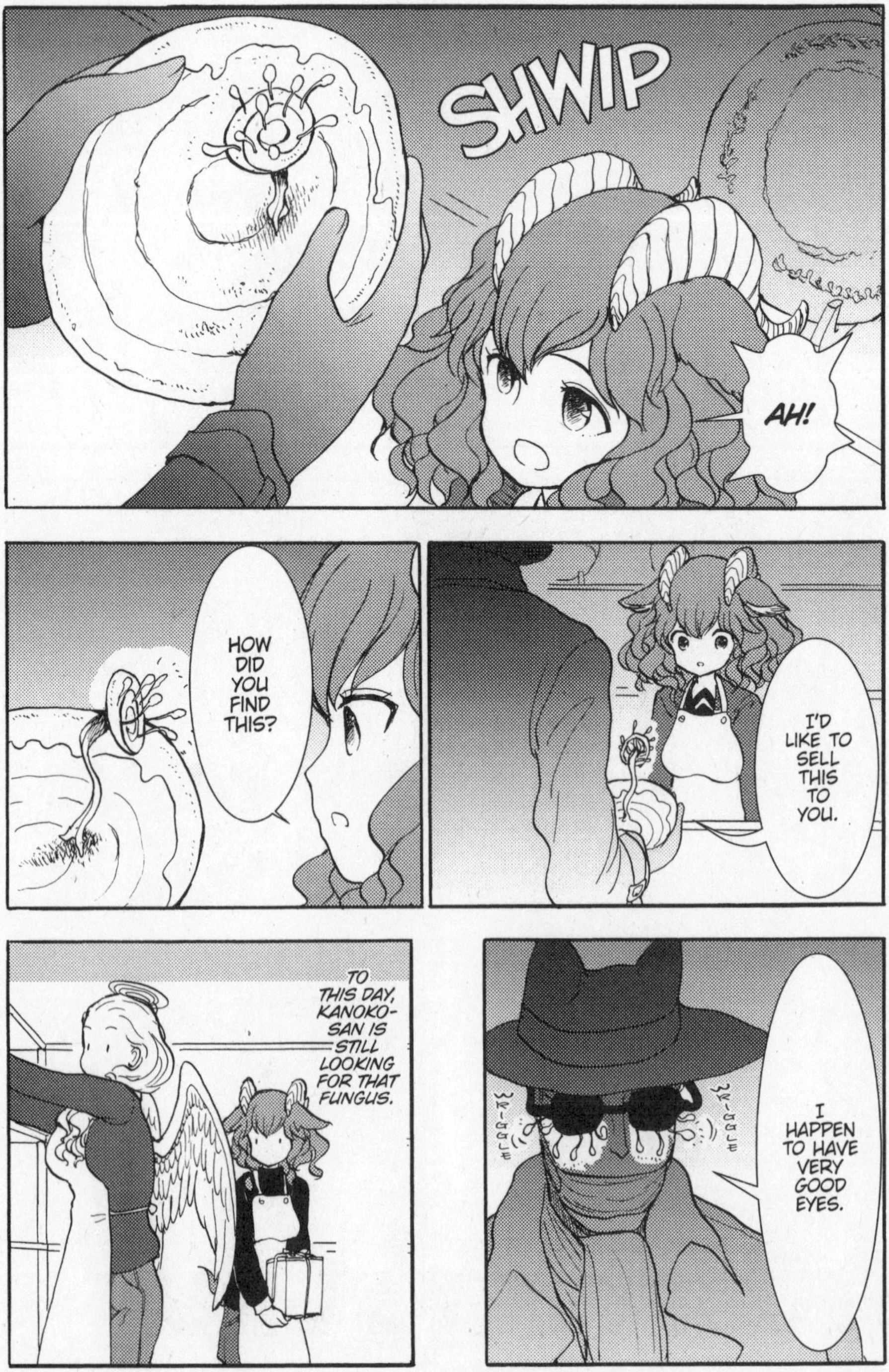
SHWIP
AH!
I'D LIKE TO SELL THIS TO YOU.
HOW DID YOU FIND THIS?
I HAPPEN TO HAVE VERY GOOD EYES.
WRIGGLE
WRIGGLE
TO THIS DAY, KANOKO-SAN IS STILL LOOKING FOR THAT FUNGUS.

A Centaur's Life

HISTORY OF ARCHITECTURE IN JAPAN AND OTHER COUNTRIES: ⟨1⟩ PIT HOUSE

A PIT HOUSE, WHICH IS BUILT OVER A SHALLOW PIT WITH WALLS AND ROOF MADE OF GRASS, IS CONSIDERED TO BE THE OLDEST FORM OF RESIDENTIAL ARCHITECTURE IN JAPAN. IT MAY APPEAR ARCHAIC, BUT IT WAS USED AS A DWELLING FOR COMMON PEOPLE UNTIL THE HEIAN PERIOD. THE LAYOUT OF A PIT HOUSE, SPECIFICALLY THE HEARTH AT THE CENTER OF A DWELLING, CONTINUES TO BE USED IN MORE MODERN HOUSING TO THIS DAY.

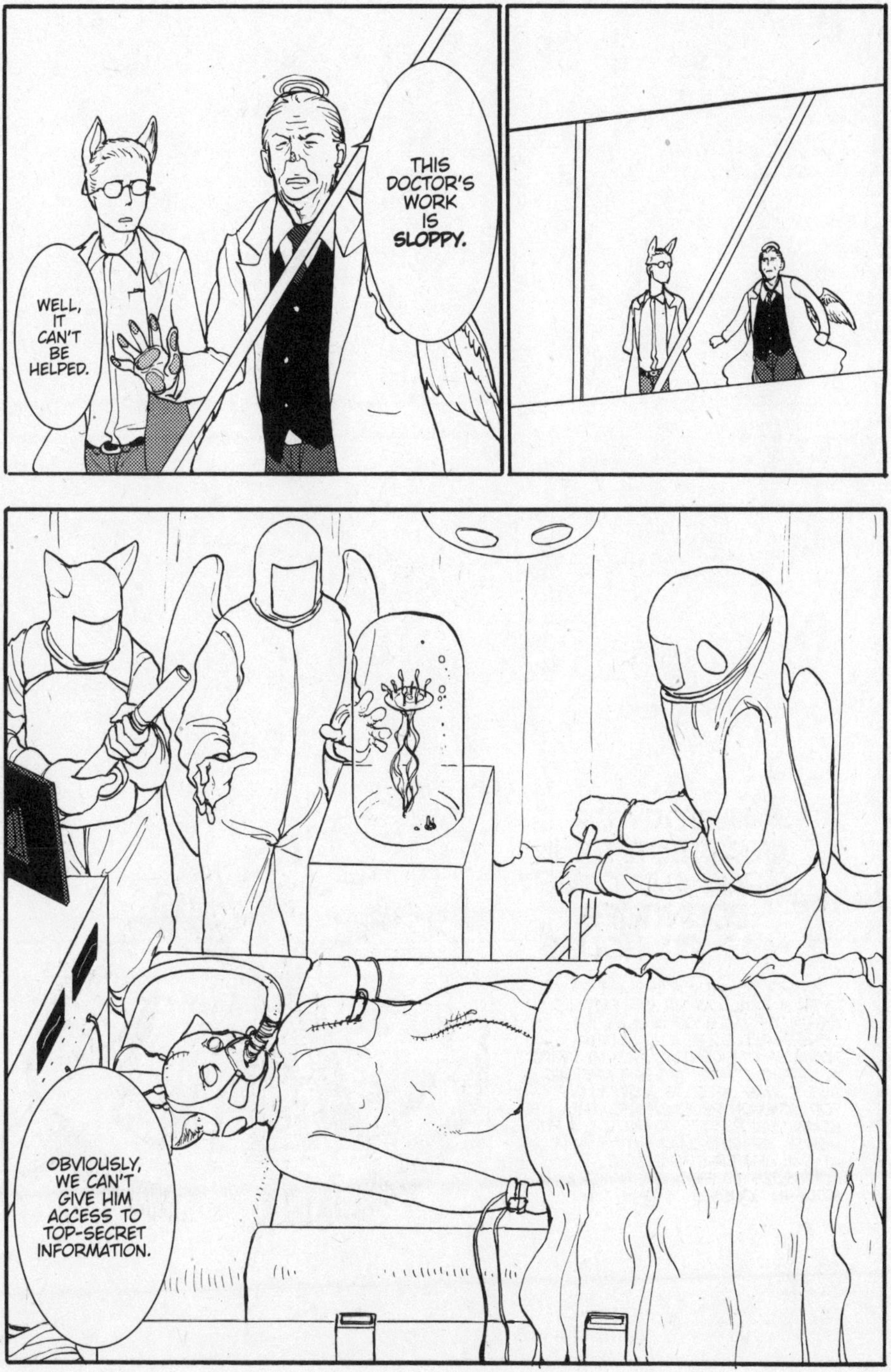
THIS DOCTOR'S WORK IS **SLOPPY.**
WELL, IT CAN'T BE HELPED.
OBVIOUSLY, WE CAN'T GIVE HIM ACCESS TO TOP-SECRET INFORMATION.

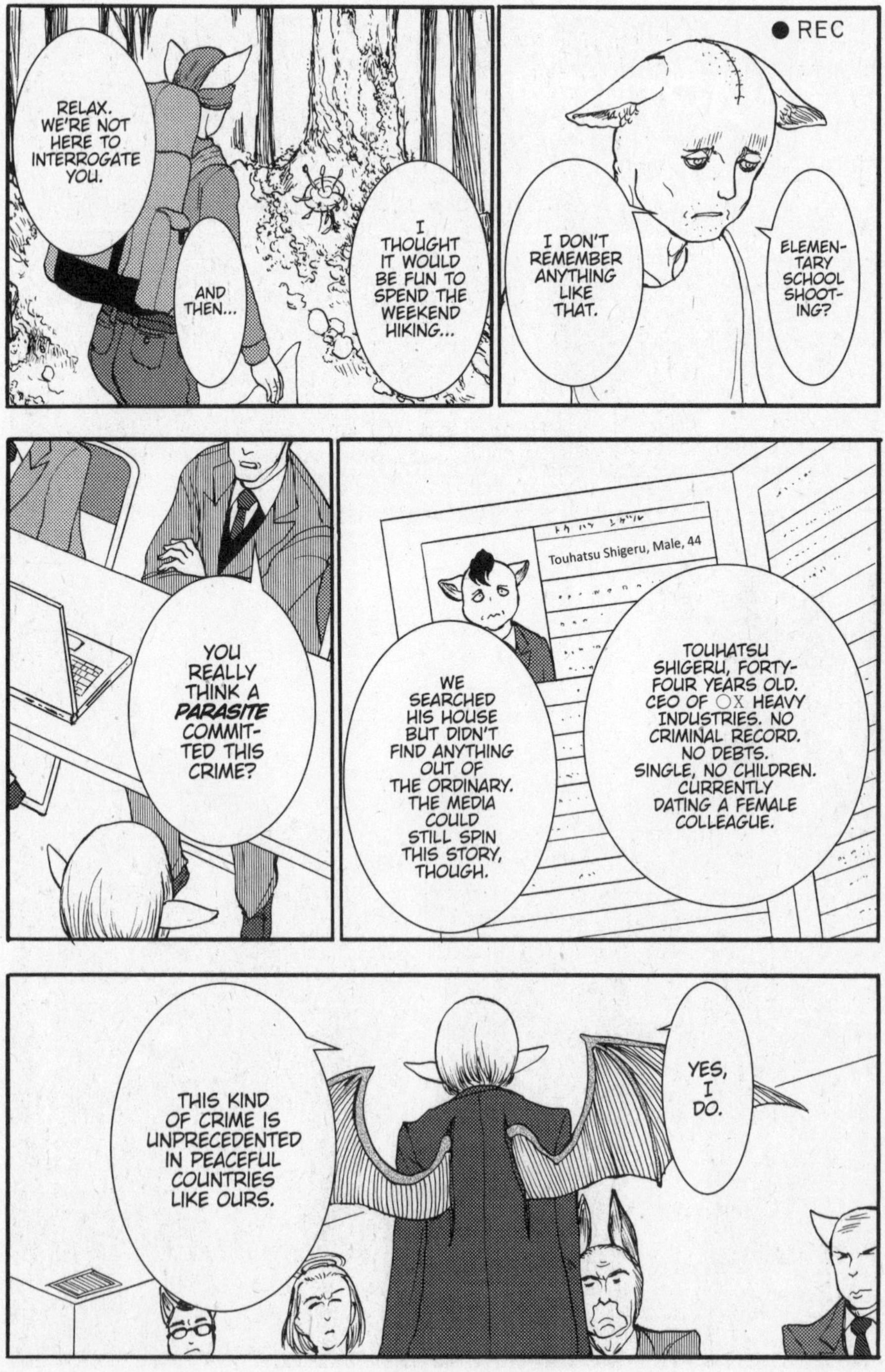
REC
ELEMENTARY SCHOOL SHOOTING?
I DON'T REMEMBER ANYTHING LIKE THAT.
I THOUGHT IT WOULD BE FUN TO SPEND THE WEEKEND HIKING...
AND THEN...
RELAX. WE'RE NOT HERE TO INTERROGATE YOU.
Touhatsu Shigeru, Male, 44
TOUHATSU SHIGERU, FORTY-FOUR YEARS OLD. CEO OF ○X HEAVY INDUSTRIES. NO CRIMINAL RECORD. NO DEBTS. SINGLE, NO CHILDREN. CURRENTLY DATING A FEMALE COLLEAGUE.
WE SEARCHED HIS HOUSE BUT DIDN'T FIND ANYTHING OUT OF THE ORDINARY. THE MEDIA COULD STILL SPIN THIS STORY, THOUGH.
YOU REALLY THINK A *PARASITE* COMMITTED THIS CRIME?
YES, I DO.
THIS KIND OF CRIME IS UNPRECEDENTED IN PEACEFUL COUNTRIES LIKE OURS.

CHAPTER 129

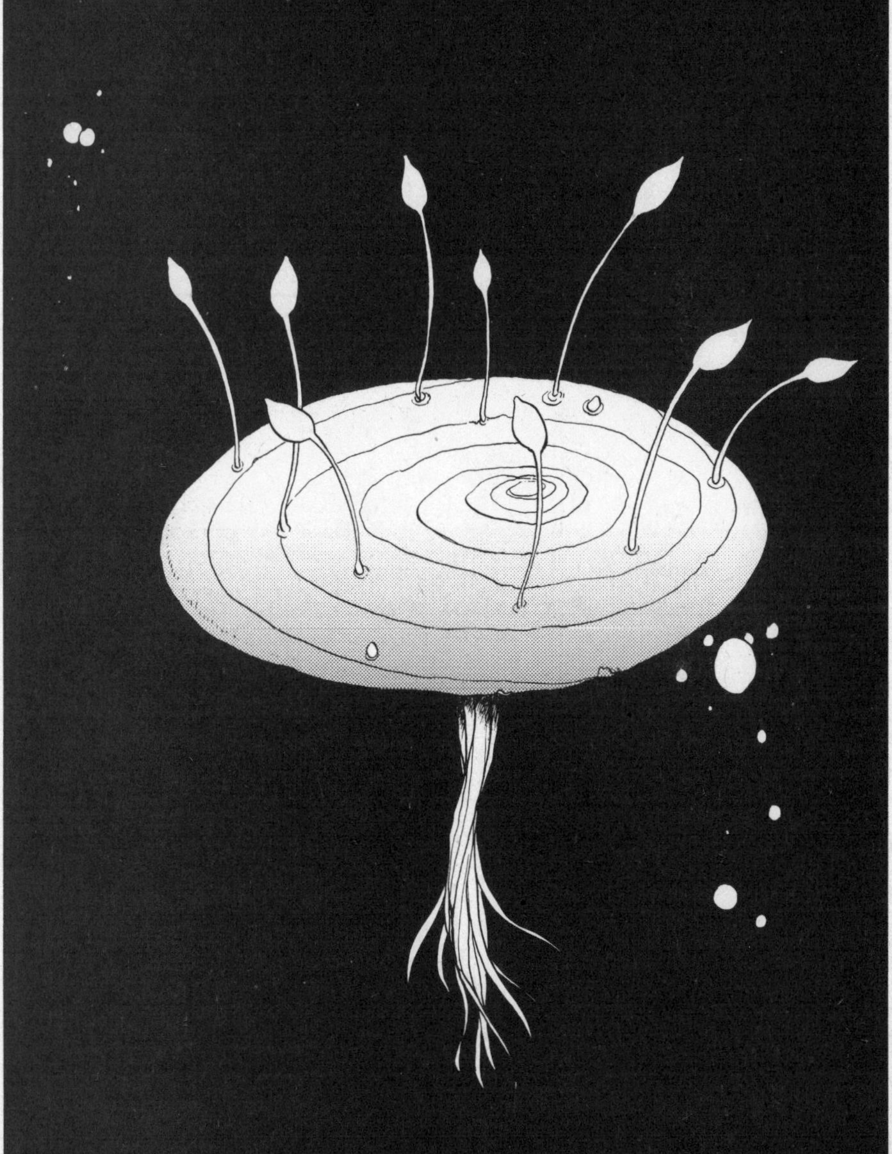

CLACK

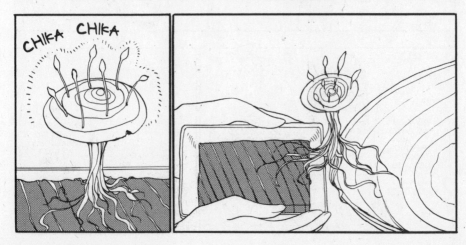

CHIKA CHIKA

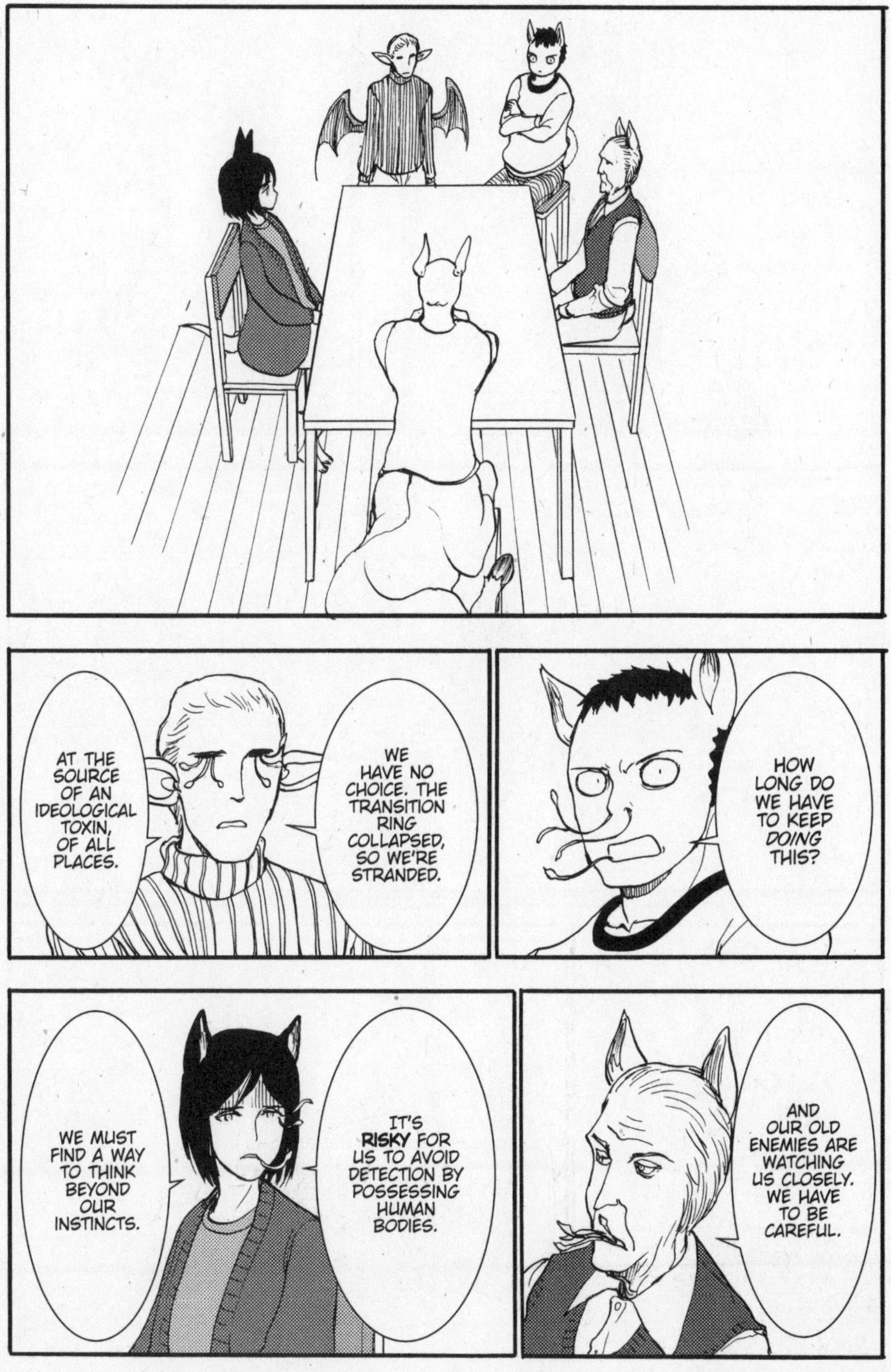
HOW LONG DO WE HAVE TO KEEP *DOING* THIS?
WE HAVE NO CHOICE. THE TRANSITION RING COLLAPSED, SO WE'RE STRANDED.
AT THE SOURCE OF AN IDEOLOGICAL TOXIN, OF ALL PLACES.
AND OUR OLD ENEMIES ARE WATCHING US CLOSELY. WE HAVE TO BE CAREFUL.
IT'S **RISKY** FOR US TO AVOID DETECTION BY POSSESSING HUMAN BODIES.
WE MUST FIND A WAY TO THINK BEYOND OUR INSTINCTS.

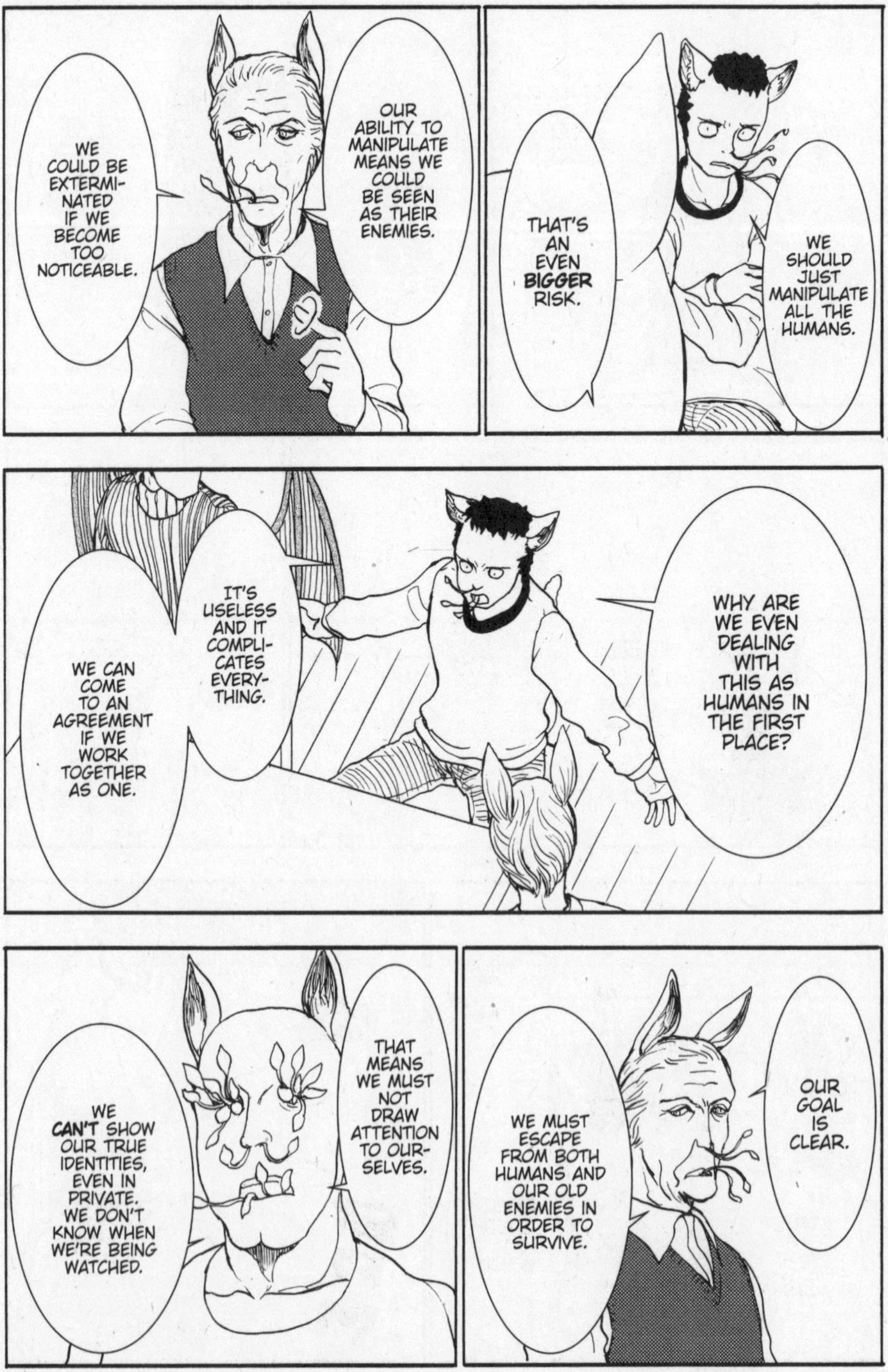
WE SHOULD JUST MANIPULATE ALL THE HUMANS.
THAT'S AN EVEN **BIGGER** RISK.
OUR ABILITY TO MANIPULATE MEANS WE COULD BE SEEN AS THEIR ENEMIES.
WE COULD BE EXTERMI-NATED IF WE BECOME TOO NOTICEABLE.
WHY ARE WE EVEN DEALING WITH THIS AS HUMANS IN THE FIRST PLACE?
IT'S USELESS AND IT COMPLI-CATES EVERY-THING.
WE CAN COME TO AN AGREEMENT IF WE WORK TOGETHER AS ONE.
OUR GOAL IS CLEAR.
WE MUST ESCAPE FROM BOTH HUMANS AND OUR OLD ENEMIES IN ORDER TO SURVIVE.
THAT MEANS WE MUST NOT DRAW ATTENTION TO OUR-SELVES.
WE **CAN'T** SHOW OUR TRUE IDENTITIES, EVEN IN PRIVATE. WE DON'T KNOW WHEN WE'RE BEING WATCHED.

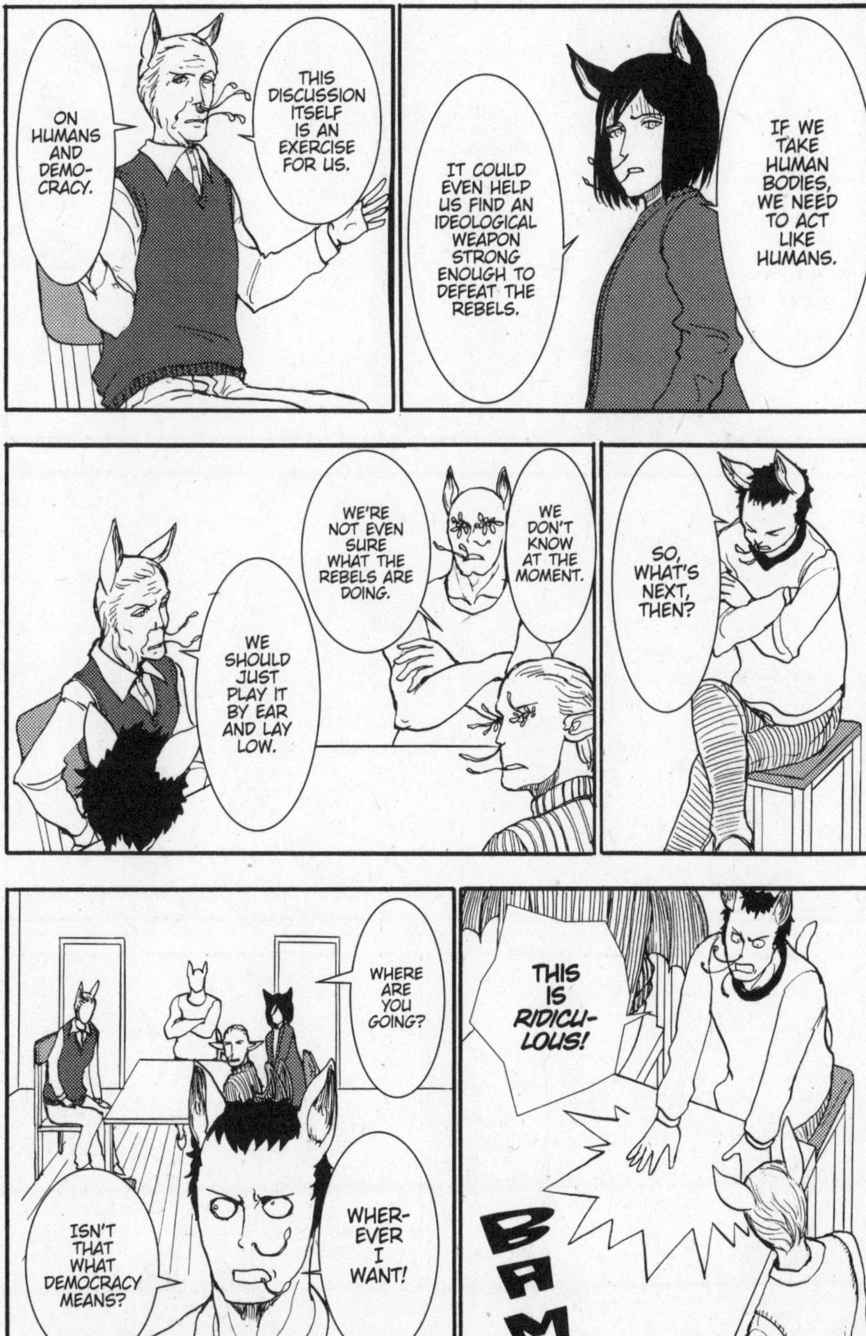
IF WE TAKE HUMAN BODIES, WE NEED TO ACT LIKE HUMANS.
IT COULD EVEN HELP US FIND AN IDEOLOGICAL WEAPON STRONG ENOUGH TO DEFEAT THE REBELS.
THIS DISCUSSION ITSELF IS AN EXERCISE FOR US.
ON HUMANS AND DEMO-CRACY.
SO, WHAT'S NEXT, THEN?
WE DON'T KNOW AT THE MOMENT.
WE'RE NOT EVEN SURE WHAT THE REBELS ARE DOING.
WE SHOULD JUST PLAY IT BY EAR AND LAY LOW.
THIS IS *RIDICU-LOUS!*
BAM
WHERE ARE YOU GOING?
WHER-EVER I WANT!
ISN'T THAT WHAT DEMOCRACY MEANS?

SLAM
REFUSING TO ACCEPT A MAJORITY DECISION GOES *AGAINST* DEMOCRACY, RIGHT?
IT *WAS* A MAJORITY VOTE, BUT THERE ARE OTHER WAYS TO MAKE DECISIONS.
BUT DON'T HUMANS ELIMINATE THOSE WHO IGNORE THEIR DECISIONS?
IF WE'RE TRYING TO ACT AS **THEY** DO...
NO, LET'S FOLLOW THE TRUE DEMOCRATIC WAY.
WE CAN DEAL WITH THIS LATER.
DISAGREEMENT AND REBELLION ARE ALL PART OF LEARNING.

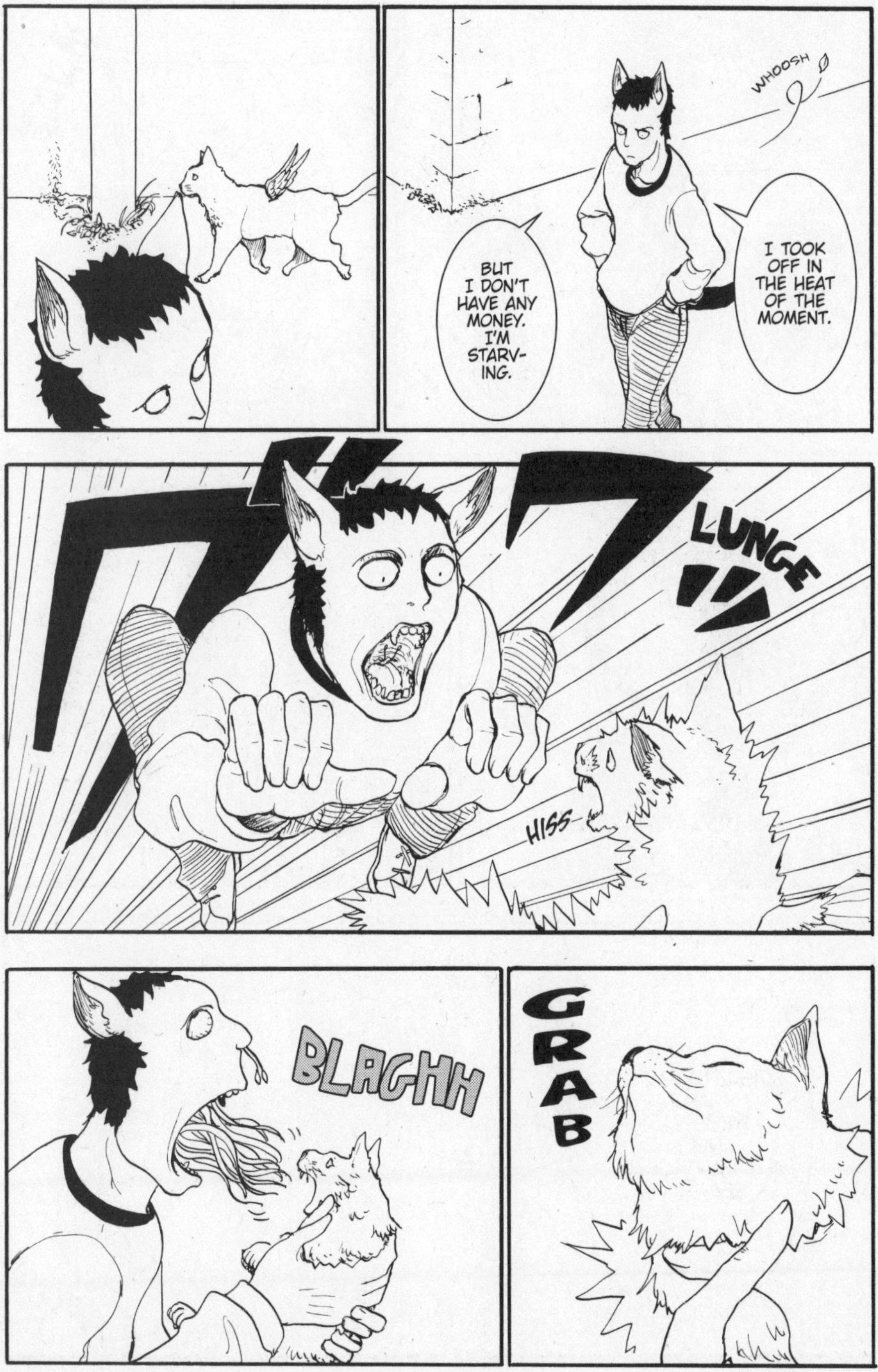
WHOOSH
I TOOK OFF IN THE HEAT OF THE MOMENT.
BUT I DON'T HAVE ANY MONEY. I'M STARV- ING.
LUNGE
HISS
GRAB
BLAGHH

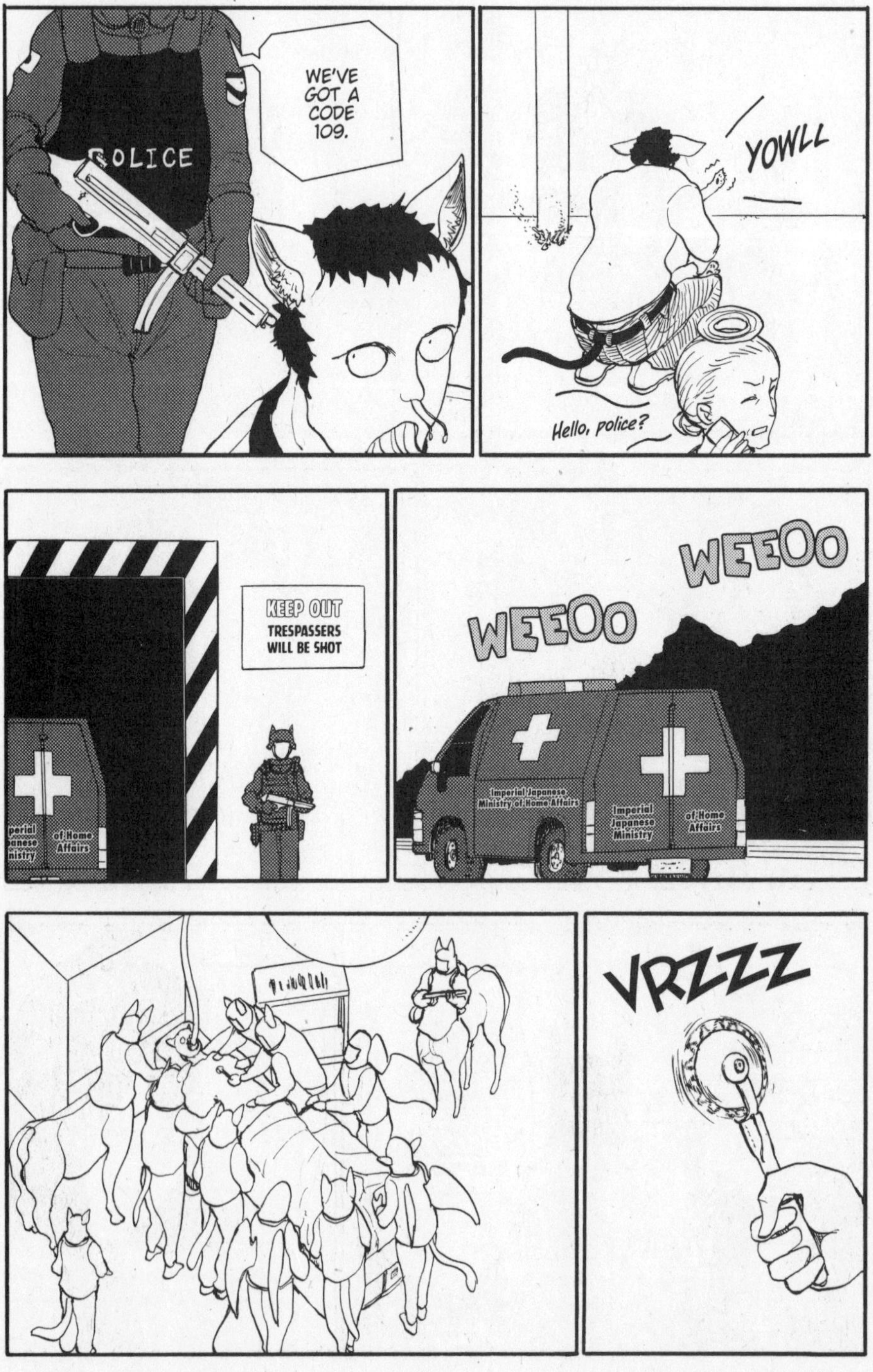
YOWLL
Hello, police?
WE'VE GOT A CODE 109.
POLICE
WEEOO
WEEOO
Imperial Japanese Ministry of Home Affairs
Imperial Japanese Ministry
of Home Affairs
KEEP OUT
TRESPASSERS WILL BE SHOT
of Home Affairs
VRZZZ

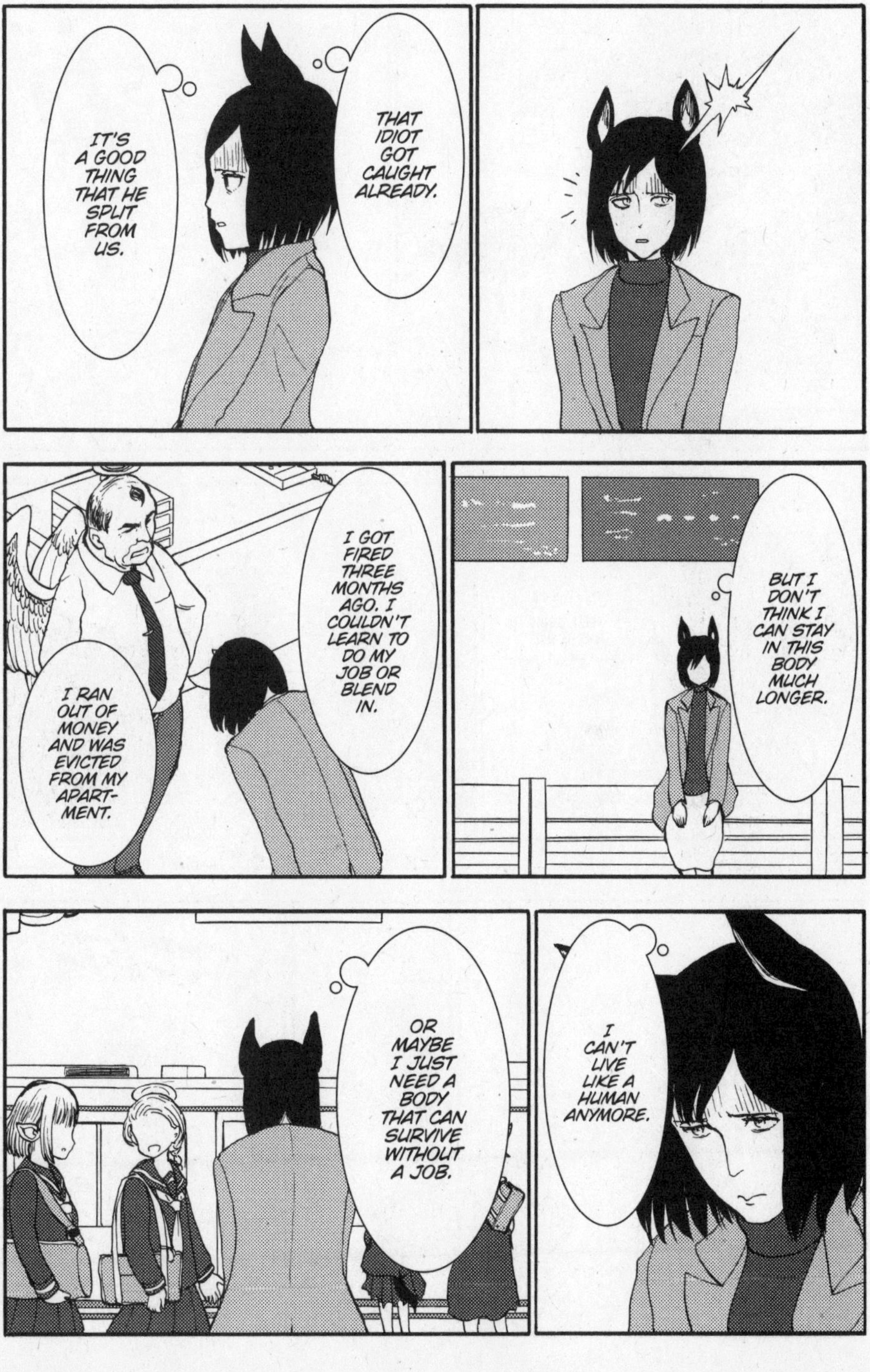
THAT IDIOT GOT CAUGHT ALREADY.
IT'S A GOOD THING THAT HE SPLIT FROM US.
BUT I DON'T THINK I CAN STAY IN THIS BODY MUCH LONGER.
I GOT FIRED THREE MONTHS AGO. I COULDN'T LEARN TO DO MY JOB OR BLEND IN.
I RAN OUT OF MONEY AND WAS EVICTED FROM MY APARTMENT.
I CAN'T LIVE LIKE A HUMAN ANYMORE.
OR MAYBE I JUST NEED A BODY THAT CAN SURVIVE WITHOUT A JOB.

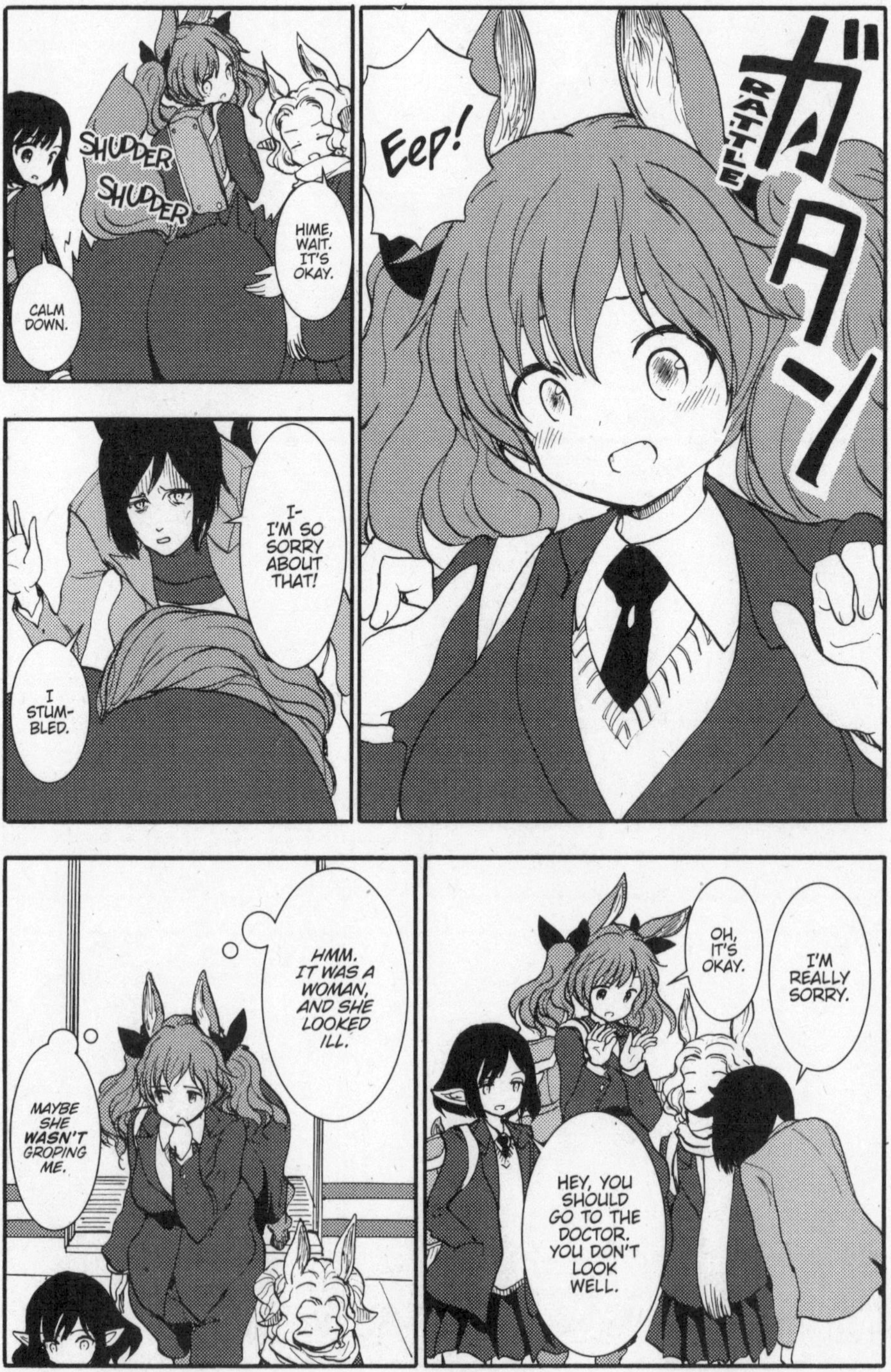
ガタン
RATTLE
Eep!
HIME, WAIT. IT'S OKAY.
SHUDDER SHUDDER
CALM DOWN.
I- I'M SO SORRY ABOUT THAT!
I STUMBLED.
I'M REALLY SORRY.
OH, IT'S OKAY.
HEY, YOU SHOULD GO TO THE DOCTOR. YOU DON'T LOOK WELL.
HMM. IT WAS A WOMAN, AND SHE LOOKED ILL.
MAYBE SHE WASN'T GROPING ME.

A Centaur's Life

HISTORY OF ARCHITECTURE IN JAPAN AND OTHER COUNTRIES: <2> ELEVATED STOREHOUSE

JAPAN'S HOT AND HUMID CLIMATE MADE IT DIFFICULT TO STORE THE REWARDS OF THE HARVEST, WHICH WERE PRONE TO PEST DAMAGE FROM MICE AND OTHER CREATURES. THESE ISSUES HAVE BEEN ADDRESSED SINCE ANCIENT TIMES BY ELEVATING STOREHOUSES OFF THE GROUND.

IT WAS BELIEVED FOR MANY YEARS THAT CENTAURS COULD NOT USE ELEVATED STOREHOUSES BECAUSE IT WOULD BE TOO DIFFICULT FOR THEM TO ENTER. WHEN THIS THEORY WAS FINALLY TESTED, HOWEVER, HEALTHY CENTAURS WITH GOOD COORDINATION AND AVERAGE STRENGTH PROVED CAPABLE OF MANEUVERING INTO THE ENTRIES, WHICH WERE LOWER THAN THEIR NATURAL HEIGHT. ASSISTIVE DEVICES SUCH AS STAIRS OR RAMPS WOULD HAVE RESOLVED ANY ACCESSIBILITY ISSUES. UNFORTUNATELY, THESE PLAUSIBLE SOLUTIONS WERE LEFT UNTESTED, AND UNFOUNDED ASSUMPTIONS WERE ACCEPTED AS FACT FOR MANY YEARS.

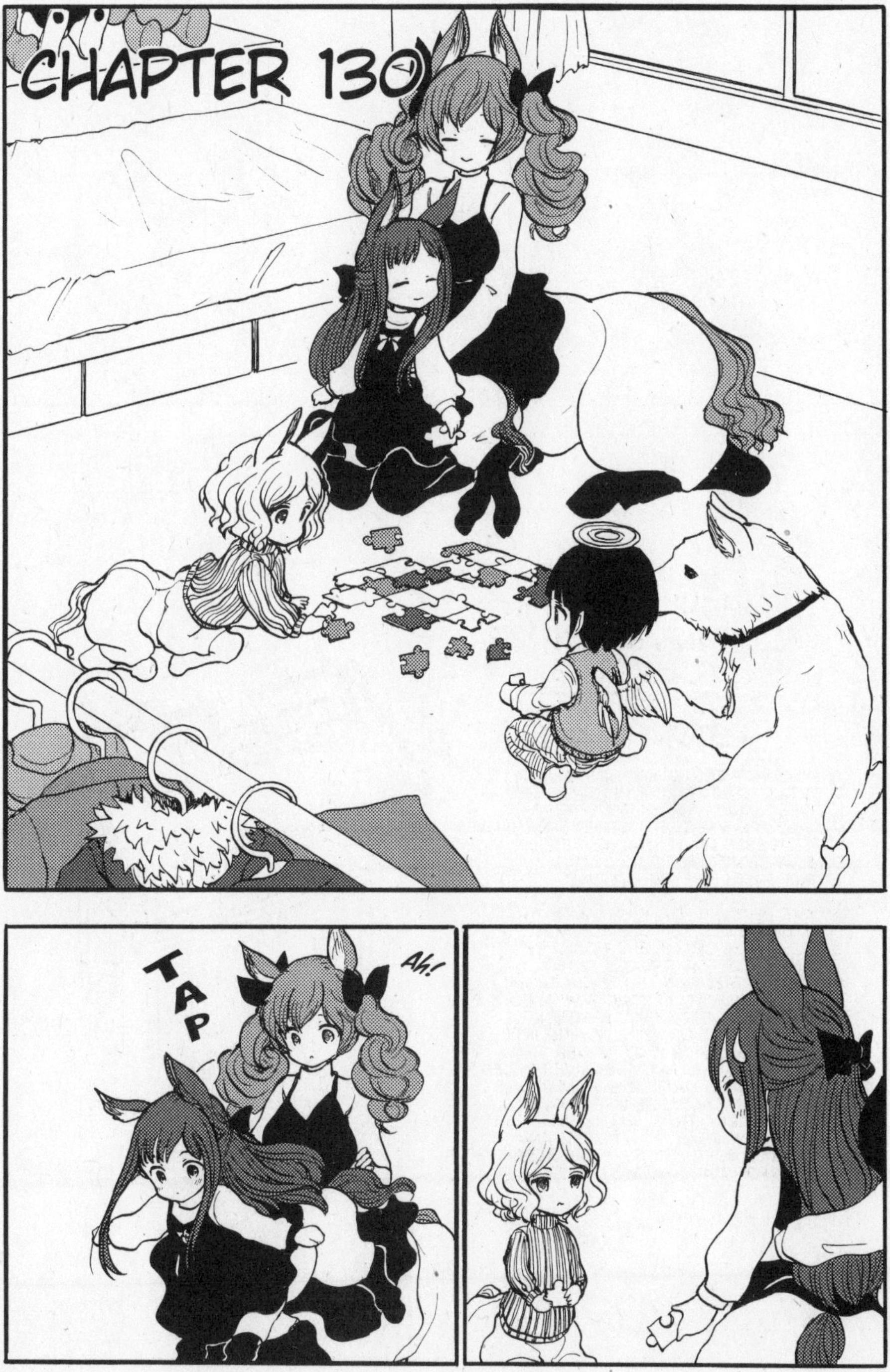
CHAPTER 130
Ah!
TAP

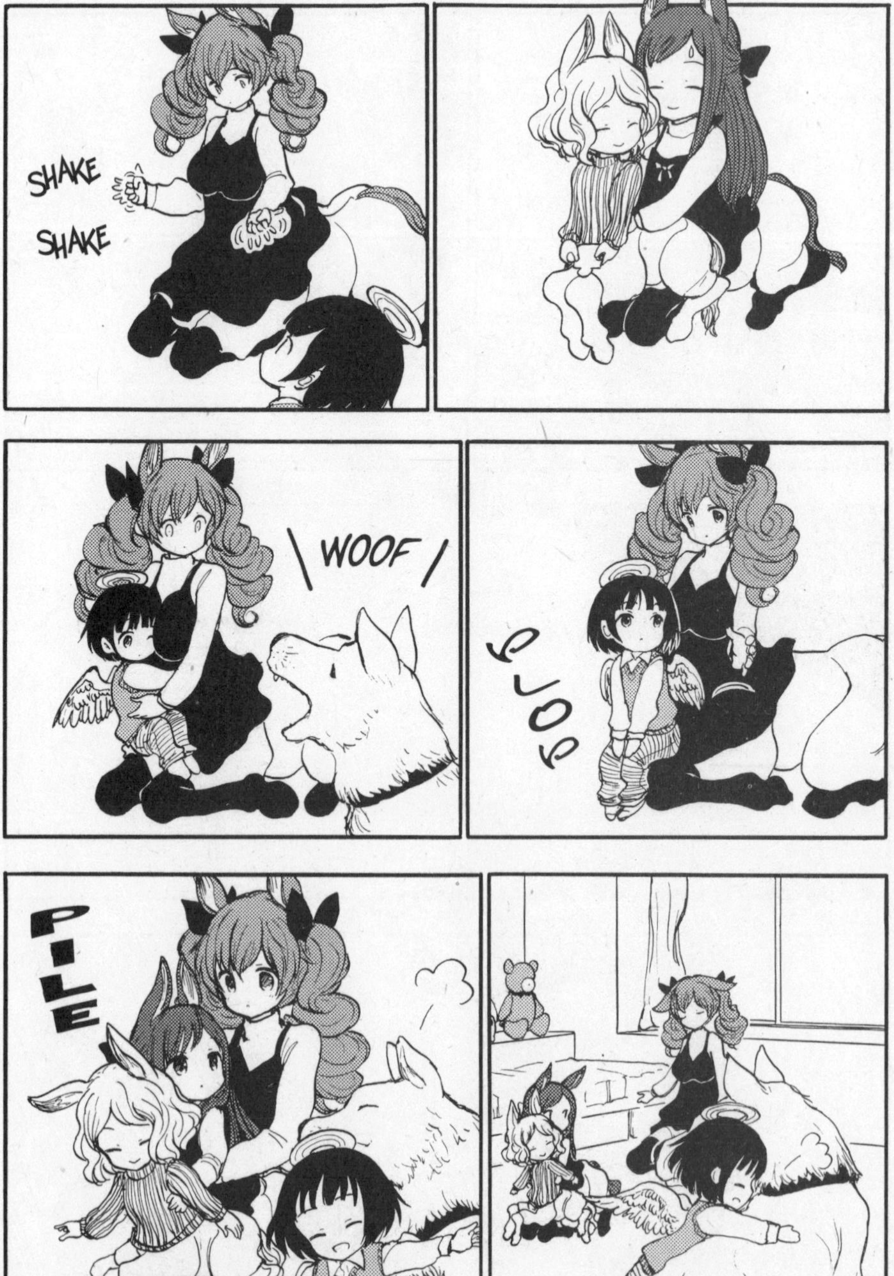
SHAKE
SHAKE
PLOP
WOOF
PILE

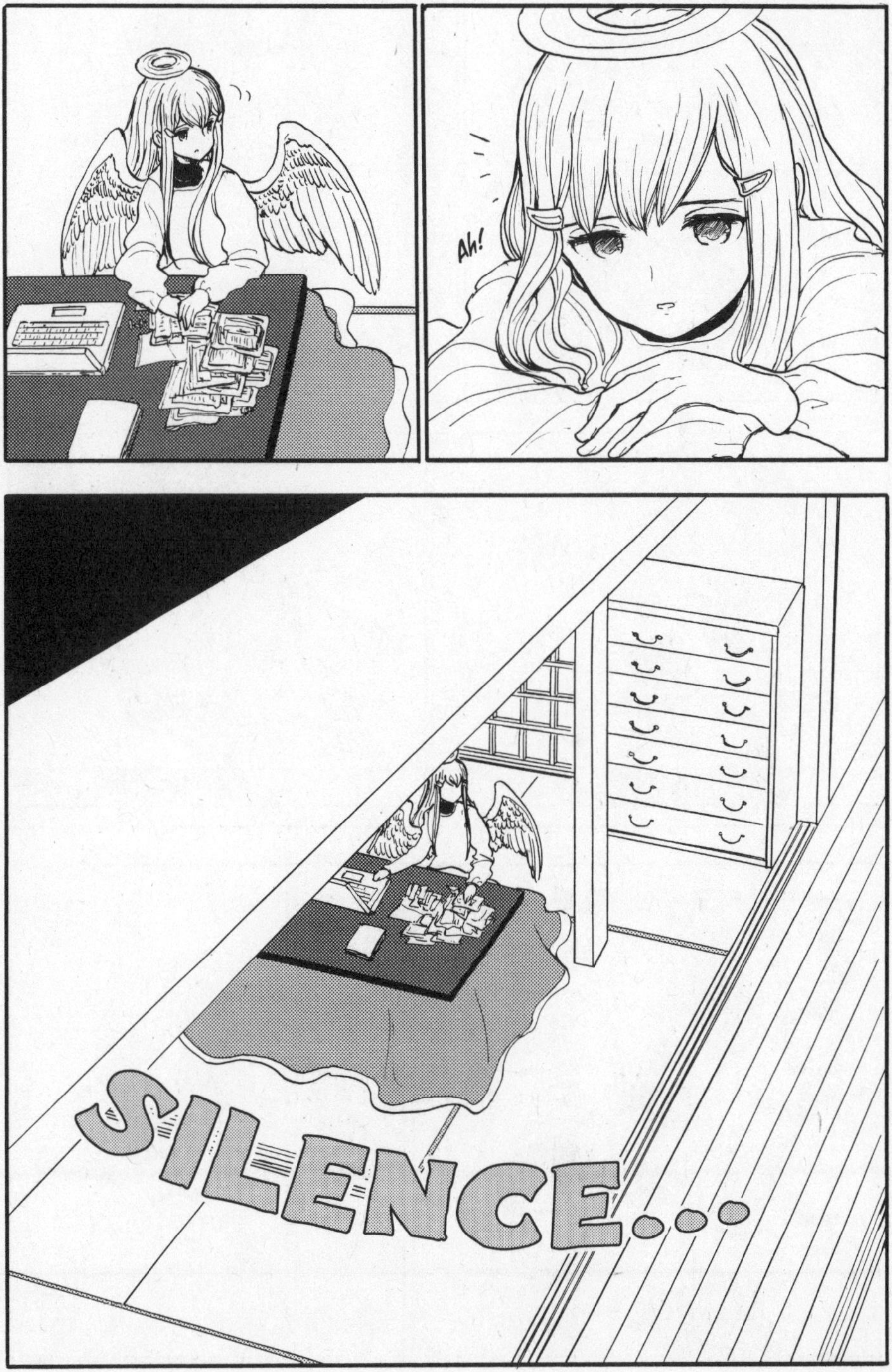
Ah!
SILENCE...

SILENCE...
Ah!
BIG SIS!
SISSY!
PHEW!
SQUELCH
We caught some loaches!
Isn't this great?
HEY...
WHERE'VE YOU BEEN?

A Centaur's Life

HISTORY OF ARCHITECTURE IN JAPAN AND OTHER COUNTRIES: < 3 > UNDERWATER PALACE

MERFOLK, WHO PLAYED A LARGE ROLE IN BOTH THE SPIRITUALITY AND THE DISTRIBUTION OF GOODS IN THE JAPANESE ARCHIPELAGO, CREATED AN ARISTOCRATIC HIERARCHY IN THE CLASSICAL PERIOD. OVER TIME, GENUINE MERFOLK ARISTOCRACY DECLINED, AND THEY BECAME A MINORITY BY THE ASUKA PERIOD. DESPITE THIS, ARCHITECTURE AND CULTURE IN THE ARISTOCRATIC SOCIETY STILL CONFORMED TO MERFOLK STANDARDS. ONE EXAMPLE IS THE UNDERWATER PALACE, AN ARISTOCRATIC RESIDENCE FROM THE CLASSICAL PERIOD WITH A NETWORK OF WATERWAYS AND STEPPING STONES THROUGHOUT ITS INTERIOR AND GARDEN. THE GARDEN'S LANDSCAPE WAS REPLACED WITH PONDS AND WATERWAYS, AND IT BECAME RENOWNED FOR ITS BEAUTY AND SERENITY. SACRED WATER RITUALS WERE A SIGNIFICANT PART OF LIFE DURING THE CLASSICAL PERIOD, AND THE GARDEN WAS A PROMINENT PLACE FOR THOSE RITUALS.

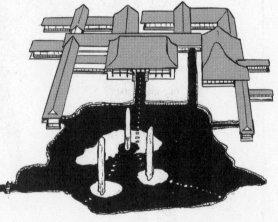

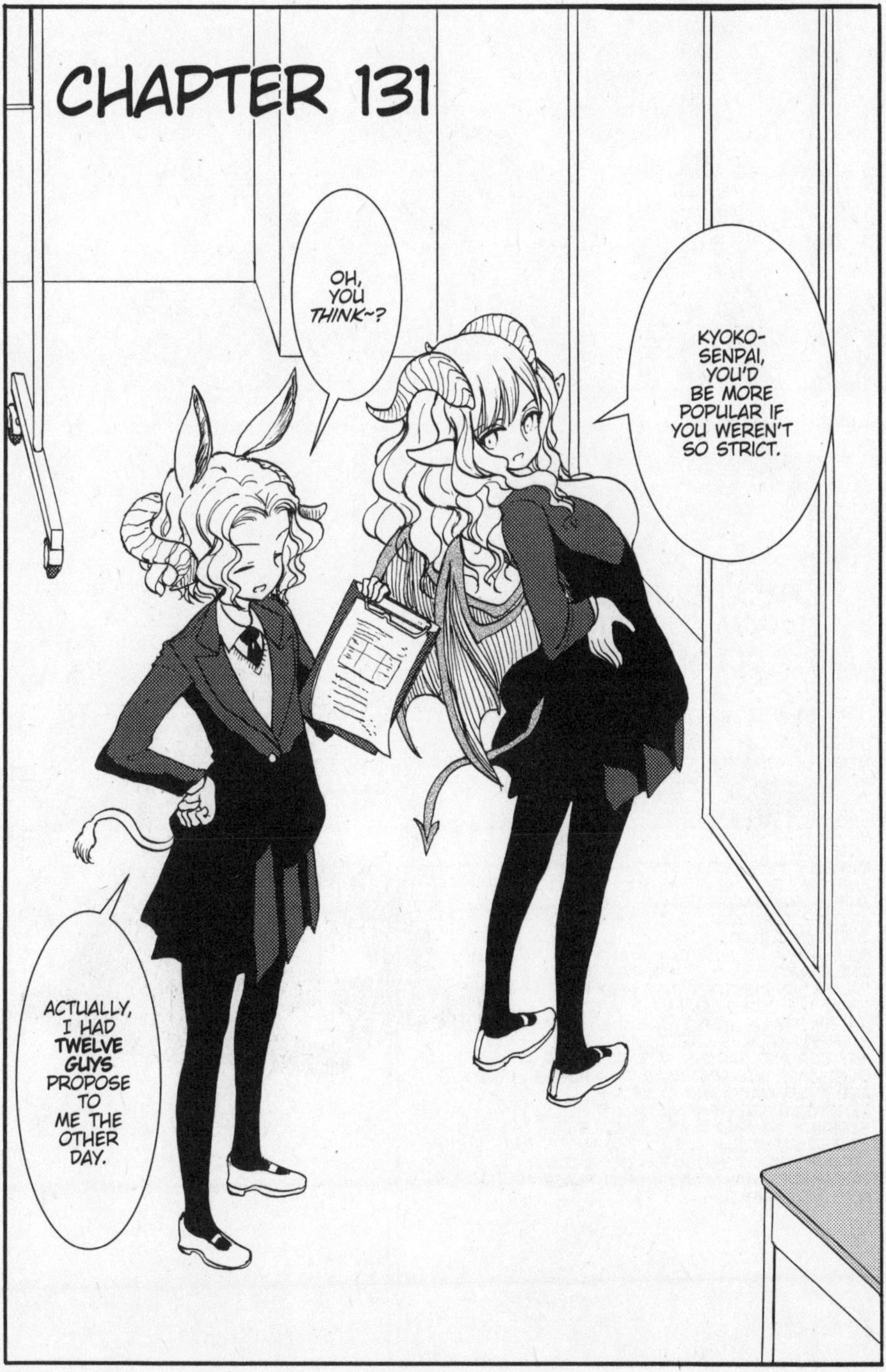
CHAPTER 131
KYOKO-SENPAI, YOU'D BE MORE POPULAR IF YOU WEREN'T SO STRICT.
OH, YOU *THINK~?*
ACTUALLY, I HAD **TWELVE GUYS** PROPOSE TO ME THE OTHER DAY.

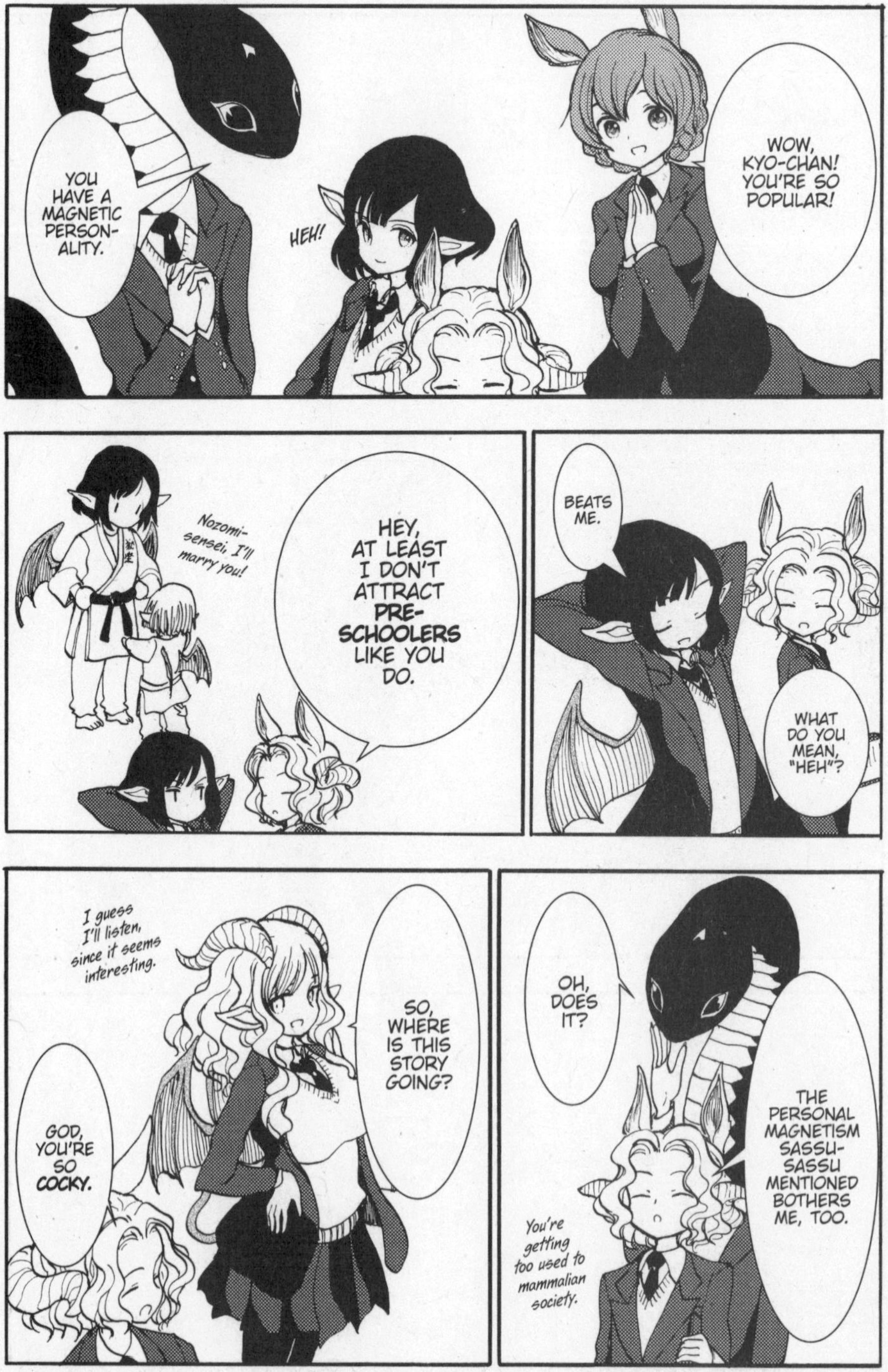
WOW, KYO-CHAN! YOU'RE SO POPULAR!
YOU HAVE A MAGNETIC PERSON-ALITY.
HEH!
WHAT DO YOU MEAN, "HEH"?
BEATS ME.
HEY, AT LEAST I DON'T ATTRACT PRE-SCHOOLERS LIKE YOU DO.
Nozomi-sensei, I'll marry you!
THE PERSONAL MAGNETISM SASSU-SASSU MENTIONED BOTHERS ME, TOO.
OH, DOES IT?
You're getting too used to mammalian society.
SO, WHERE IS THIS STORY GOING?
GOD, YOU'RE SO COCKY.
I guess I'll listen, since it seems interesting.

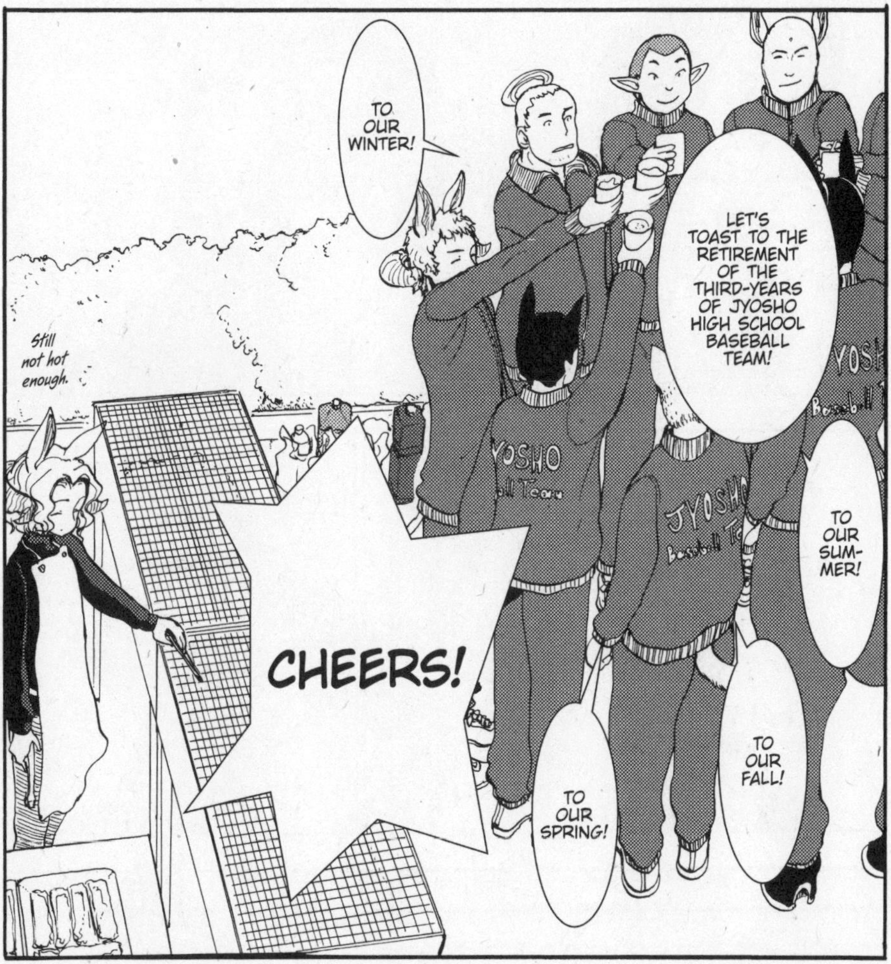
LET'S TOAST TO THE RETIREMENT OF THE THIRD-YEARS OF JYOSHO HIGH SCHOOL BASEBALL TEAM!
TO OUR SUMMER!
TO OUR FALL!
TO OUR SPRING!
TO OUR WINTER!
CHEERS!
Still not hot enough.

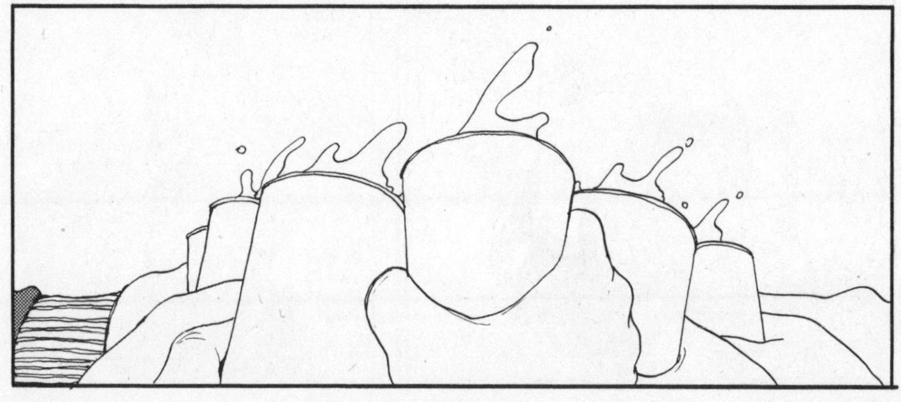

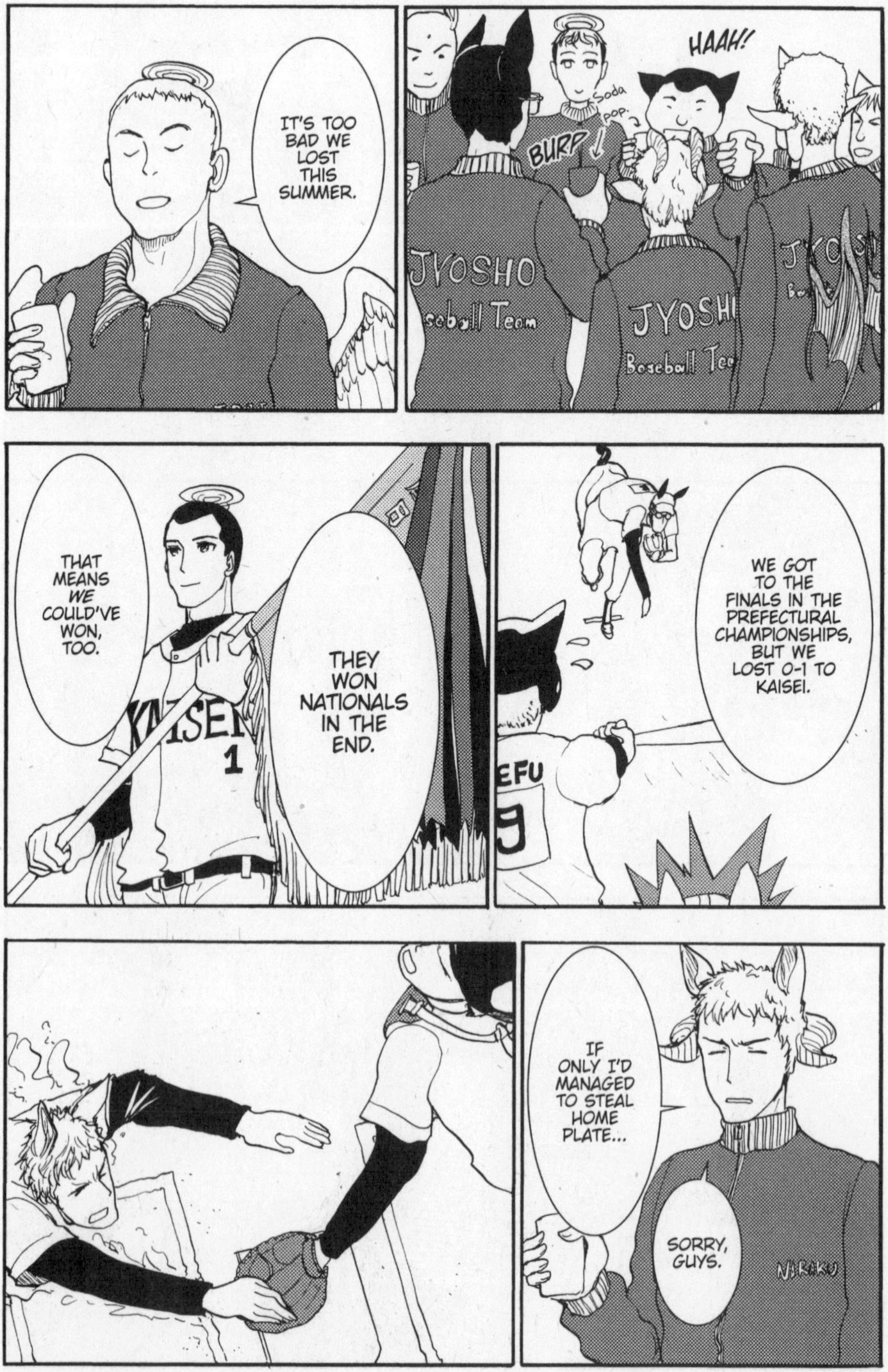
HAAH!
Soda pop.
BURP
JYOSHO Baseball Team
JYOSHO Baseball Team
IT'S TOO BAD WE LOST THIS SUMMER.
WE GOT TO THE FINALS IN THE PREFECTURAL CHAMPIONSHIPS, BUT WE LOST 0-1 TO KAISEI.
THEY WON NATIONALS IN THE END.
THAT MEANS WE COULD'VE WON, TOO.
KAISEI 1
IF ONLY I'D MANAGED TO STEAL HOME PLATE...
SORRY, GUYS.
NARAKU

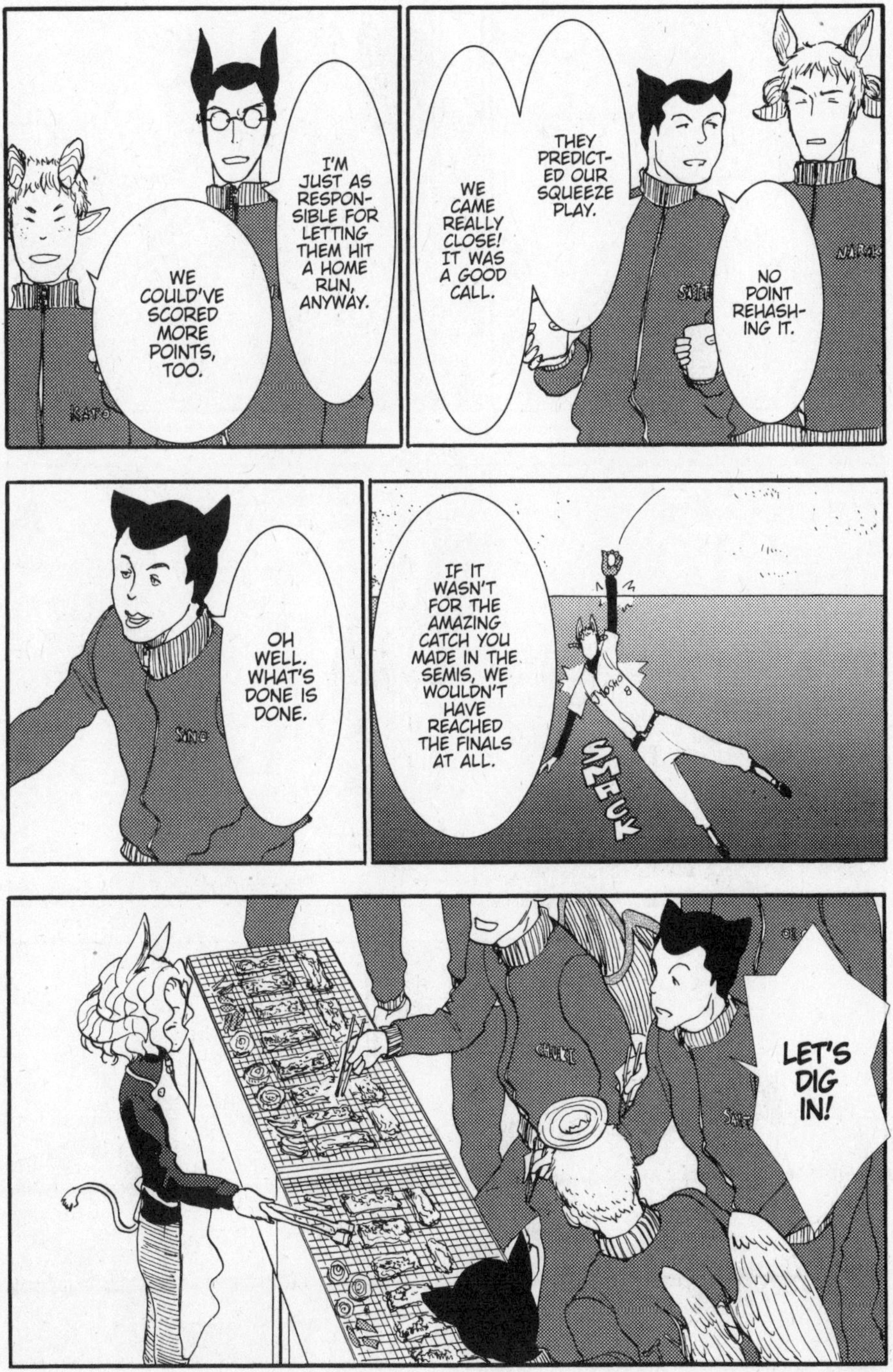
WE CAME REALLY CLOSE! IT WAS A GOOD CALL.
THEY PREDICTED OUR SQUEEZE PLAY.
NO POINT REHASHING IT.
I'M JUST AS RESPONSIBLE FOR LETTING THEM HIT A HOME RUN, ANYWAY.
WE COULD'VE SCORED MORE POINTS, TOO.
IF IT WASN'T FOR THE AMAZING CATCH YOU MADE IN THE SEMIS, WE WOULDN'T HAVE REACHED THE FINALS AT ALL.
SMACK
OH WELL. WHAT'S DONE IS DONE.
LET'S DIG IN!

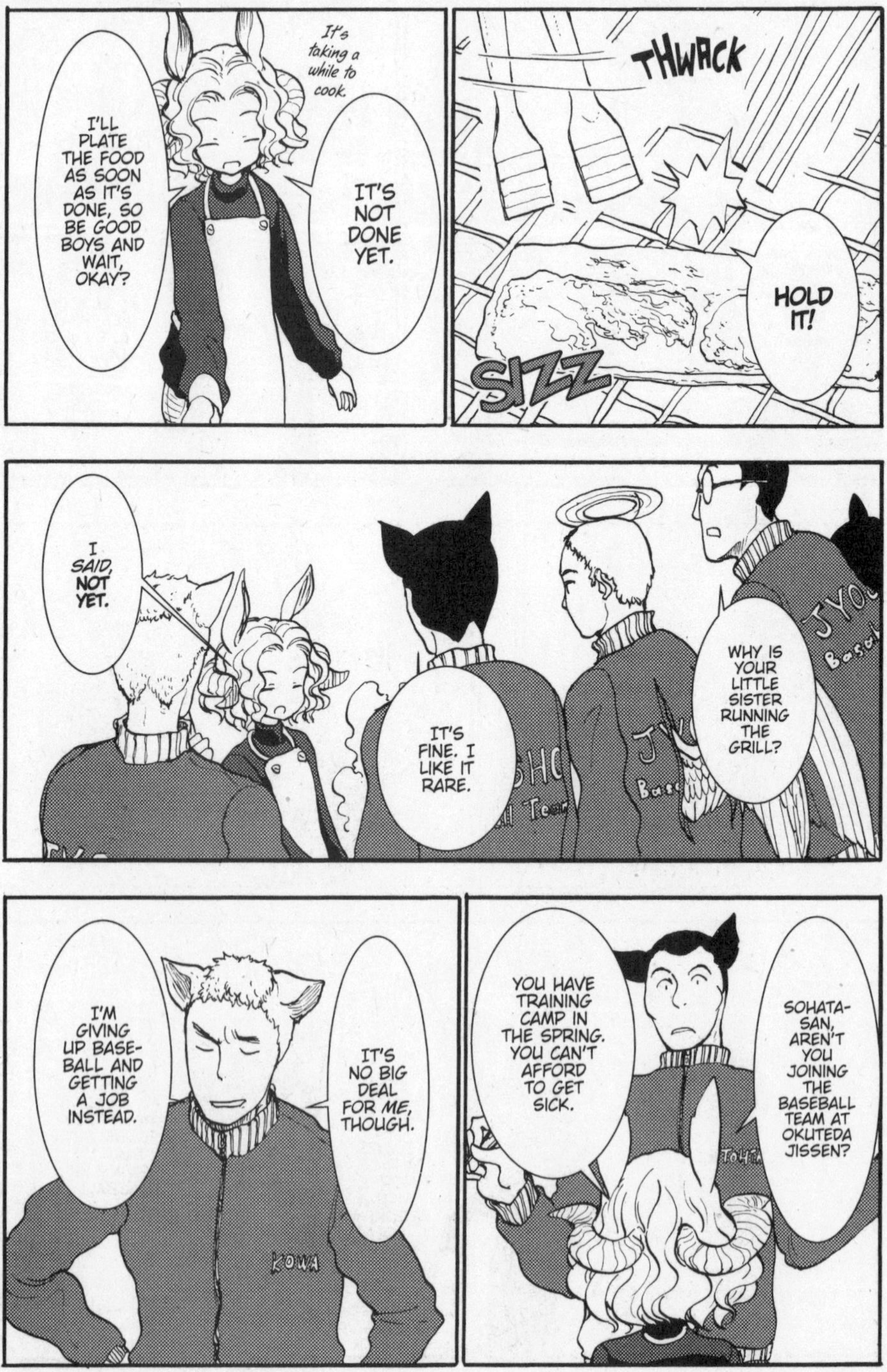
THWACK
HOLD IT!
SIZZ
It's taking a while to cook.
IT'S NOT DONE YET.
I'LL PLATE THE FOOD AS SOON AS IT'S DONE, SO BE GOOD BOYS AND WAIT, OKAY?
WHY IS YOUR LITTLE SISTER RUNNING THE GRILL?
IT'S FINE. I LIKE IT RARE.
I *SAID*, **NOT YET.**
SOHATA-SAN, AREN'T YOU JOINING THE BASEBALL TEAM AT OKUTEDA JISSEN?
YOU HAVE TRAINING CAMP IN THE SPRING. YOU CAN'T AFFORD TO GET SICK.
IT'S NO BIG DEAL FOR *ME*, THOUGH.
I'M GIVING UP BASEBALL AND GETTING A JOB INSTEAD.

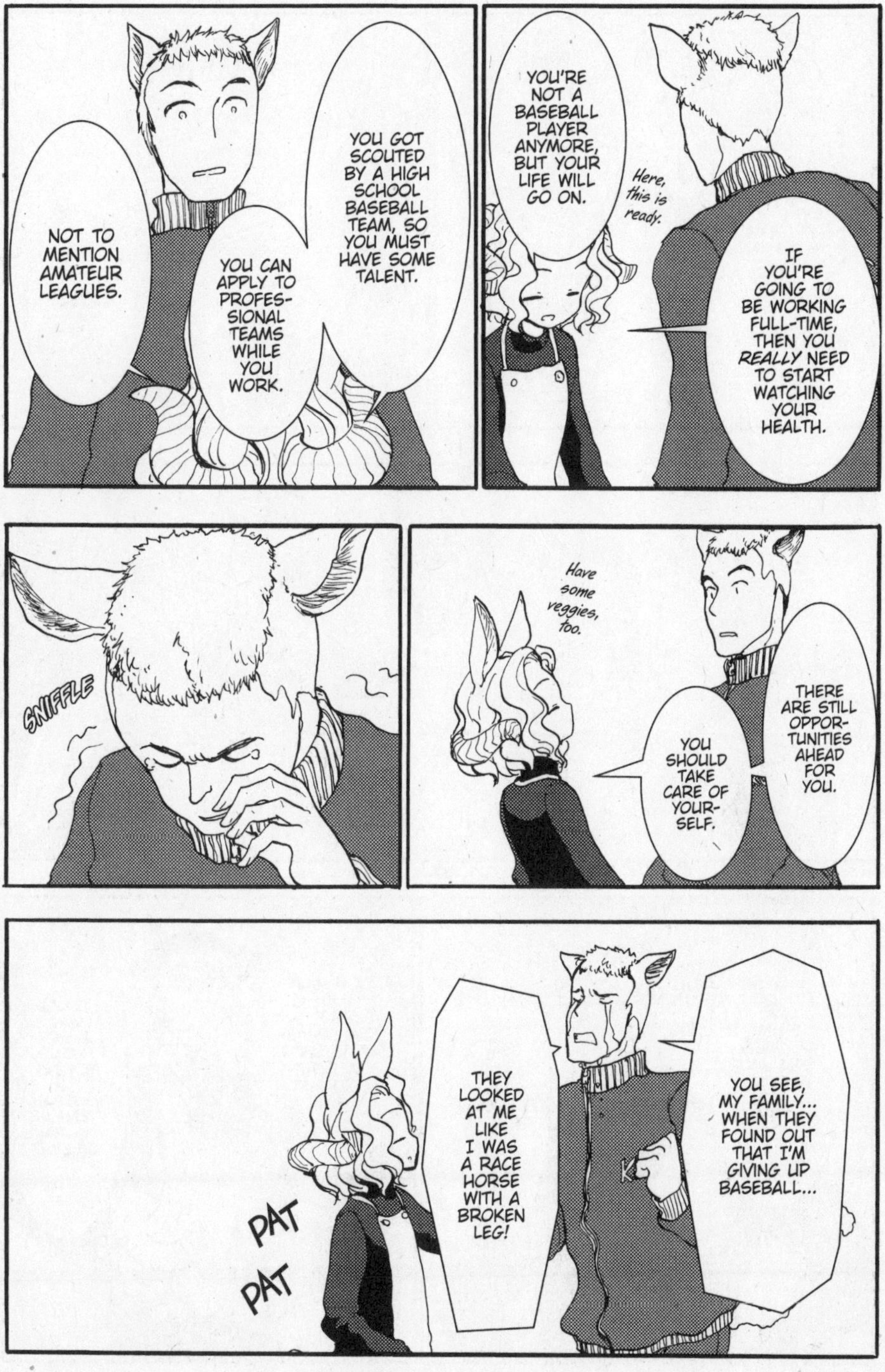
YOU'RE NOT A BASEBALL PLAYER ANYMORE, BUT YOUR LIFE WILL GO ON.
Here, this is ready.
IF YOU'RE GOING TO BE WORKING FULL-TIME, THEN YOU *REALLY* NEED TO START WATCHING YOUR HEALTH.
YOU GOT SCOUTED BY A HIGH SCHOOL BASEBALL TEAM, SO YOU MUST HAVE SOME TALENT.
YOU CAN APPLY TO PROFES-SIONAL TEAMS WHILE YOU WORK.
NOT TO MENTION AMATEUR LEAGUES.
Have some veggies, too.
THERE ARE STILL OPPOR-TUNITIES AHEAD FOR YOU.
YOU SHOULD TAKE CARE OF YOUR-SELF.
SNIFFLE
YOU SEE, MY FAMILY... WHEN THEY FOUND OUT THAT I'M GIVING UP BASEBALL...
THEY LOOKED AT ME LIKE I WAS A RACE HORSE WITH A BROKEN LEG!
PAT
PAT

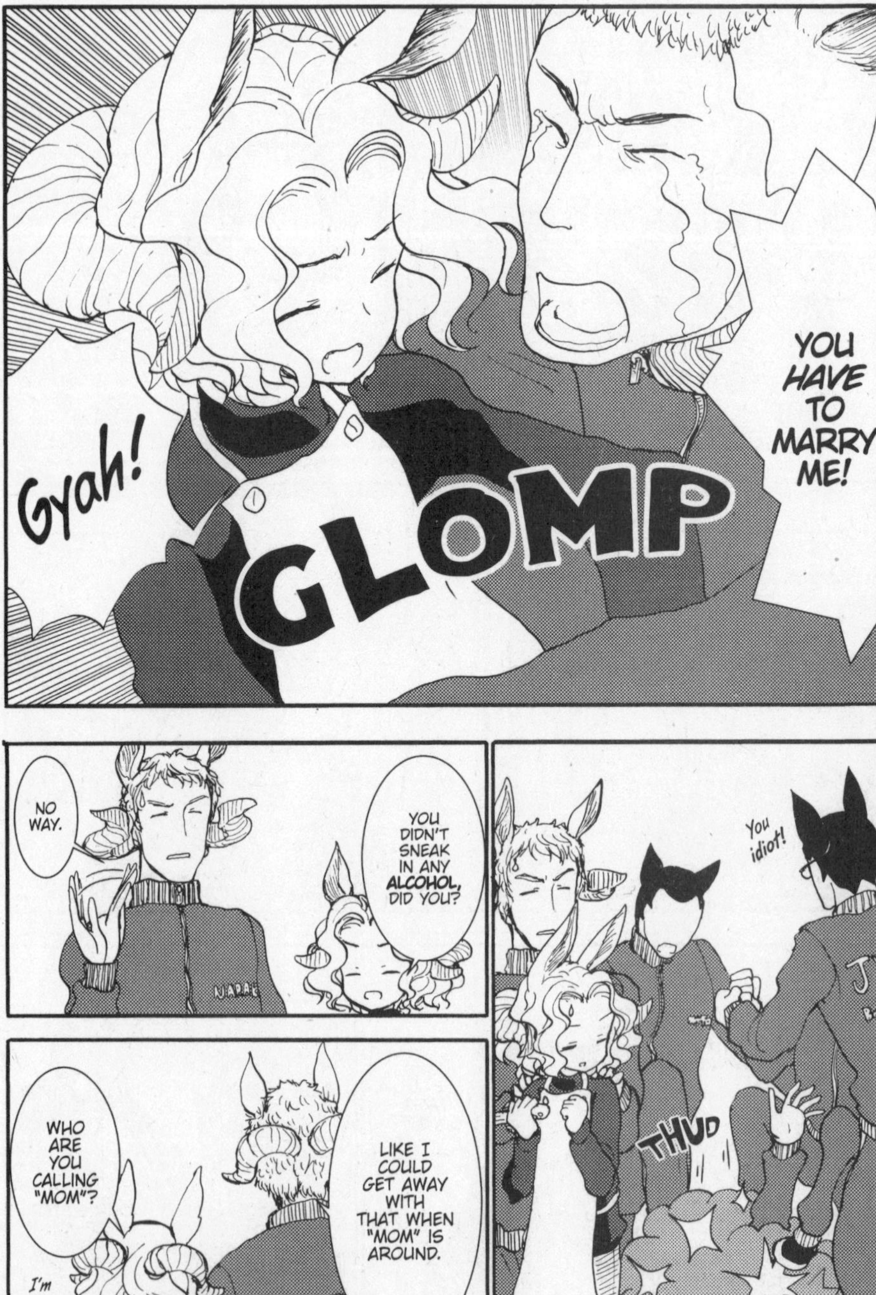
YOU HAVE TO MARRY ME!
GLOMP
Gyah!
You idiot!
THUD
WHACK
YOU DIDN'T SNEAK IN ANY **ALCOHOL**, DID YOU?
NO WAY.
LIKE I COULD GET AWAY WITH THAT WHEN "MOM" IS AROUND.
WHO ARE YOU CALLING "MOM"?
I'm still in high school!

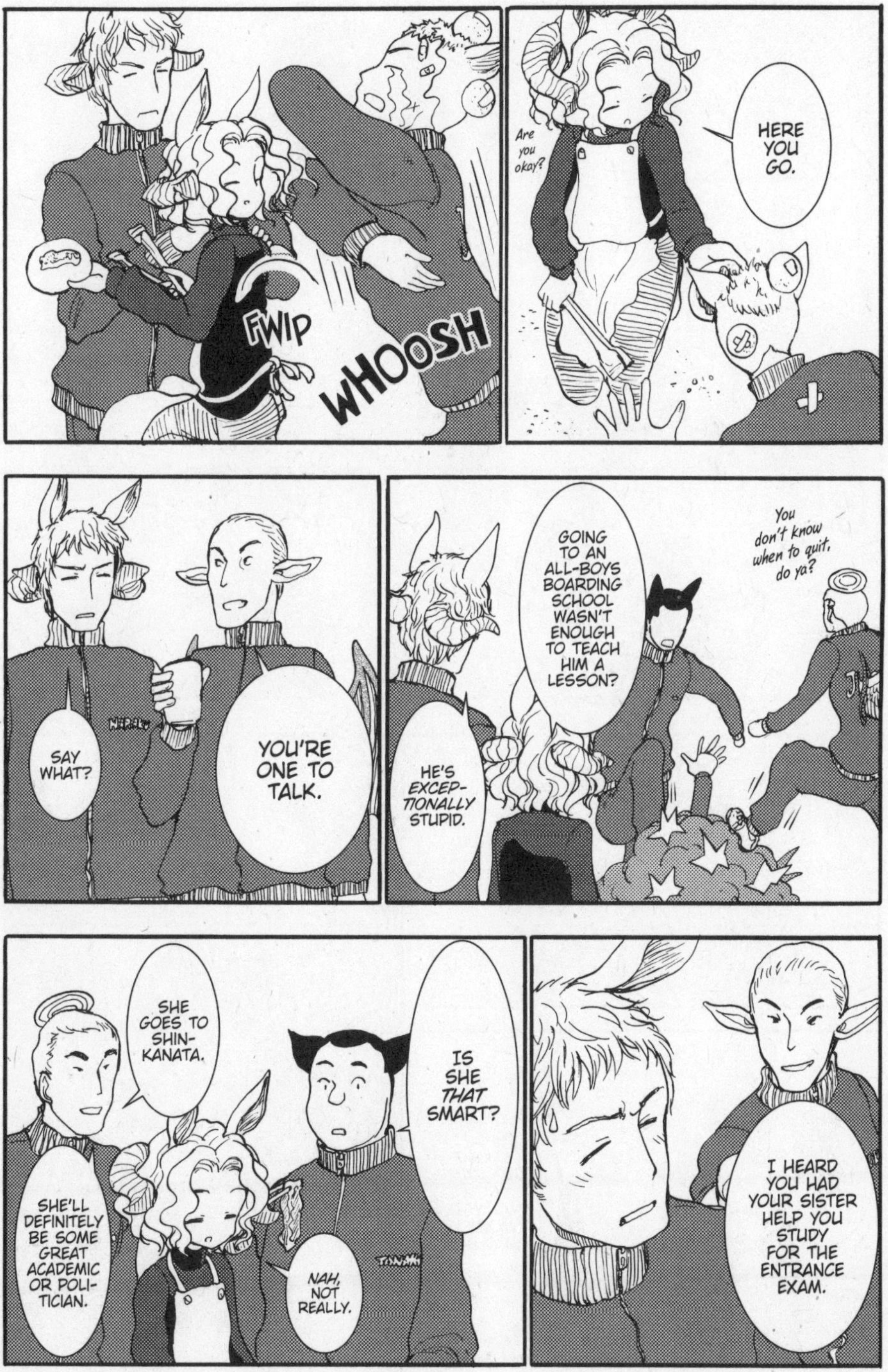
Are you okay?
HERE YOU GO.
FWIP
WHOOSH
You don't know when to quit, do ya?
GOING TO AN ALL-BOYS BOARDING SCHOOL WASN'T ENOUGH TO TEACH HIM A LESSON?
HE'S *EXCEPTIONALLY* STUPID.
YOU'RE ONE TO TALK.
SAY WHAT?
I HEARD YOU HAD YOUR SISTER HELP YOU STUDY FOR THE ENTRANCE EXAM.
IS SHE *THAT* SMART?
NAH, NOT REALLY.
SHE GOES TO SHIN-KANATA.
SHE'LL DEFINITELY BE SOME GREAT ACADEMIC OR POLITICIAN.

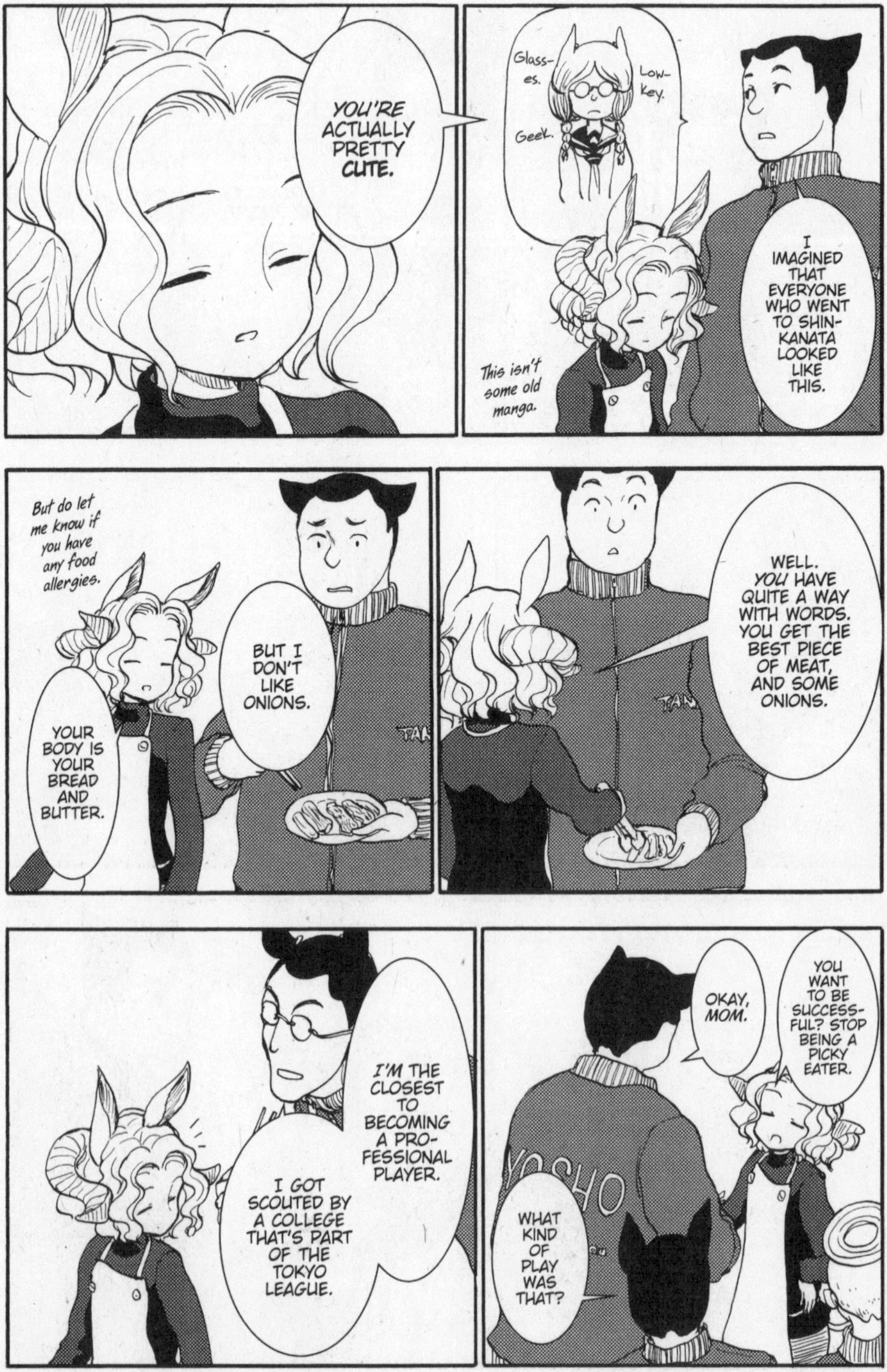
Glass-es.
Low-key.
Geek.
I IMAGINED THAT EVERYONE WHO WENT TO SHIN-KANATA LOOKED LIKE THIS.
This isn't some old manga.
YOU'RE ACTUALLY PRETTY CUTE.
WELL. YOU HAVE QUITE A WAY WITH WORDS. YOU GET THE BEST PIECE OF MEAT, AND SOME ONIONS.
BUT I DON'T LIKE ONIONS.
YOUR BODY IS YOUR BREAD AND BUTTER.
But do let me know if you have any food allergies.
YOU WANT TO BE SUCCESS-FUL? STOP BEING A PICKY EATER.
OKAY, MOM.
WHAT KIND OF PLAY WAS THAT?
I'M THE CLOSEST TO BECOMING A PRO-FESSIONAL PLAYER.
I GOT SCOUTED BY A COLLEGE THAT'S PART OF THE TOKYO LEAGUE.

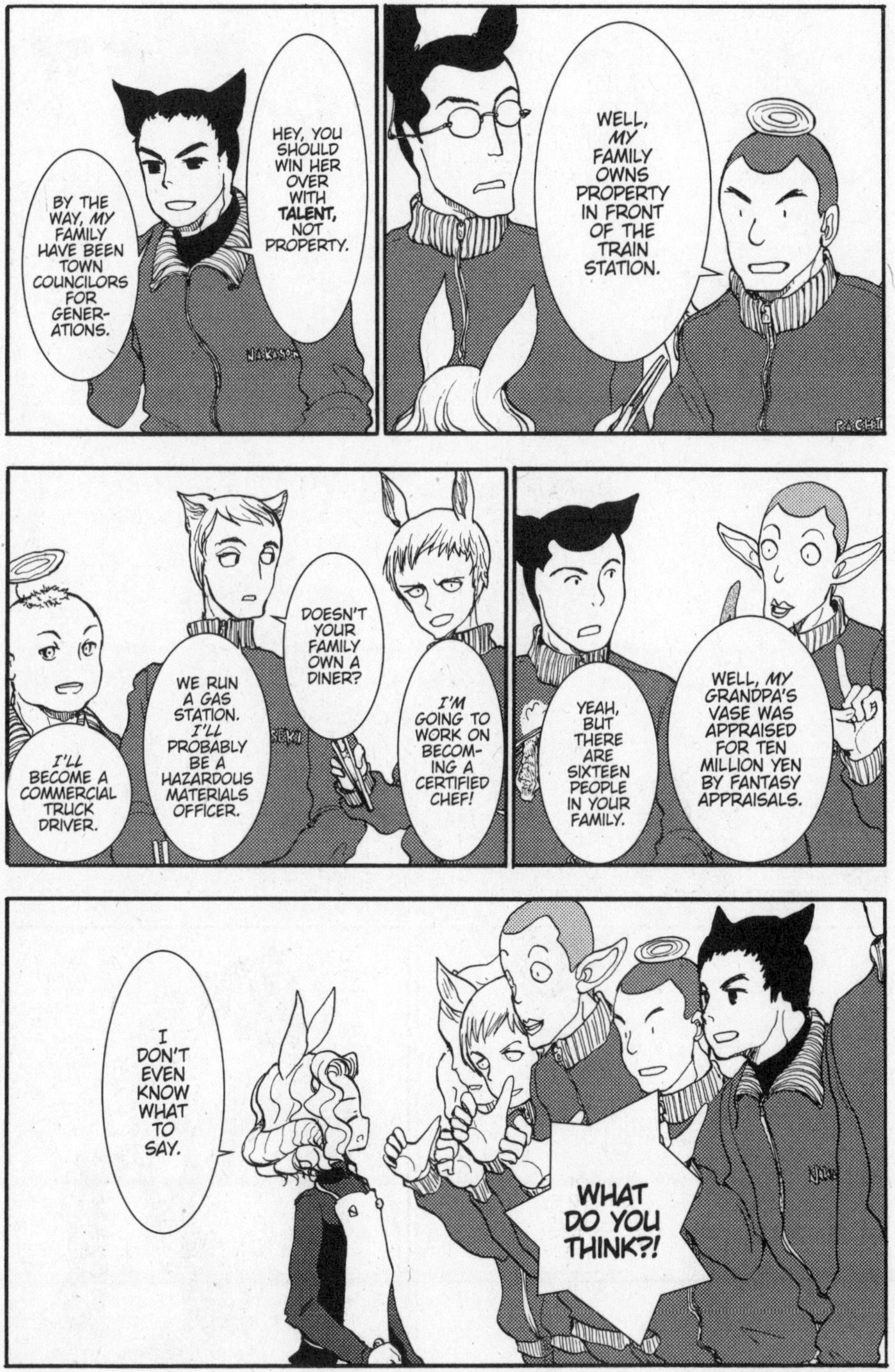
WELL, MY FAMILY OWNS PROPERTY IN FRONT OF THE TRAIN STATION.
PACHI
HEY, YOU SHOULD WIN HER OVER WITH TALENT, NOT PROPERTY.
BY THE WAY, MY FAMILY HAVE BEEN TOWN COUNCILORS FOR GENERATIONS.
WELL, MY GRANDPA'S VASE WAS APPRAISED FOR TEN MILLION YEN BY FANTASY APPRAISALS.
YEAH, BUT THERE ARE SIXTEEN PEOPLE IN YOUR FAMILY.
DOESN'T YOUR FAMILY OWN A DINER?
I'M GOING TO WORK ON BECOMING A CERTIFIED CHEF!
WE RUN A GAS STATION. I'LL PROBABLY BE A HAZARDOUS MATERIALS OFFICER.
I'LL BECOME A COMMERCIAL TRUCK DRIVER.
WHAT DO YOU THINK?!
I DON'T EVEN KNOW WHAT TO SAY.

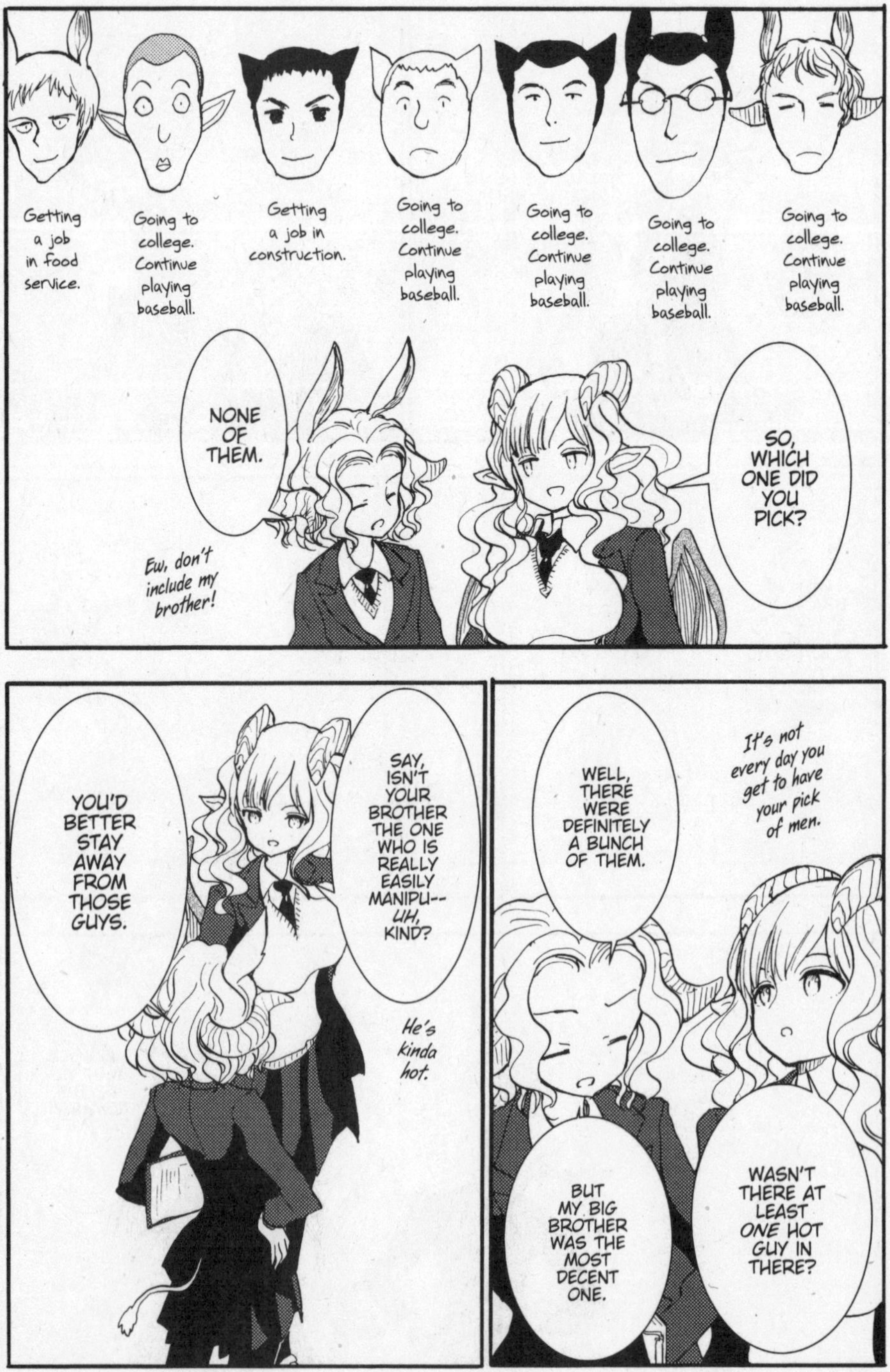
Going to college. Continue playing baseball.
Going to college. Continue playing baseball.
Going to college. Continue playing baseball.
Going to college. Continue playing baseball.
Getting a job in construction.
Going to college. Continue playing baseball.
Getting a job in food service.
SO, WHICH ONE DID YOU PICK?
NONE OF THEM.
Ew, don't include my brother!
It's not every day you get to have your pick of men.
WELL, THERE WERE DEFINITELY A BUNCH OF THEM.
WASN'T THERE AT LEAST ONE HOT GUY IN THERE?
BUT MY BIG BROTHER WAS THE MOST DECENT ONE.
SAY, ISN'T YOUR BROTHER THE ONE WHO IS REALLY EASILY MANIPU-- UH, KIND?
He's kinda hot.
YOU'D BETTER STAY AWAY FROM THOSE GUYS.

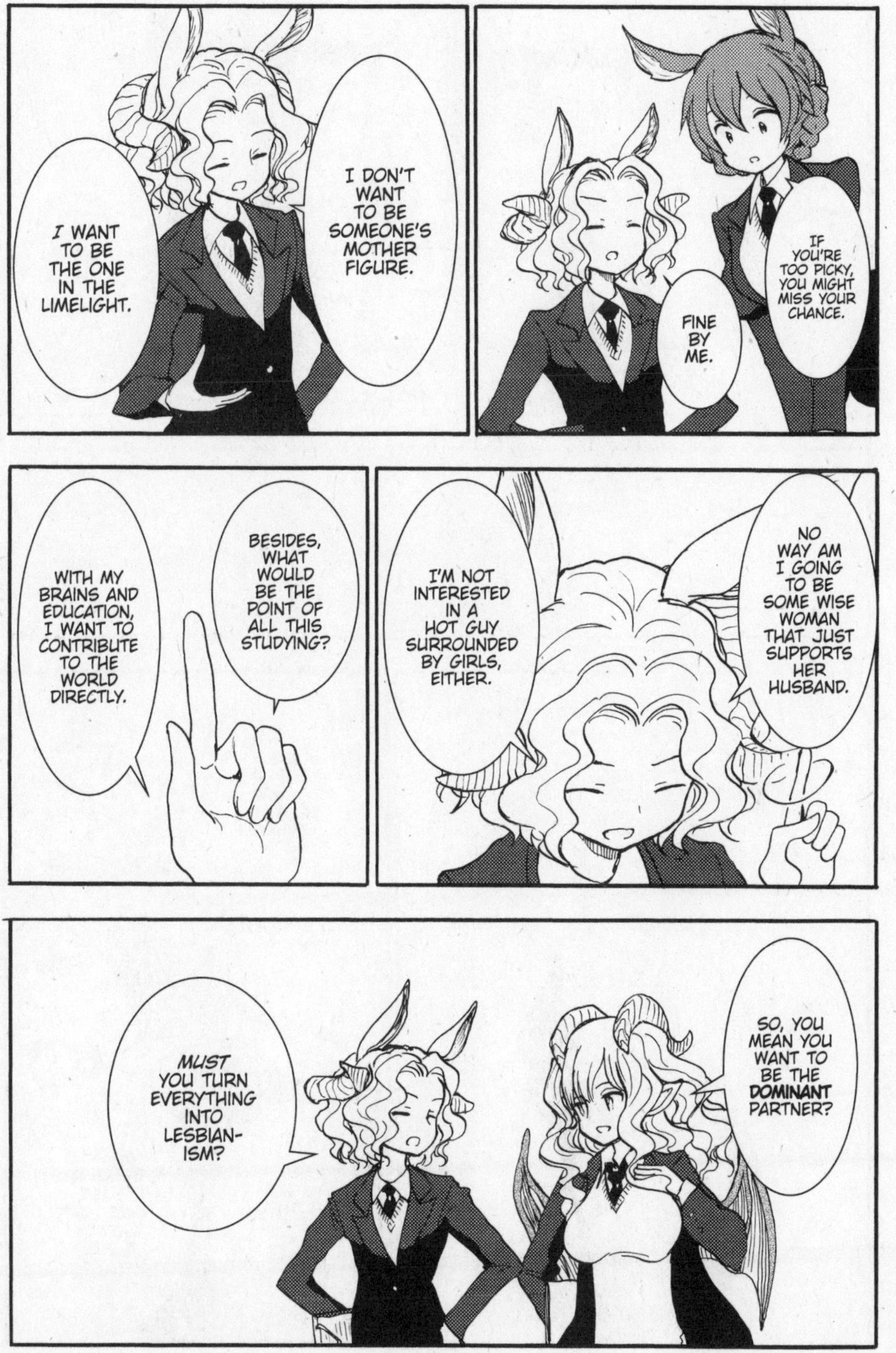
IF YOU'RE TOO PICKY, YOU MIGHT MISS YOUR CHANCE.
FINE BY ME.
I DON'T WANT TO BE SOMEONE'S MOTHER FIGURE.
I WANT TO BE THE ONE IN THE LIMELIGHT.
NO WAY AM I GOING TO BE SOME WISE WOMAN THAT JUST SUPPORTS HER HUSBAND.
I'M NOT INTERESTED IN A HOT GUY SURROUNDED BY GIRLS, EITHER.
BESIDES, WHAT WOULD BE THE POINT OF ALL THIS STUDYING?
WITH MY BRAINS AND EDUCATION, I WANT TO CONTRIBUTE TO THE WORLD DIRECTLY.
SO, YOU MEAN YOU WANT TO BE THE **DOMINANT** PARTNER?
MUST YOU TURN EVERYTHING INTO LESBIAN-ISM?

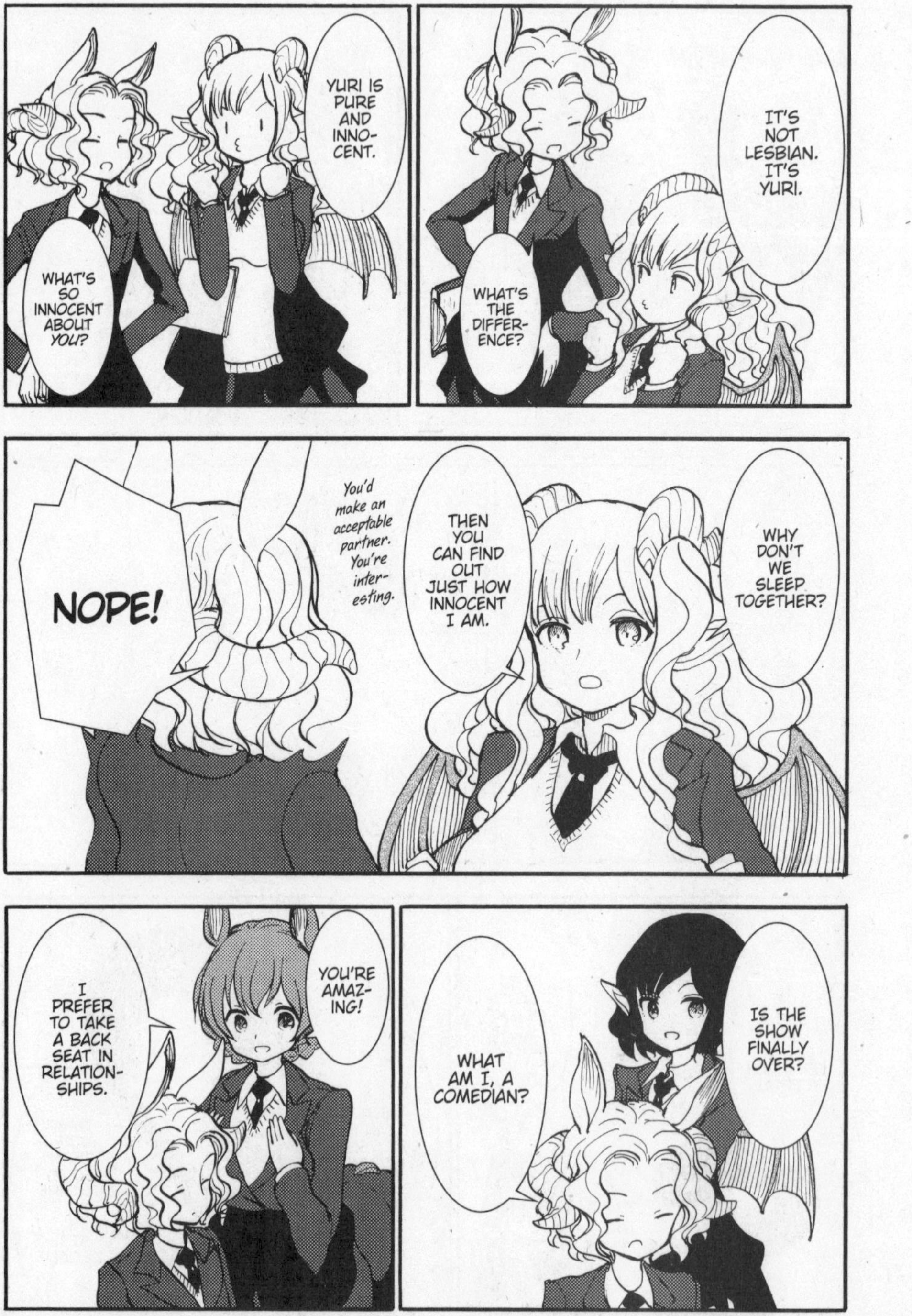
IT'S NOT LESBIAN. IT'S YURI.
WHAT'S THE DIFFERENCE?
YURI IS PURE AND INNOCENT.
WHAT'S SO INNOCENT ABOUT YOU?
WHY DON'T WE SLEEP TOGETHER?
THEN YOU CAN FIND OUT JUST HOW INNOCENT I AM.
You'd make an acceptable partner. You're interesting.
NOPE!
IS THE SHOW FINALLY OVER?
WHAT AM I, A COMEDIAN?
YOU'RE AMAZING!
I PREFER TO TAKE A BACK SEAT IN RELATIONSHIPS.

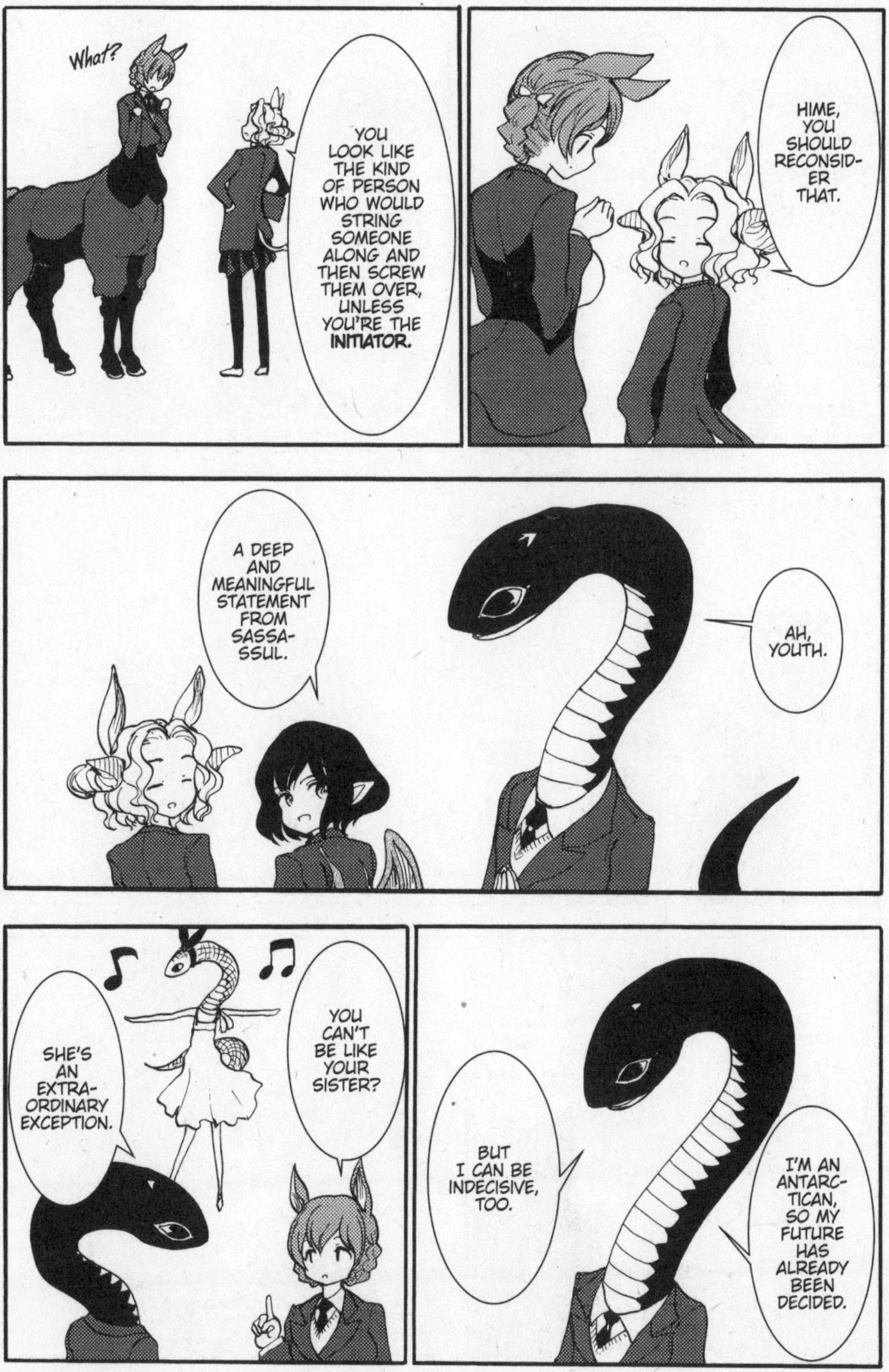
HIME, YOU SHOULD RECONSIDER THAT.
YOU LOOK LIKE THE KIND OF PERSON WHO WOULD STRING SOMEONE ALONG AND THEN SCREW THEM OVER, UNLESS YOU'RE THE **INITIATOR.**
What?
AH, YOUTH.
A DEEP AND MEANINGFUL STATEMENT FROM SASSASSUL.
I'M AN ANTARCTICAN, SO MY FUTURE HAS ALREADY BEEN DECIDED.
BUT I CAN BE INDECISIVE, TOO.
YOU CAN'T BE LIKE YOUR SISTER?
SHE'S AN EXTRAORDINARY EXCEPTION.

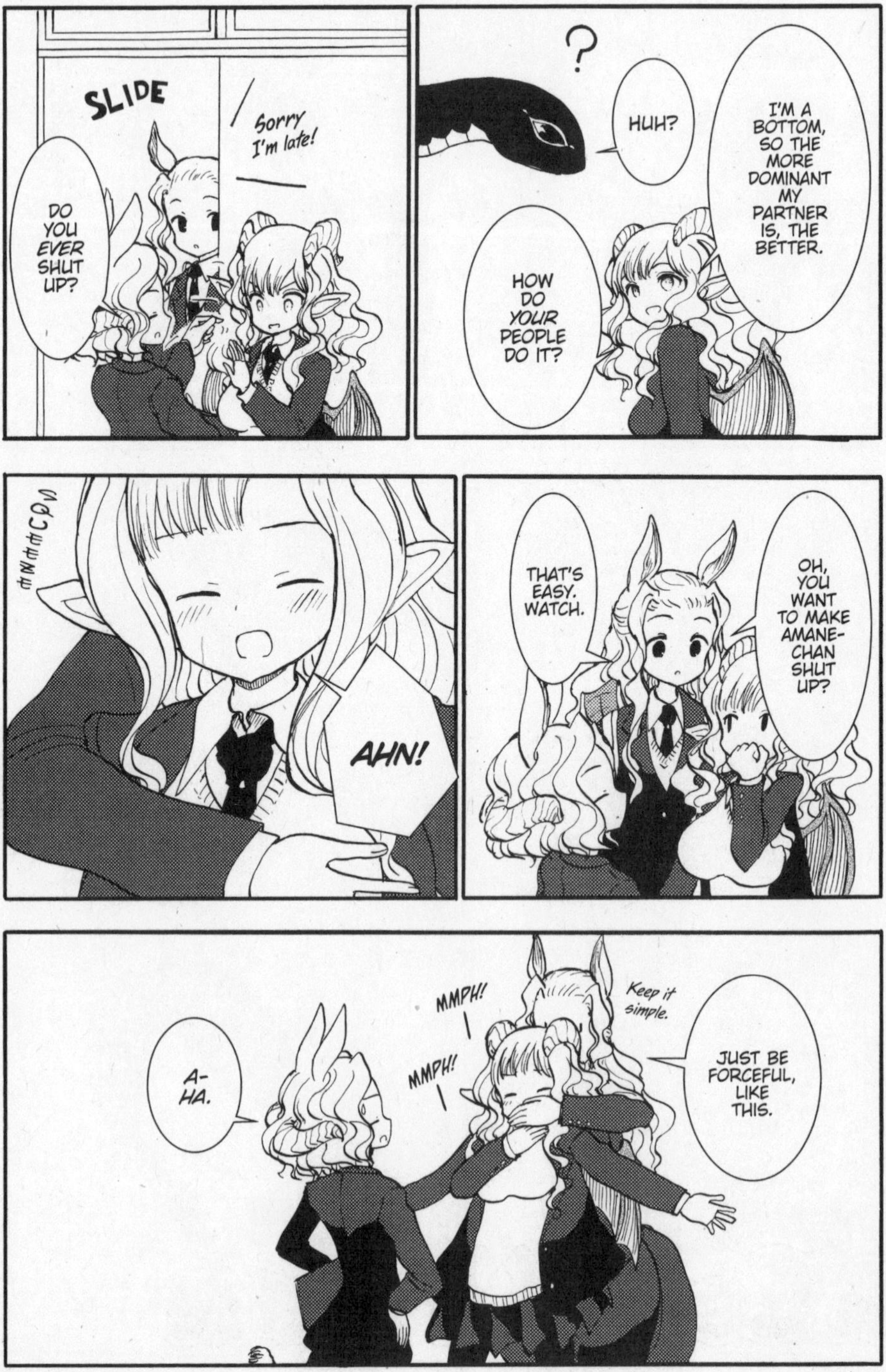
I'M A BOTTOM, SO THE MORE DOMINANT MY PARTNER IS, THE BETTER.
?
HUH?
HOW DO YOUR PEOPLE DO IT?
Sorry I'm late!
SLIDE
DO YOU EVER SHUT UP?
OH, YOU WANT TO MAKE AMANE-CHAN SHUT UP?
THAT'S EASY. WATCH.
AHN!
Keep it simple.
JUST BE FORCEFUL, LIKE THIS.
MMPH!
MMPH!
A-HA.

A Centaur's Life

HISTORY OF ARCHITECTURE IN JAPAN AND OTHER COUNTRIES: <4> SUKIYA TEA HOUSE

SUKIYA TEA HOUSES WERE DESIGNED WITH ARCHITECTURAL FEATURES THAT DEFY THE AESTHETIC STATUS QUO OF CURRENT JAPANESE ARCHITECTURE. THIS IS NOT TO SAY THAT THEIR CONSTRUCTION IS SIMPLE, BUT RATHER THAT THEIR SOPHISTICATED ARCHITECTURE WAS DESIGNED TO INCORPORATE THE AESTHETIC ELEMENTS OF THE JAPANESE TEA CEREMONY FROM THE MUROMACHI PERIOD. THESE TEA HOUSES WERE REFINED PLACES THAT OMITTED EVERYTHING EXCEPT THAT WHICH WAS NECESSARY FOR THE APPRECIATION OF TEA AND BEAUTY.

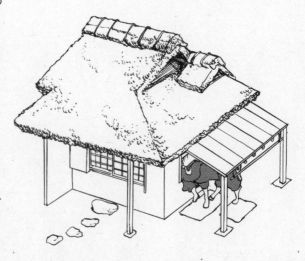

THE JAPANESE TEA CEREMONY BECAME WIDELY POPULAR WITH THE SAMURAI CLASS, AND ITS PRACTICE WAS NECESSARY FOR DIPLOMACY REGARDLESS OF INTEREST IN ITS CULTURAL ASPECTS. IT'S IMPORTANT TO NOTE, HOWEVER, THAT MANY TRADITIONAL SAMURAI FAMILIES CONSISTED OF CENTAURS. BECAUSE OF THEIR SIZE, THESE CENTAURS REQUIRED EXTENSIVE SPECIAL TRAINING TO CARRY THEMSELVES GRACEFULLY INSIDE THE SMALL SPACE OF A TEA HOUSE, AND BEING ABLE TO DO SO WAS CONSIDERED A STATUS SYMBOL FOR SAMURAI. AS JAPAN ENTERED THE WARRING STATES PERIOD, WHICH WAS MARKED BY CONSTANT REBELLIONS, IT WAS COMMON TO SEE THE DOWNFALL OF FEUDAL CLANS, EVEN DOMINANT ONES. AS SUCH, IT WAS NOT RARE TO FIND DESCENDANTS OF FALLEN CLANS TRAINED IN CENTAUR TEA CEREMONIES MAKING THEIR OWN WAYS IN THE WORLD.

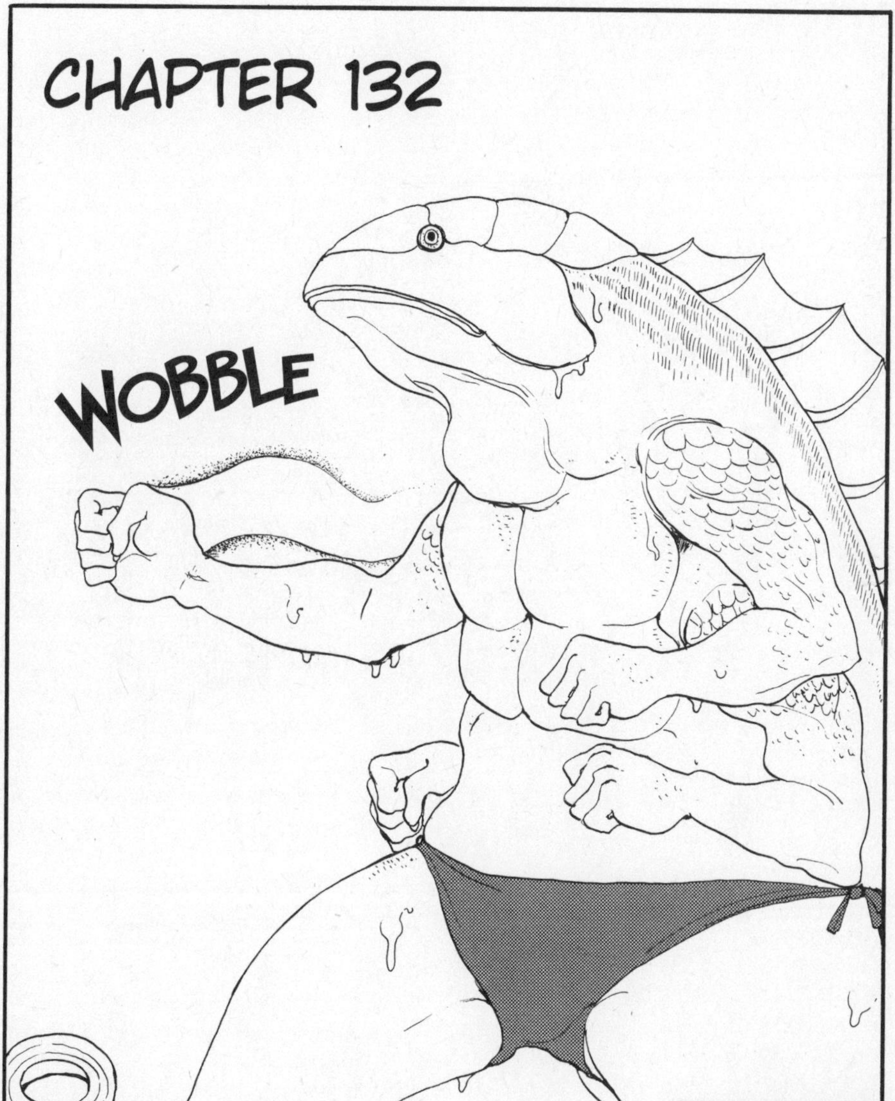
CHAPTER 132
WOBBLE
TAGON

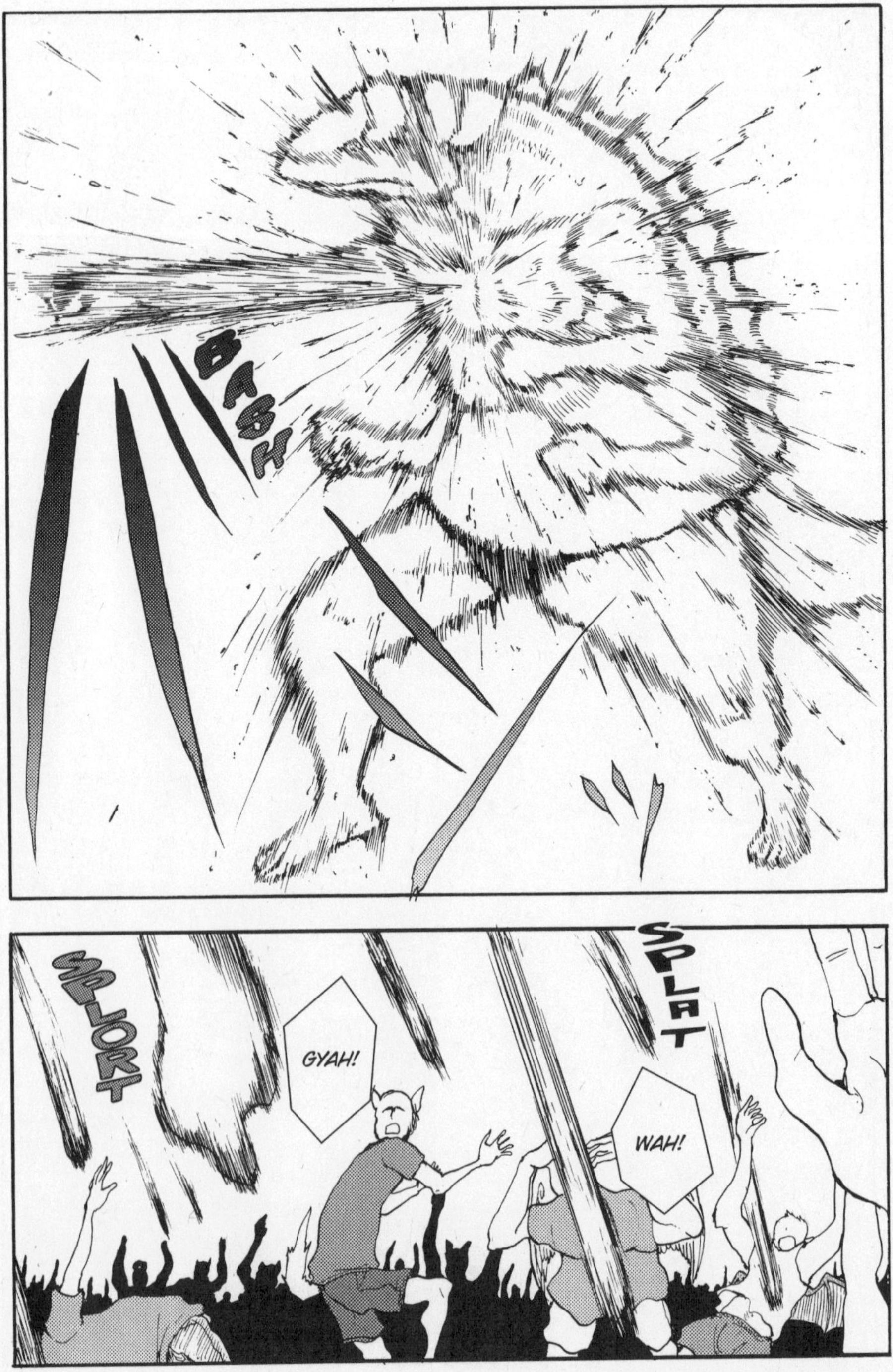
BASH
SPLAT
WAH!
GYAH!
SPLORT

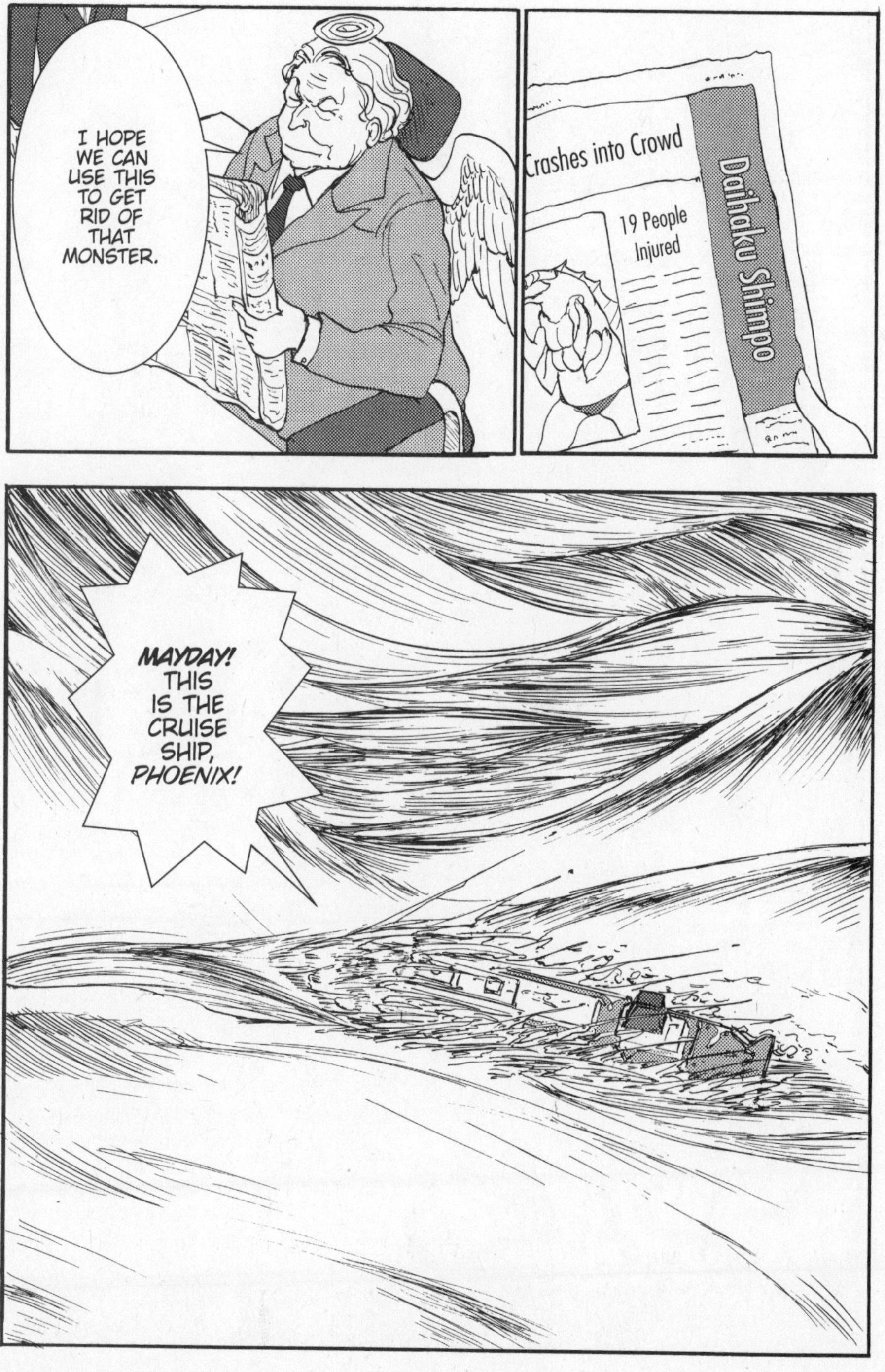
Daihoku Shimpo
Crashes into Crowd
19 People Injured
I HOPE WE CAN USE THIS TO GET RID OF THAT MONSTER.
MAYDAY! THIS IS THE CRUISE SHIP, PHOENIX!

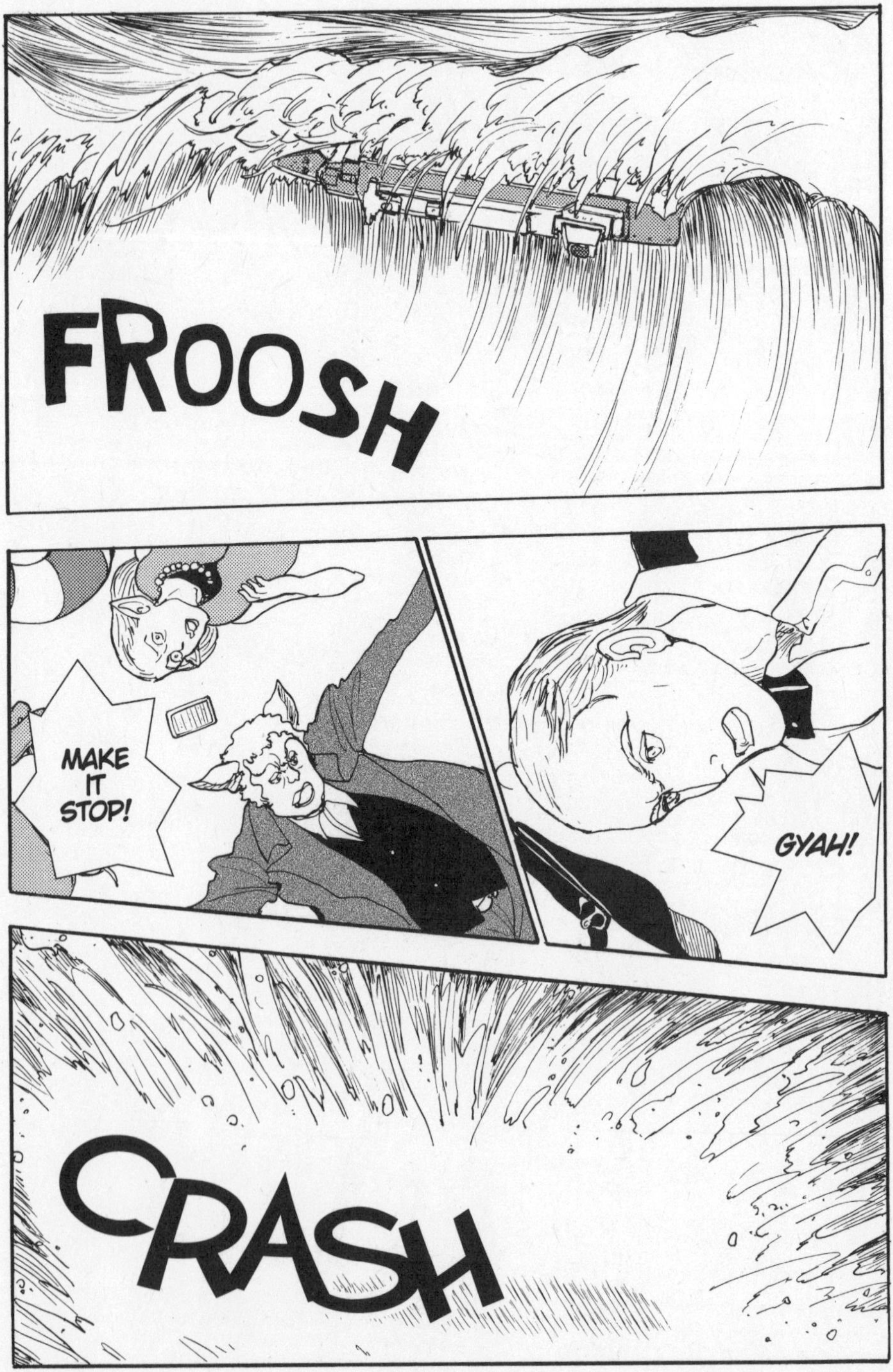
FROOSH
GYAH!
MAKE IT STOP!
CRASH

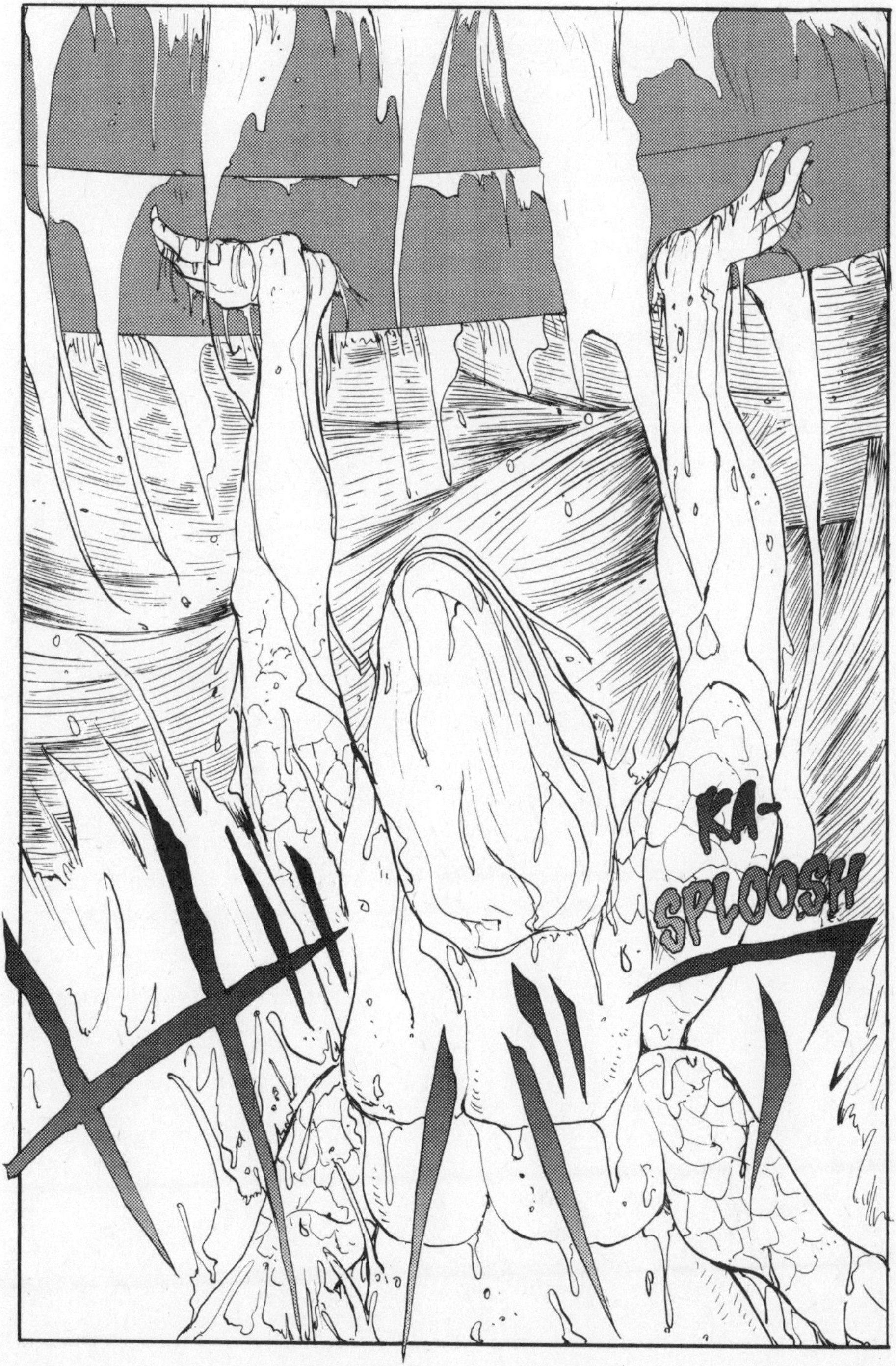
KA-
SPLOOSH

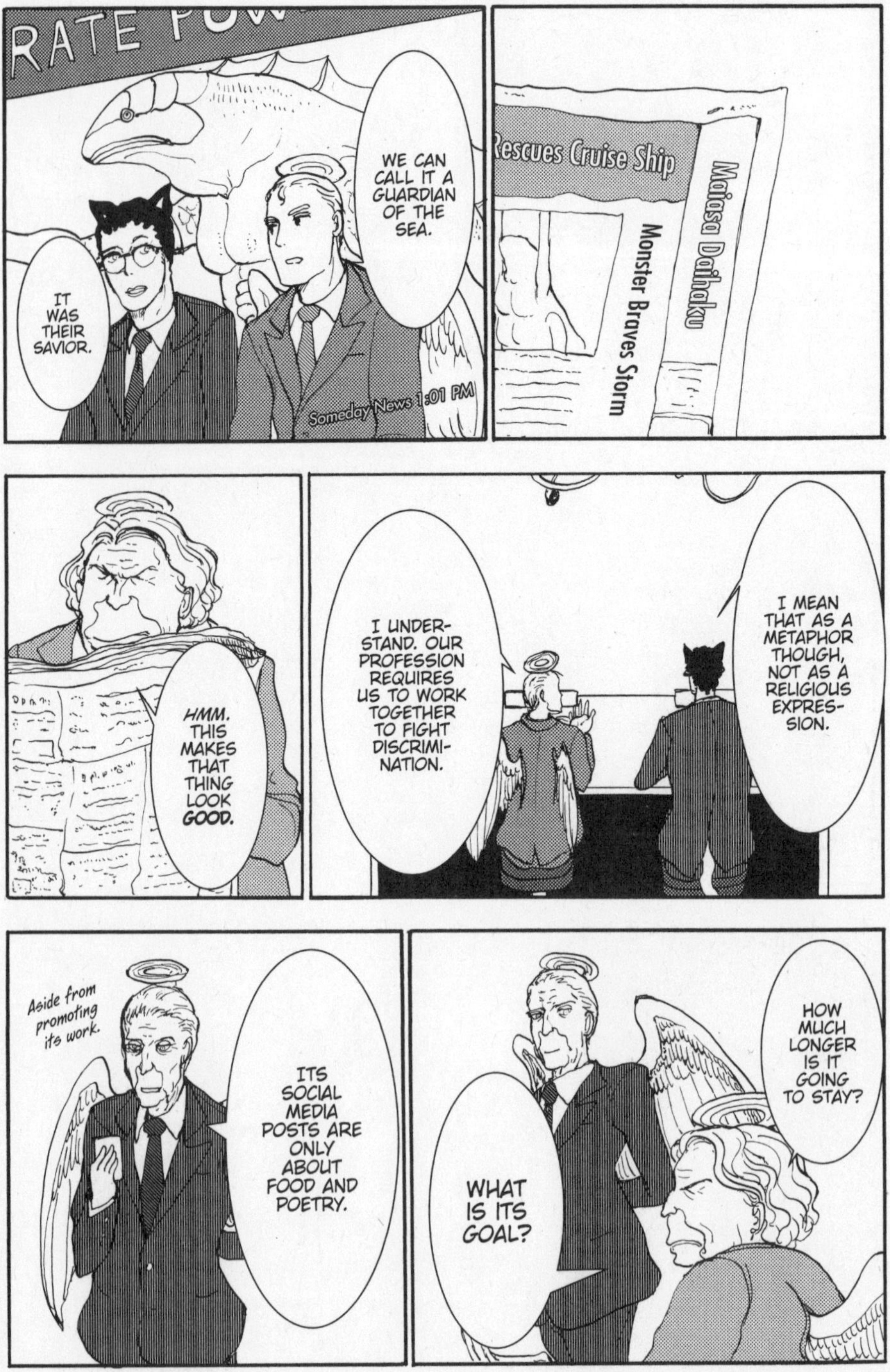
Rescues Cruise Ship
Maiasa Daihaku
Monster Braves Storm
RATE POW
WE CAN CALL IT A GUARDIAN OF THE SEA.
IT WAS THEIR SAVIOR.
Someday News 1:01 PM
I MEAN THAT AS A METAPHOR THOUGH, NOT AS A RELIGIOUS EXPRESSION.
I UNDERSTAND. OUR PROFESSION REQUIRES US TO WORK TOGETHER TO FIGHT DISCRIMINATION.
HMM. THIS MAKES THAT THING LOOK GOOD.
HOW MUCH LONGER IS IT GOING TO STAY?
WHAT IS ITS GOAL?
ITS SOCIAL MEDIA POSTS ARE ONLY ABOUT FOOD AND POETRY.
Aside from promoting its work.

YOU MEAN IT CAN USE THE *INTERNET?*
WE LIVE IN A TIME WHEN FROGS USE VIDEO-SHARING SITES TO FURTHER THEIR CAUSE.
IT WAS USING A REGULAR SMARTPHONE BEFORE SOMEONE GAVE IT A GIGANTIC ONE AS A PROMOTIONAL STUNT. IT'S PRETTY GOOD WITH ITS HEAD AND FINGERS.
WHY CAN'T IT JUST ACT LIKE A MONSTER AND LET US WIPE IT OUT?!
ACTUALLY, WE MIGHT BE ABLE TO MAKE THIS WORK FOR US.
WE CAN START PUBLIC WORKS PROJECTS UNDER THE GUISE OF STRENGTHENING OUR DEMOCRACY THROUGH OUR INFRASTRUCTURE.
WE'LL BE ABLE TO USE IT AS A PRETEXT FOR A NATIONAL DEBT INCREASE, GOVERNMENT BOND ISSUANCE, AND TAX HIKES.
The opposition will be denounced as segregationists.
THERE'S NOTHING WE OR ANY OTHER COUNTRY CAN DO AGAINST SOMEONE THAT BOASTS OF DEMOCRACY AND CAN'T BE TAKEN OUT WITH MISSILES.
ALL THAT'S LEFT IS TO MAKE THE BEST OF THE SITUATION.
THIS COULD MEAN A THIRD TERM, EVEN FOR AN UNPOPULAR PRESIDENT LIKE YOU.

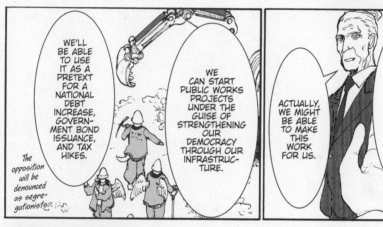

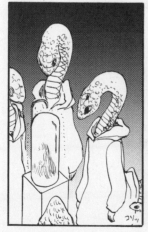

WHAT MOVE SHOULD WE MAKE WITH TAGON?
THIS INDECISIVENESS IS VERY UNUSUAL FOR US.
INDECISION ITSELF IS A RARITY WORTH RECORDING.
IT PROBABLY SHOULD HAVE BEEN RETURNED TO THE SEA, REGARDLESS OF CONTEXT.
SHOULD WE SEND IT BACK ONCE UNIVERSAL HEALTH INSURANCE IS IMPLEMENTED?
THAT WOULD GIVE TOO MUCH WEIGHT TO A SINGLE SYSTEM.
WHAT IF WE SIMPLY LET IT RUN ITS COURSE?
HOW CAN WE ACCOMMODATE ITS UNPRECEDENTED RARITY?
METAPHYSICALLY IT MAY SEEM LIKE A MATCH, BUT IT'S QUESTIONABLE AS A REALISTIC POLICY.
BEING UNABLE TO COME UP WITH A CLEAR DIRECTION IS PRACTICALLY THE SAME AS LETTING IT RUN ITS COURSE.
PERHAPS WE SHOULD EXPERIMENT WITH HOW MAMMALIAN DEMOCRACY CAN SUPPORT THE INCLUSION OF IMMIGRANTS.
WHAT IT COMES DOWN TO IS LETTING IT RUN ITS COURSE.

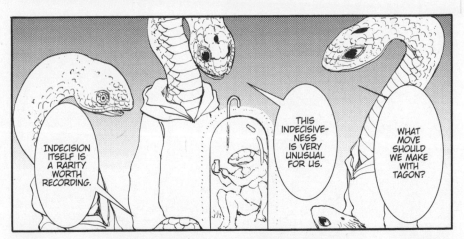

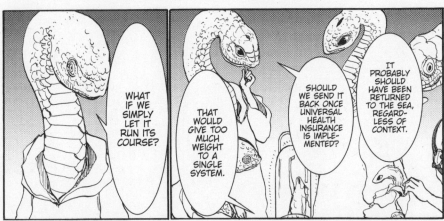

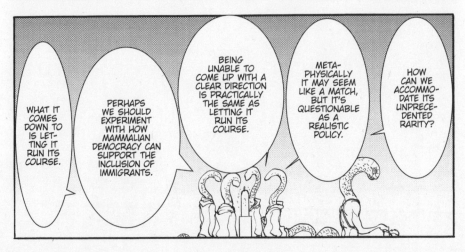

A CentaUr's Life

HISTORY OF ARCHITECTURE IN JAPAN AND OTHER COUNTRIES: < 5 > MULTI-FAMILY HOUSING

TRADITIONAL HOUSES WITH WELLS AND CHARCOAL HEARTHS BECAME INEFFICIENT AS MODERN INFRASTRUCTURE GREW MORE WIDESPREAD. IN THE PROCESS OF BUILDING METROPOLITAN AREAS, HOUSING CRISES BEGAN TO GROW AS THE POPULATION BALLOONED AND HOUSING TRADITIONALLY DESIGNED FOR LARGE FAMILIES BECAME INADEQUATE. THE CREATION OF RESIDENTIAL ZONES IN POOR SURROUNDING AREAS, SUCH AS THE ONE DESCRIBED IN *IN DARKEST CAPITAL*, BECAME A MAJOR ISSUE FOR METROPOLITAN GOVERNMENTS IN TERMS OF SANITATION AND FIRE PREVENTION. THIS WAS WHEN THE IDEA OF MULTI-FAMILY HOUSING WAS CONCEIVED. A SPRAWL OF WOODEN ONE-STORIED ROWHOUSES ON UNSUITABLE LAND WAS DEMOLISHED AND REPLACED WITH SOLID REINFORCED CONCRETE AND QUAKE-RESISTANT HIGH-RISE HOUSING TO ACCOMMODATE A LARGER POPULATION. THIS ALSO IMPROVED FIRE AND DISASTER PREVENTION WITHIN THE CITY. ADDITIONALLY, THE CREATION OF COURTYARDS AS PARKS WAS NOT JUST A SELLING POINT, BUT ALSO HELPED TO ESTABLISH QUALITY OF LIFE AND WEALTH OF CULTURE. THESE HOUSING UNITS WERE BUILT WITH UTILITIES SUCH AS INDOOR PLUMBING AND ELECTRIC AND GAS LINES AS THE PIONEER OF MODERN HOUSING.

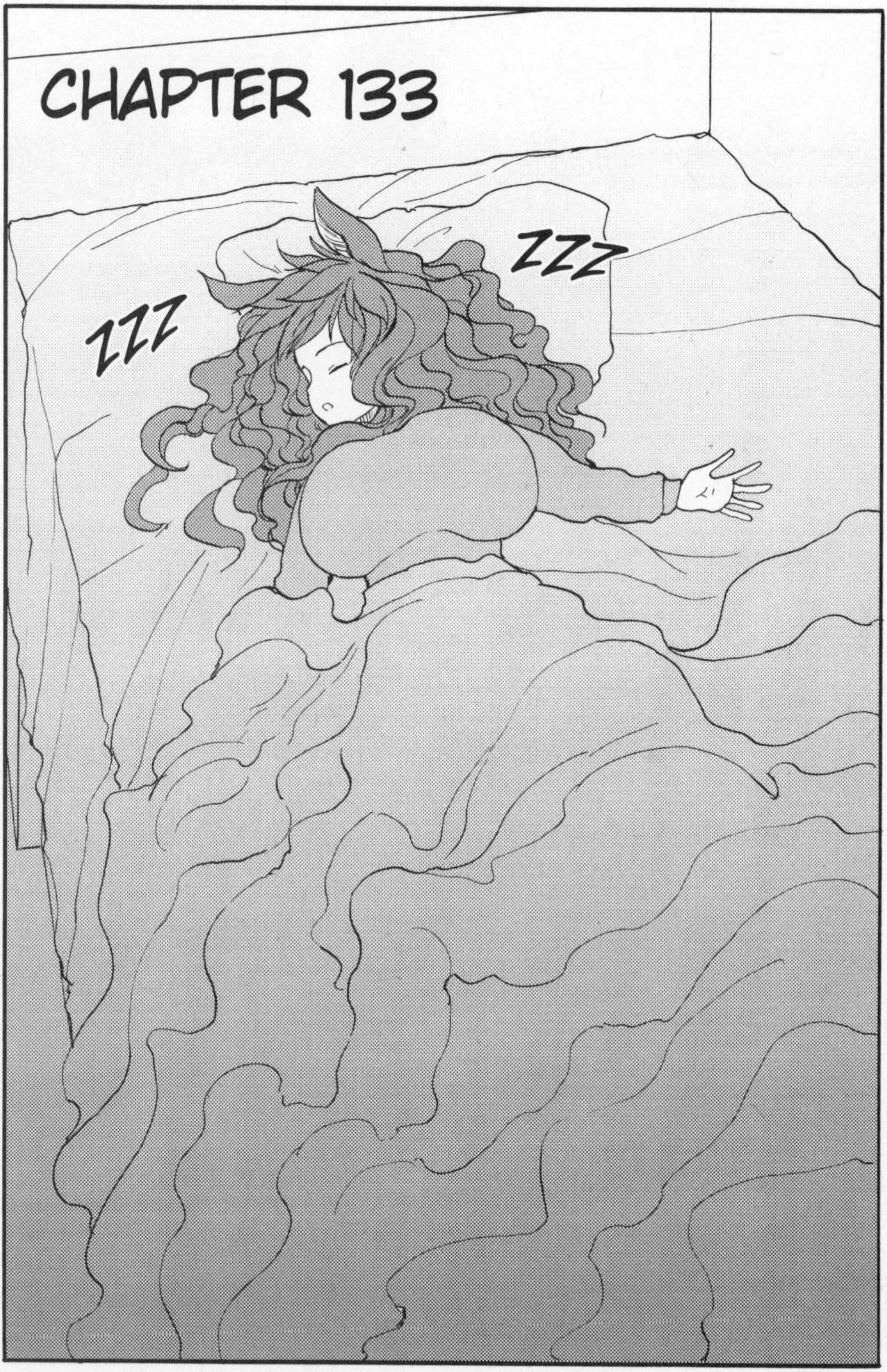
CHAPTER 133
ZZZ
ZZZ

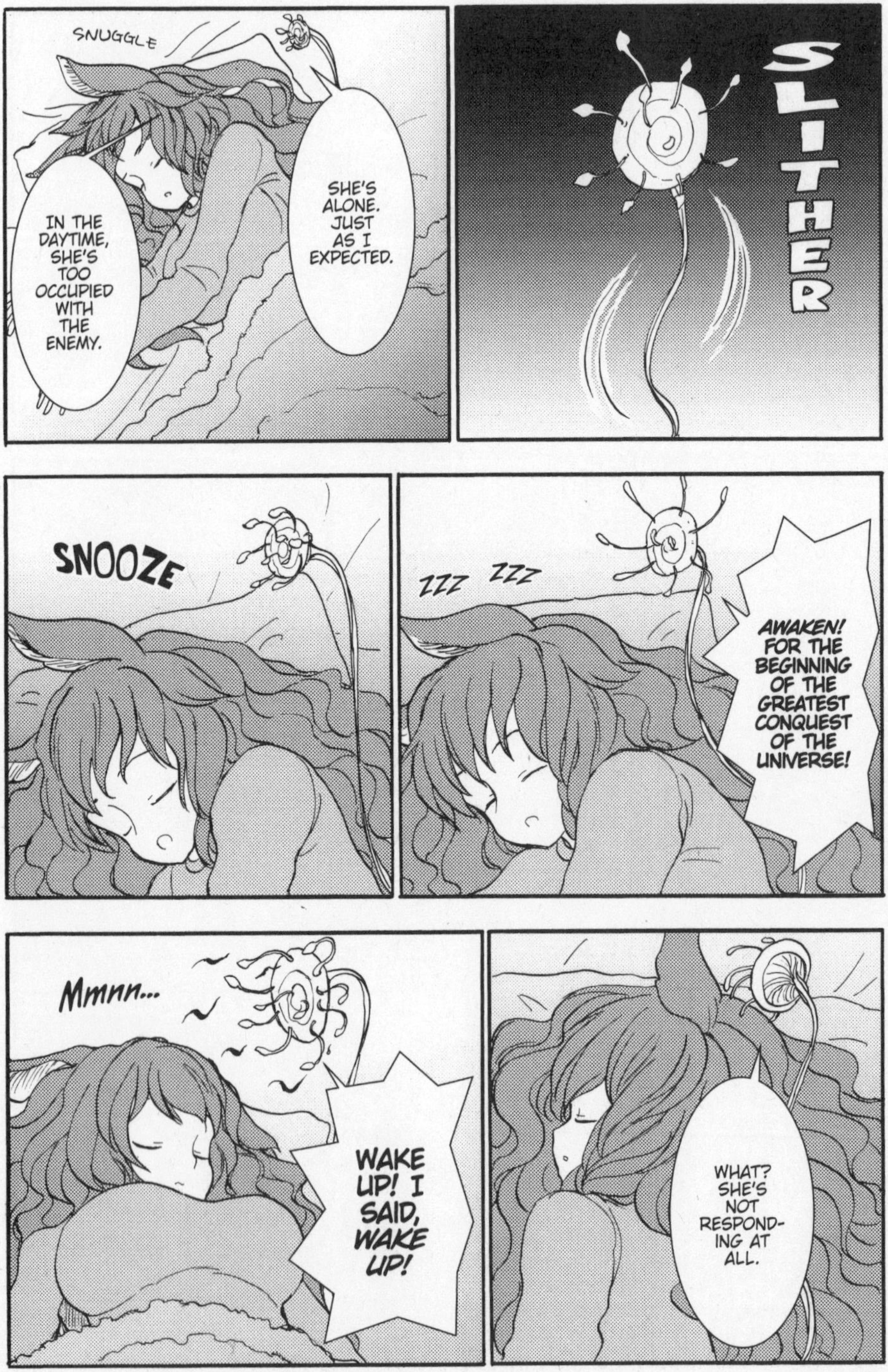
SLITHER
SNUGGLE
SHE'S ALONE. JUST AS I EXPECTED.
IN THE DAYTIME, SHE'S TOO OCCUPIED WITH THE ENEMY.
ZZZ ZZZ
AWAKEN! FOR THE BEGINNING OF THE GREATEST CONQUEST OF THE UNIVERSE!
SNOOZE
WHAT? SHE'S NOT RESPONDING AT ALL.
Mmnn...
WAKE UP! I SAID, WAKE UP!

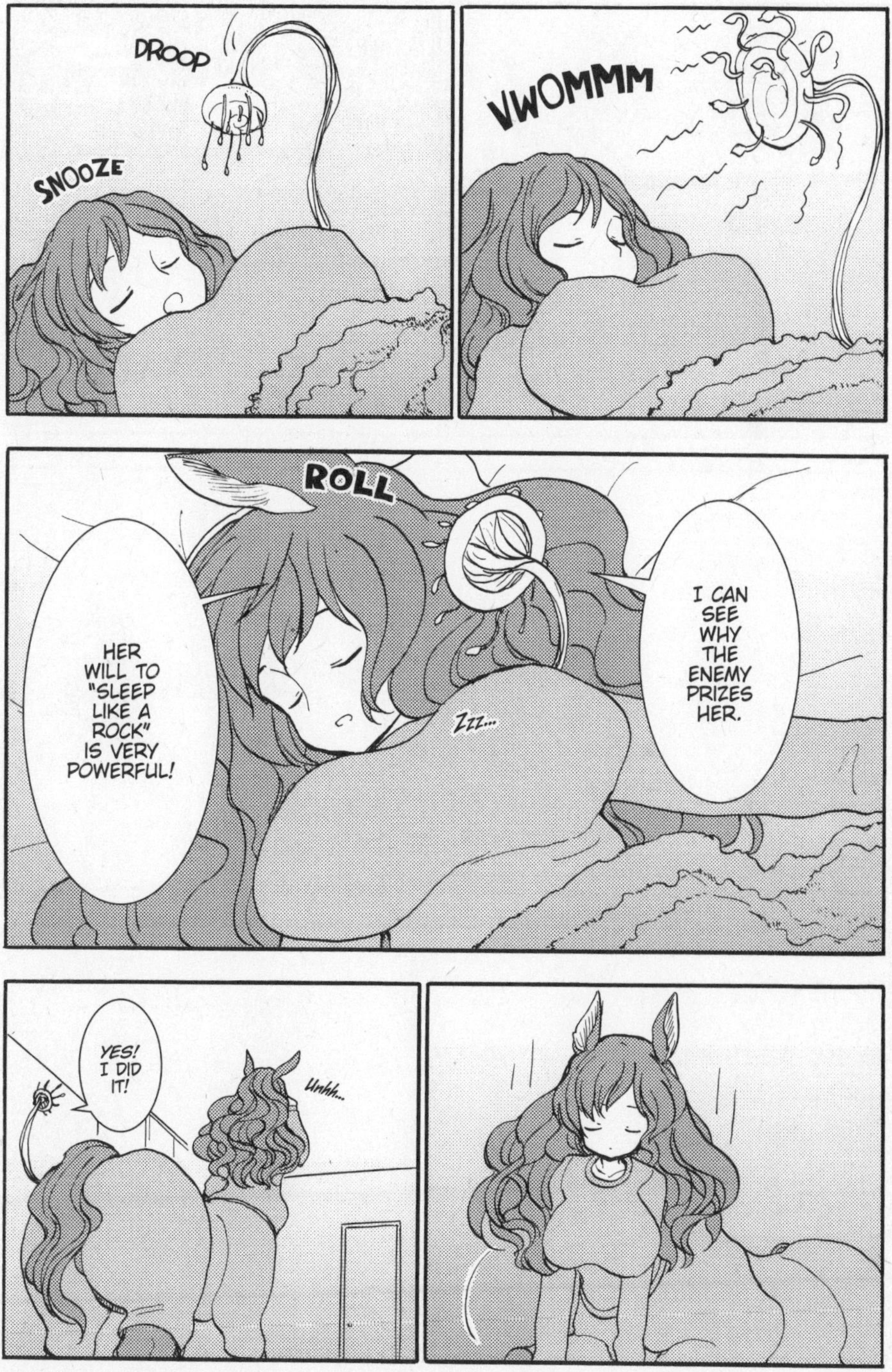
VWOMMM
DROOP
SNOOZE
ROLL
I CAN SEE WHY THE ENEMY PRIZES HER.
Zzz...
HER WILL TO "SLEEP LIKE A ROCK" IS VERY POWERFUL!
Unhh...
YES! I DID IT!

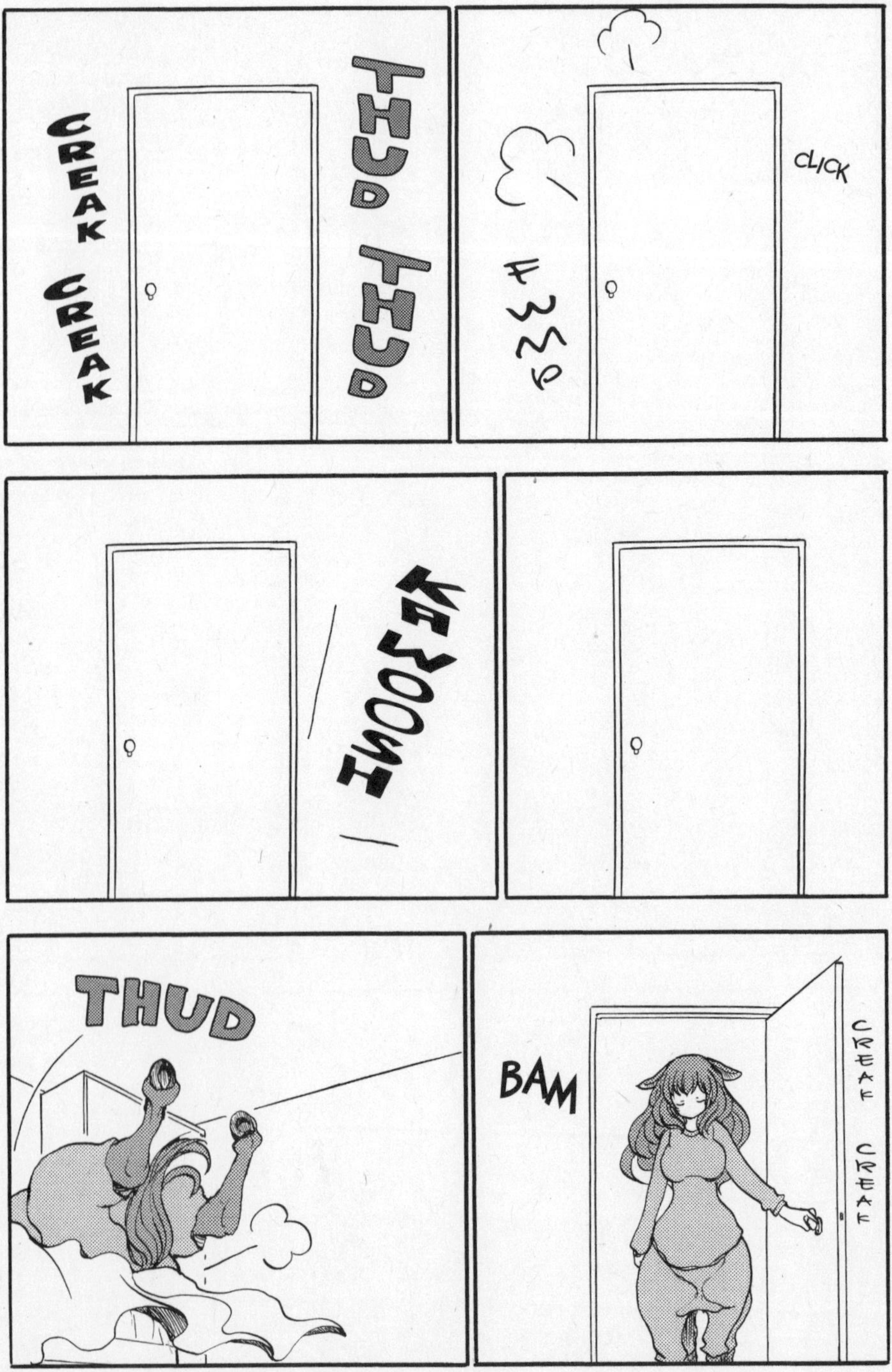
CLICK
FWMP
THUD THUD
CREAK CREAK
KAWOOSH
CREAK CREAK
BAM
THUD

BUT ALSO...

ZLURP

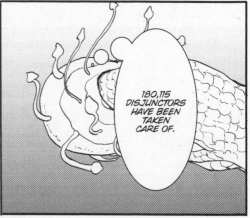

180,115 DISJUNCTORS HAVE BEEN TAKEN CARE OF.

BURP

FWP

I CAN SEE WHY OUR ENEMY WOULD EYE HER...

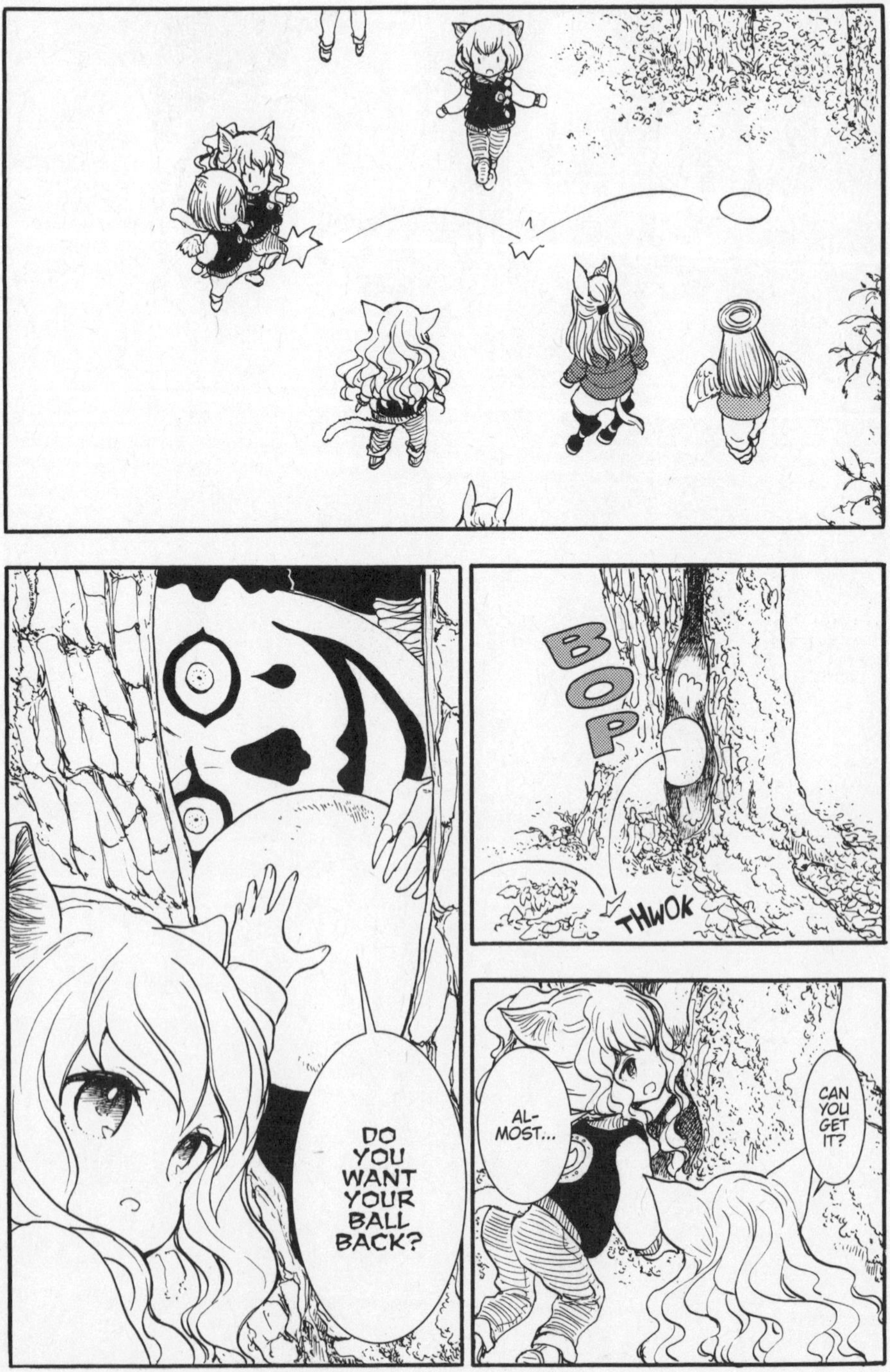
BOP
THWOK
CAN YOU GET IT?
AL-MOST...
DO YOU WANT YOUR BALL BACK?

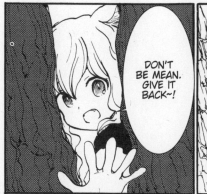

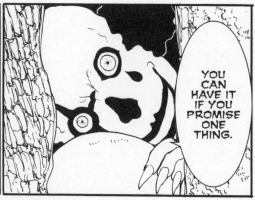

YOU CAN HAVE IT IF YOU PROMISE ONE THING.
DON'T BE MEAN. GIVE IT BACK~!
The ball came back...
THAT'S A PROMISE.
YOUR LITTLE SISTER IN EXCHANGE FOR THE BALL. I'LL COME FOR HER AT THE WITCHING HOUR.
WHAT'S WRONG?
THERE WAS A WEIRD OLD MAN IN THERE, BUT HE'S GONE NOW.

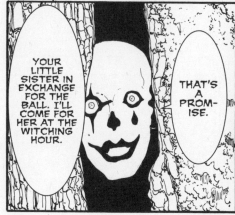

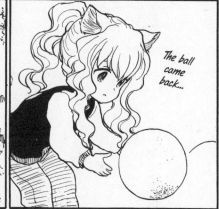

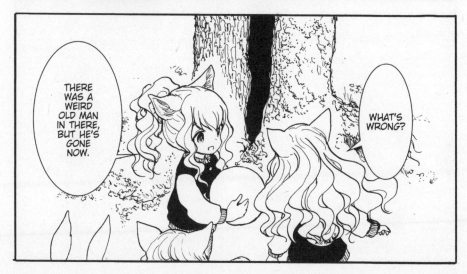

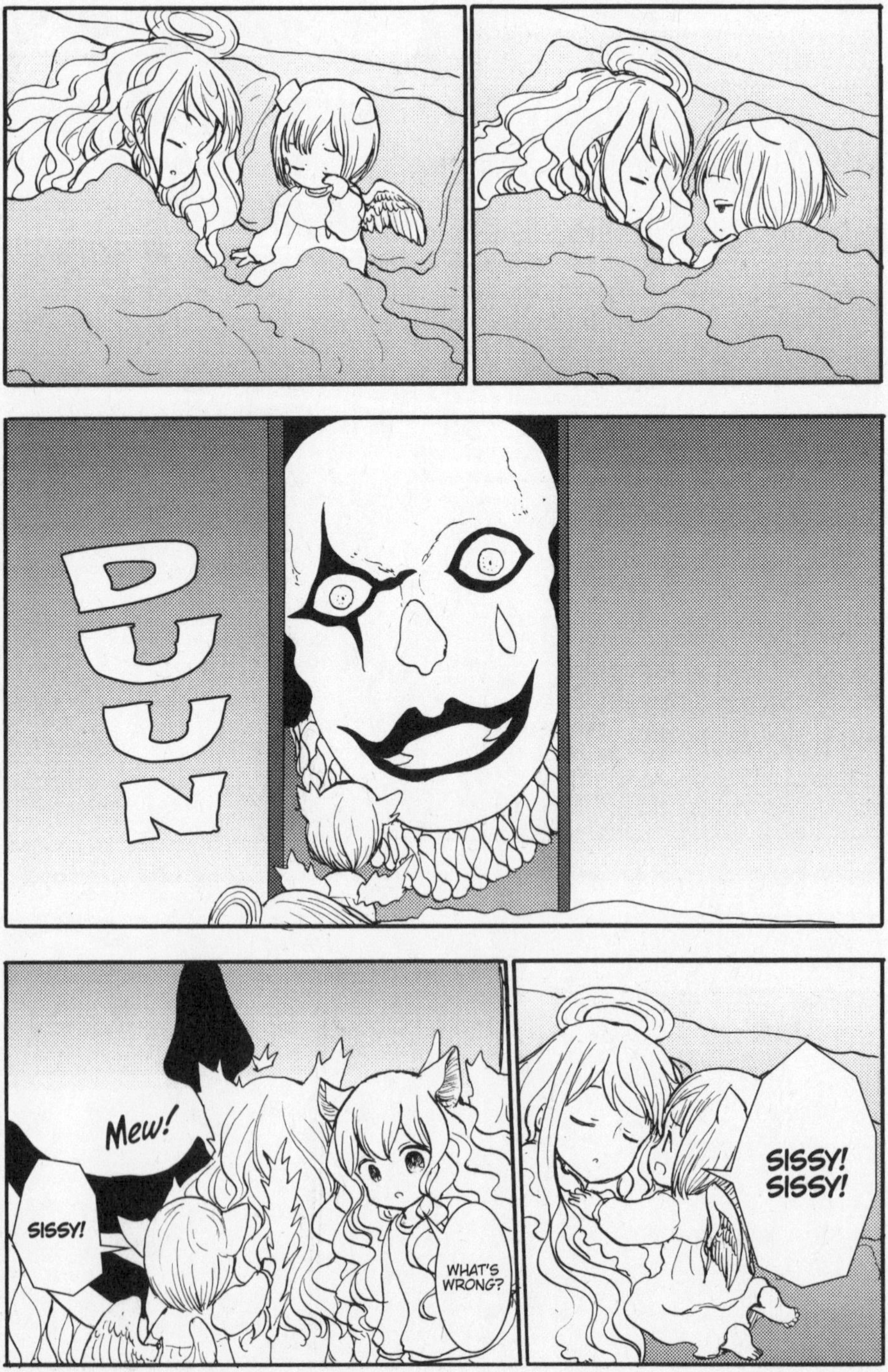
DJUN
SISSY! SISSY!
WHAT'S WRONG?
Mew!
SISSY!

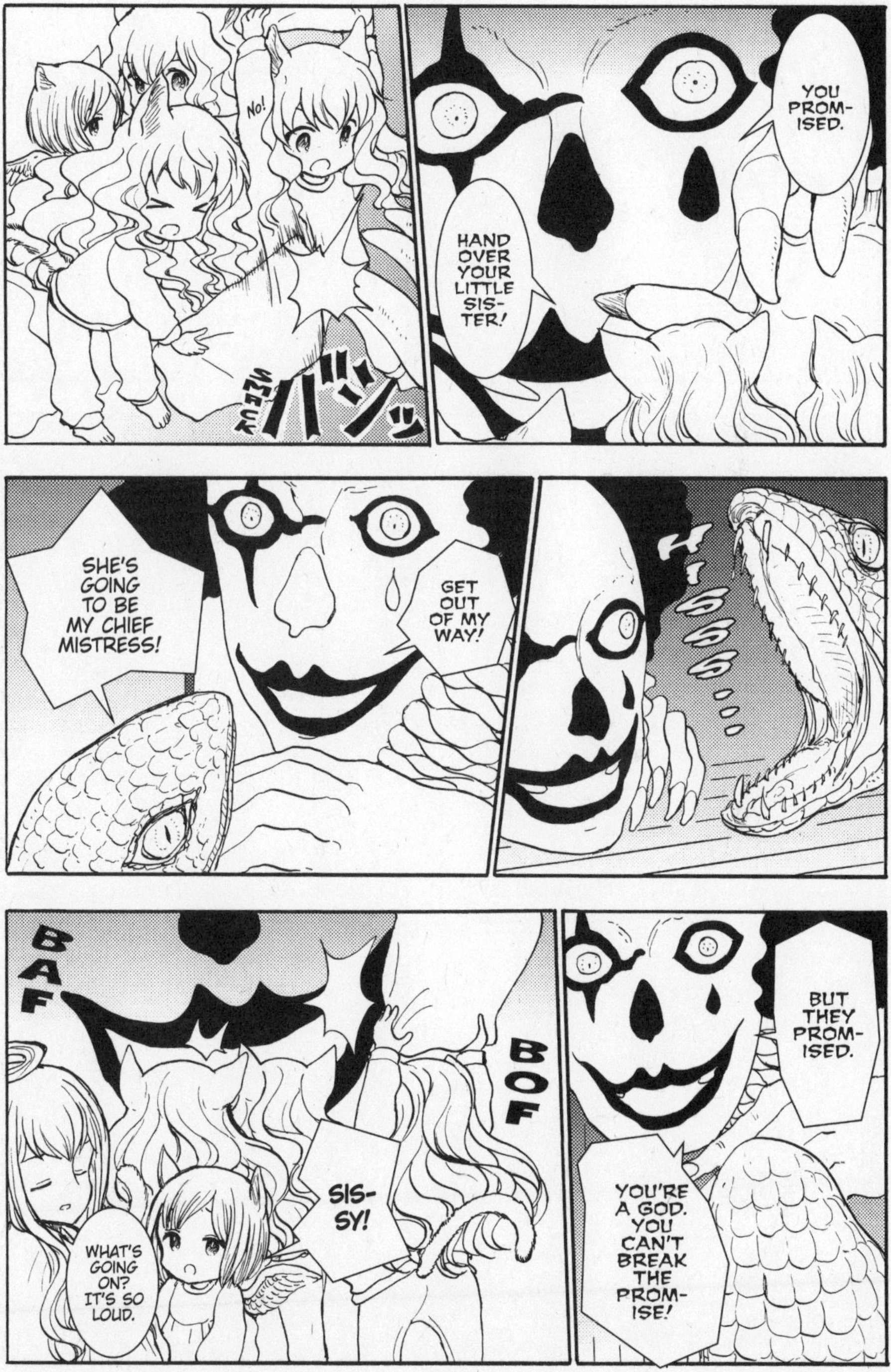
YOU PROMISED.
HAND OVER YOUR LITTLE SISTER!
No!
SMACK
HISSS...
GET OUT OF MY WAY!
SHE'S GOING TO BE MY CHIEF MISTRESS!
BUT THEY PROMISED.
YOU'RE A GOD. YOU CAN'T BREAK THE PROMISE!
BOF
BAF
SISSY!
WHAT'S GOING ON? IT'S SO LOUD.

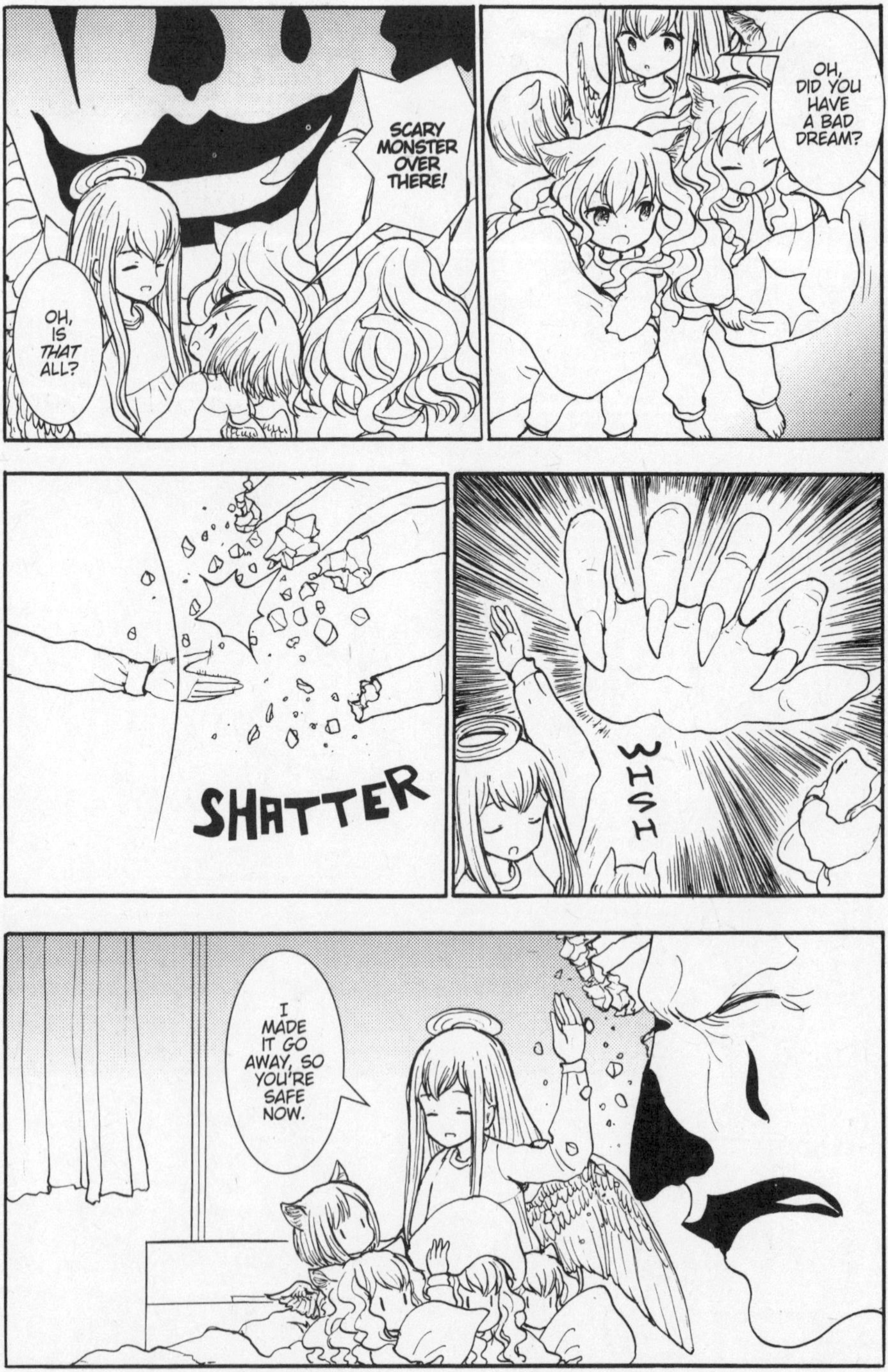
OH, DID YOU HAVE A BAD DREAM?
SCARY MONSTER OVER THERE!
OH, IS *THAT* ALL?
WHSH
SHATTER
I MADE IT GO AWAY, SO YOU'RE SAFE NOW.

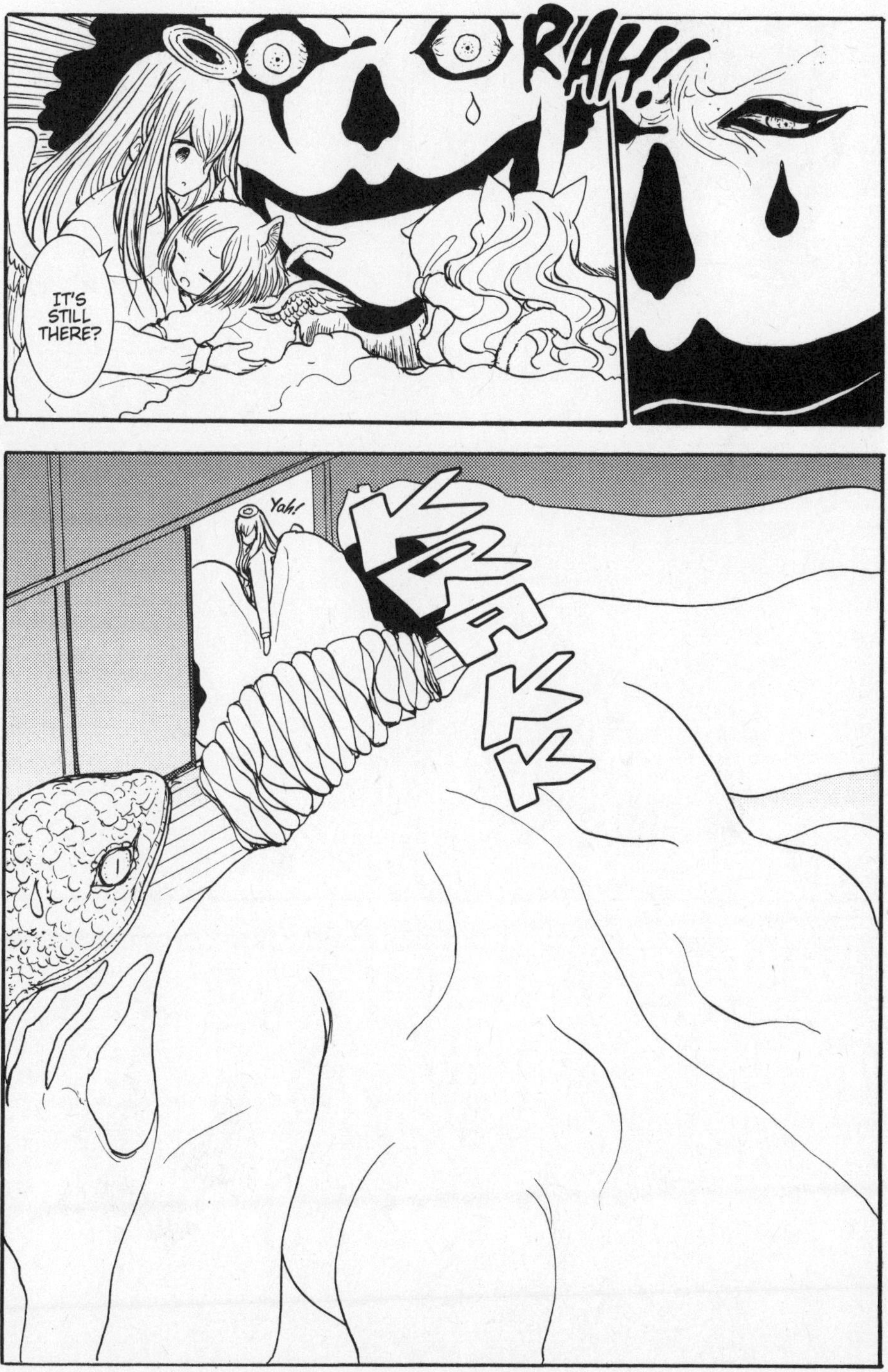
RAH!!
IT'S STILL THERE?
Yah!
WHAKK

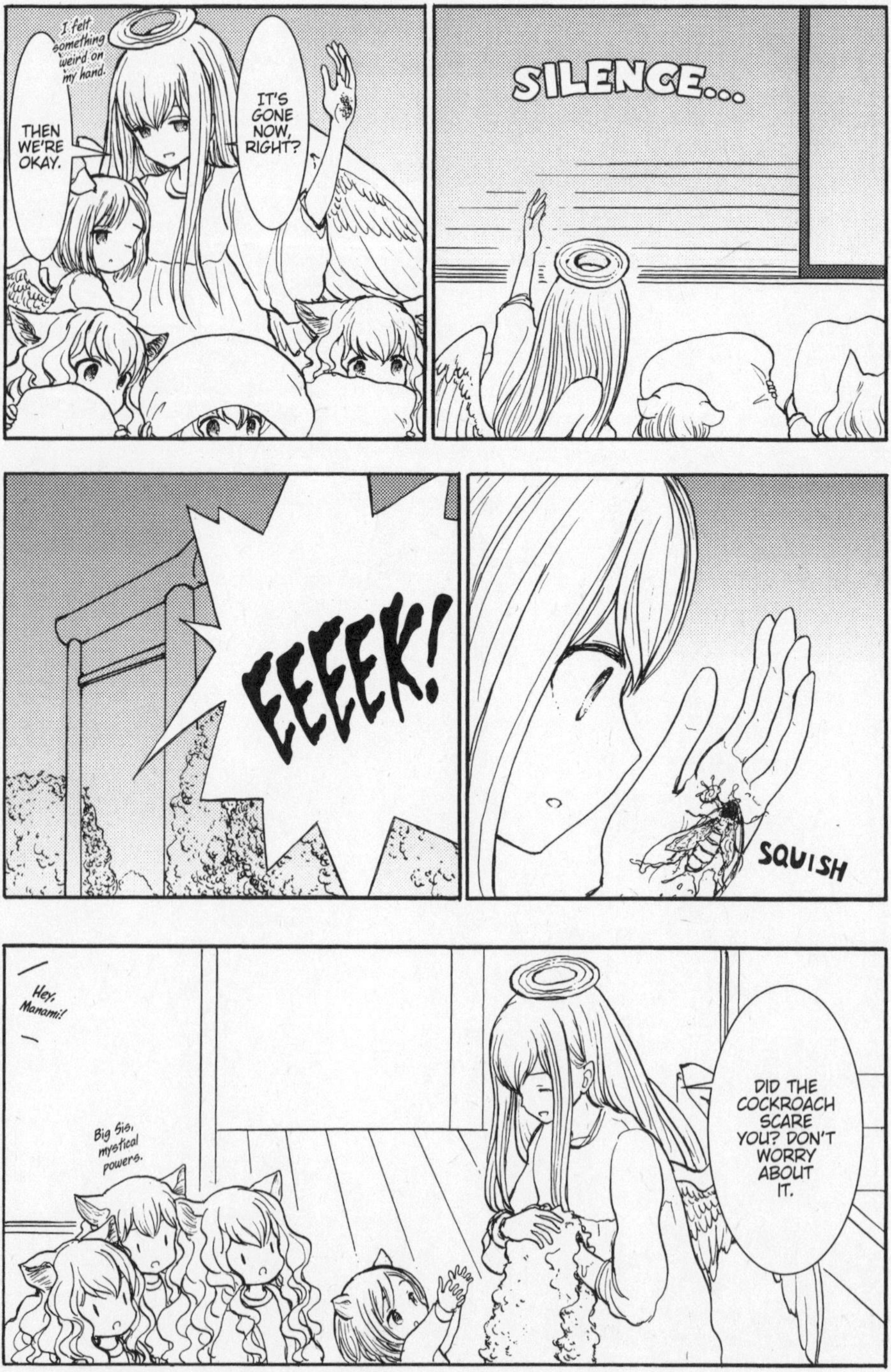
SILENCE...
IT'S GONE NOW, RIGHT?
I felt something weird on my hand.
THEN WE'RE OKAY.
SQUISH
EEEEK!
DID THE COCKROACH SCARE YOU? DON'T WORRY ABOUT IT.
Hey, Manami!
Big Sis, mystical powers.

A Centaur's Life

HISTORY OF ARCHITECTURE IN JAPAN AND OTHER COUNTRIES: < 6 > NATIONAL MUSEUM OF WESTERN ART

JAPAN IS A UTOPIA OF MULTIRACIAL COEXISTENCE, AND THE SOLE PLACE WHERE MERFOLK LIVE. HOWEVER, DURING THE WORLD WARS, MORE EMPHASIS WAS PLACED ON FUNCTIONAL FEATURES THAN ACCESSIBILITY, LEADING TO UNDENIABLE INEQUALITY. AFTER THE WAR, THE NATIONAL MUSEUM OF WESTERN ART WAS CREATED TO DEMONSTRATE THE IDEAL SYMBIOSIS OF THE RACES, AND ITS ARCHITECT, LE CORBUSIER, FOCUSED ON MERFOLK. UNDER THE BELIEF THAT THEY HAD AS MUCH RIGHT TO APPRECIATE ART AS OTHER RACES, RESEARCH WAS DONE ON TRADITIONAL UNDERWATER PALACE ARCHITECTURES, BUT IT WAS DEEMED IMPOSSIBLE TO BUILD A WATERWAY TO BRING MERFOLK TO WORKS OF ART. THIS WAS WHEN THE IDEA OF USING MACHINERY TO TRANSPORT MERFOLK WAS CONCEIVED. IN THE ACTUAL CONSTRUCTION, CORBUSIER'S JAPANESE APPRENTICES MADE REVISIONS TO THE ORIGINAL PLAN FOR FEASIBILITY, WHICH ELIMINATED SOME INITIAL ELEMENTS, SUCH AS LIMITLESS EXTENSIBILITY. DESPITE THIS, THE NATIONAL MUSEUM OF WESTERN ART WAS INSCRIBED ON THE WORLD HERITAGE LIST AS A SYMBOL OF EQUALITY.

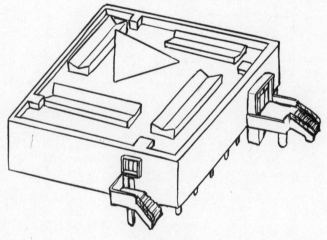

CHAPTER 134

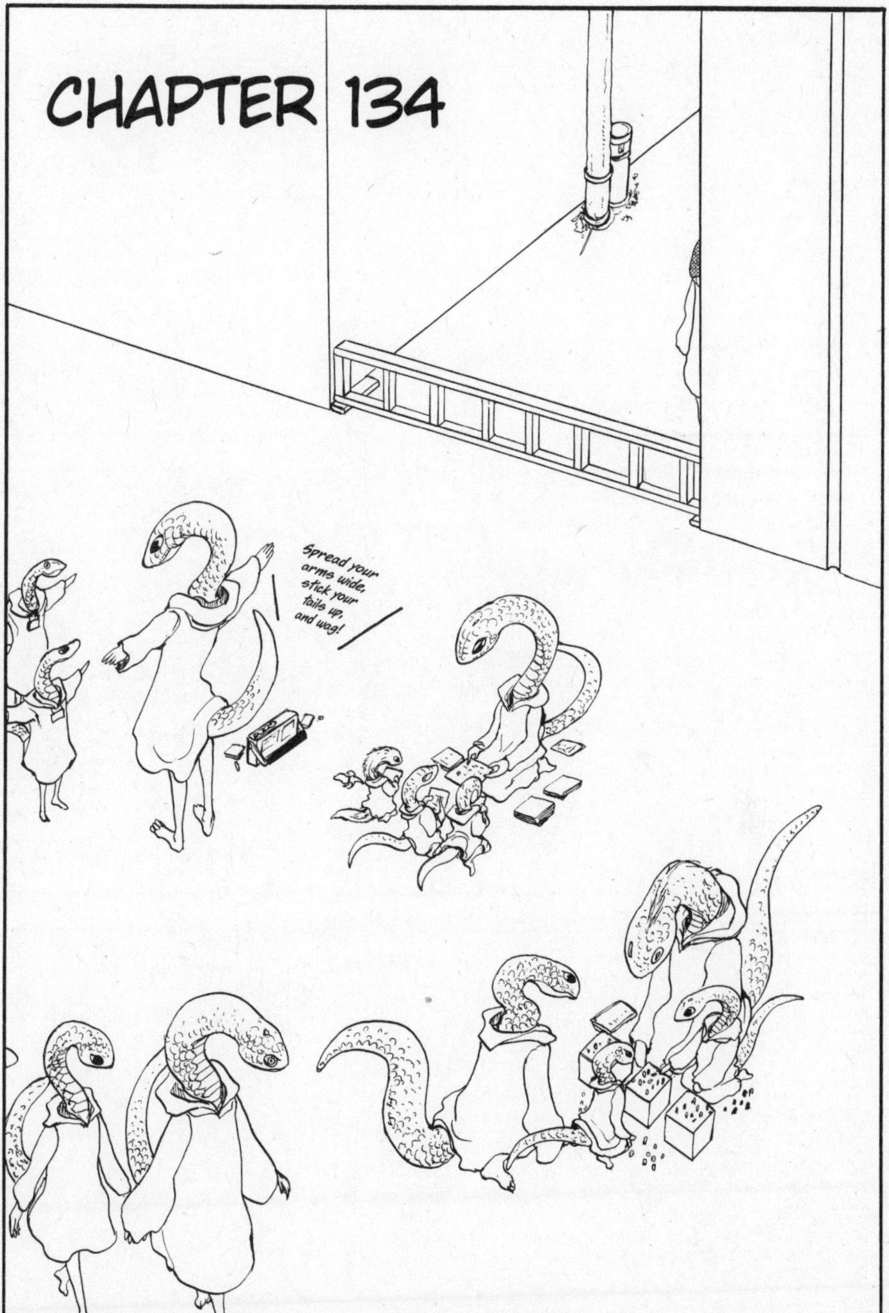
Spread your arms wide, stick your tails up, and wag!

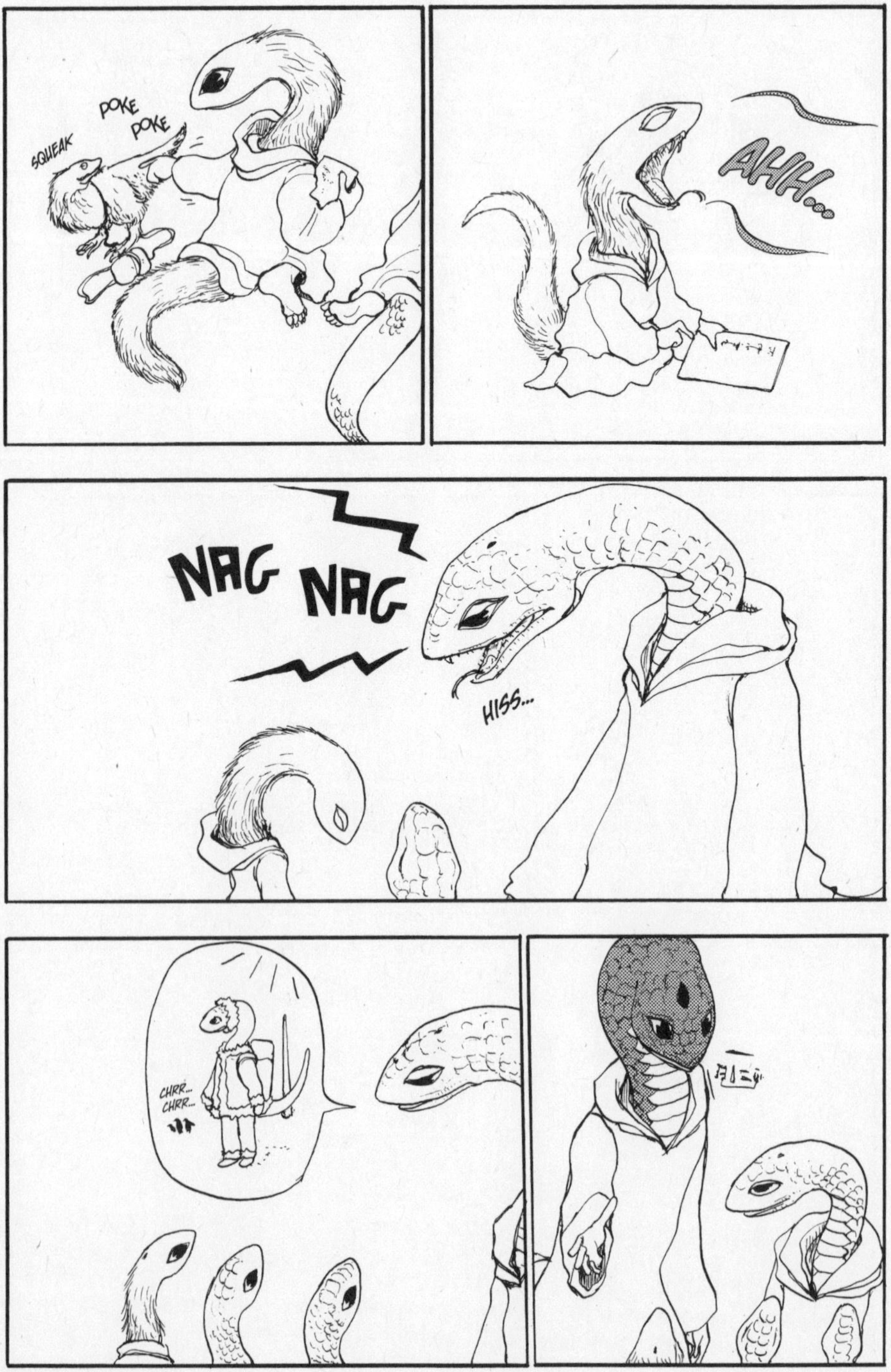
AHH...
POKE POKE
SQUEAK
NAG NAG
HISS...
CHRR... CHRR...

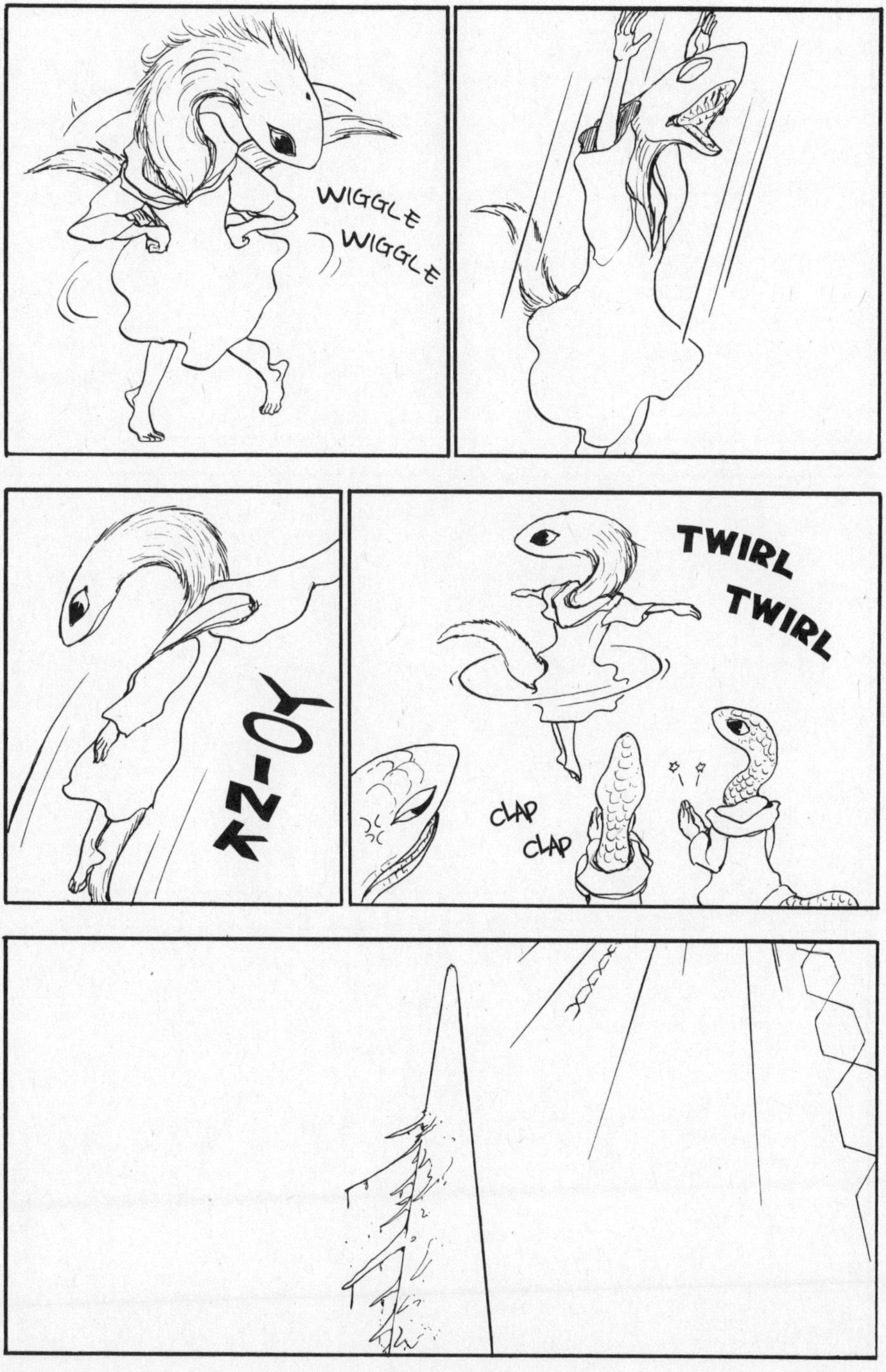
WIGGLE
WIGGLE
TWIRL
TWIRL
CLAP
CLAP
YOINK

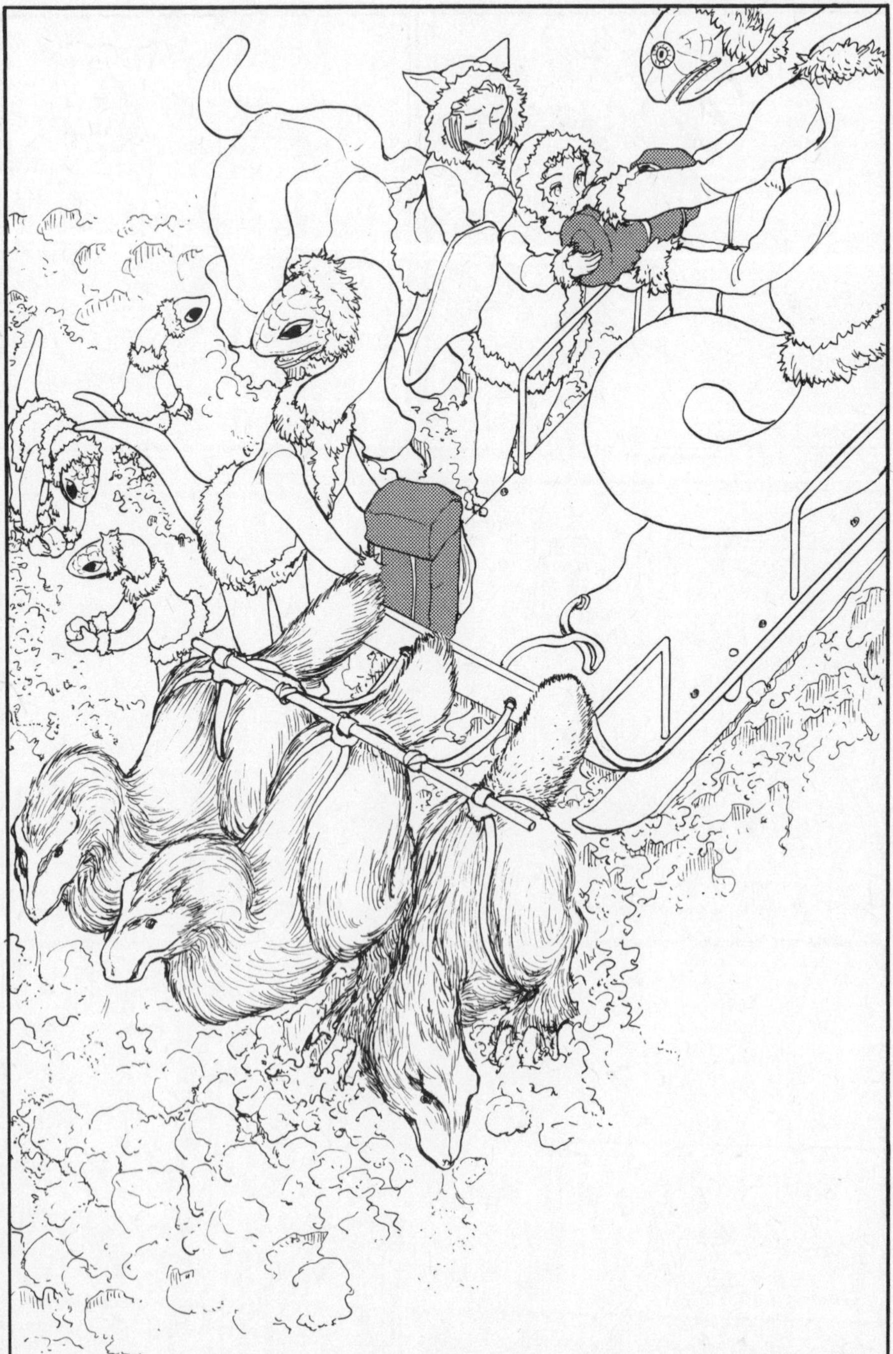

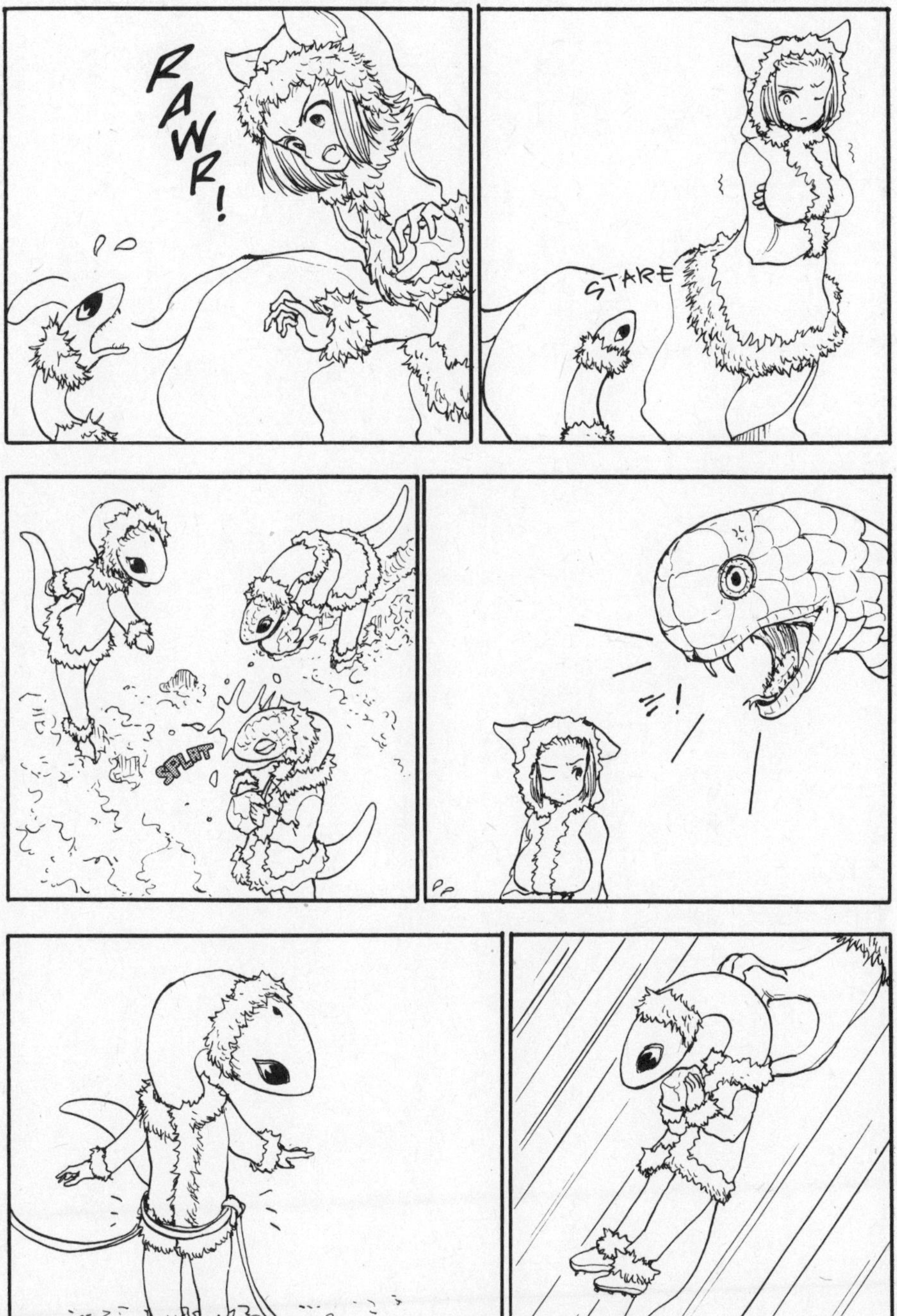
STARE
RAWR!
SPLIT

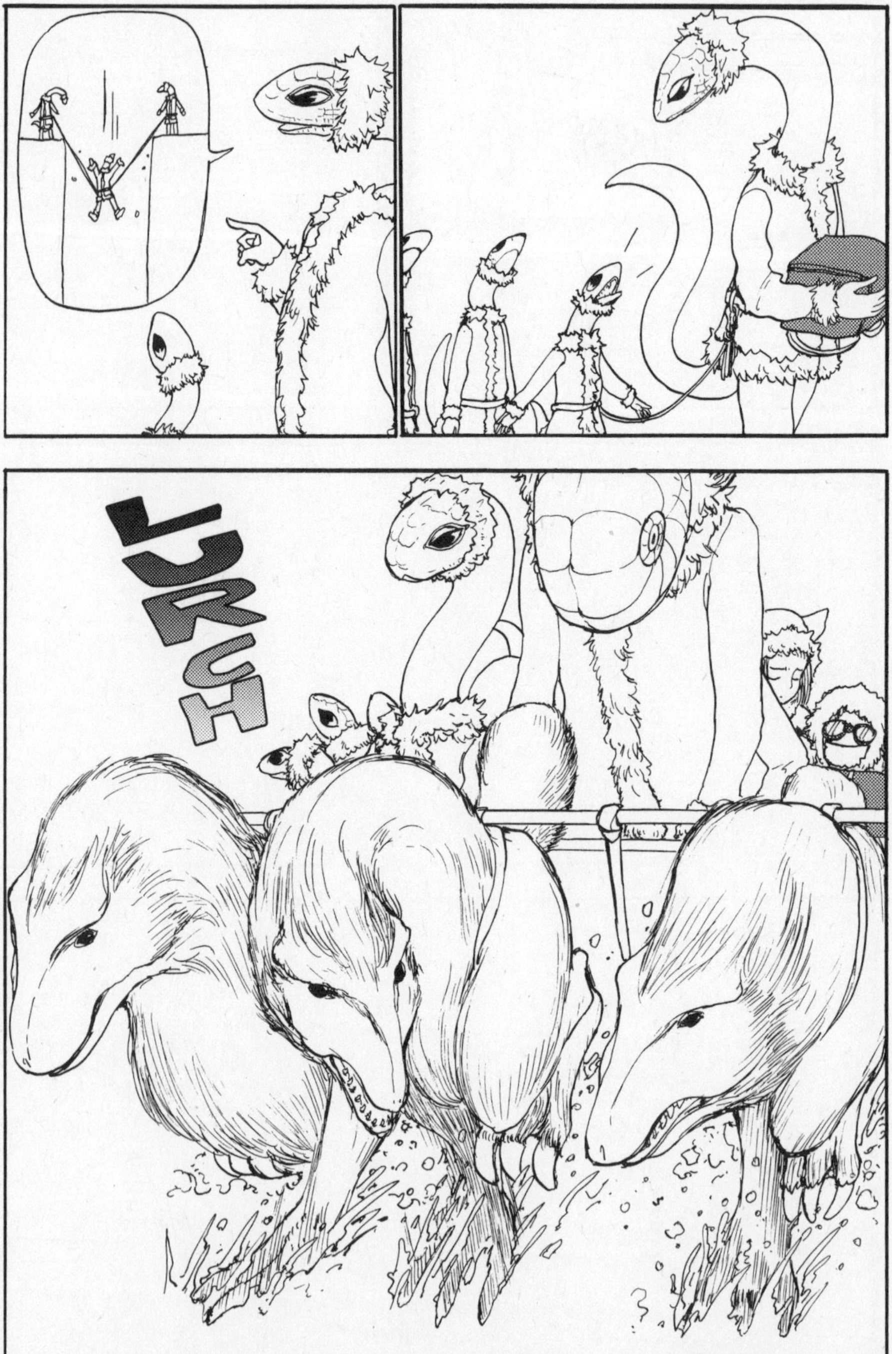
LURCH

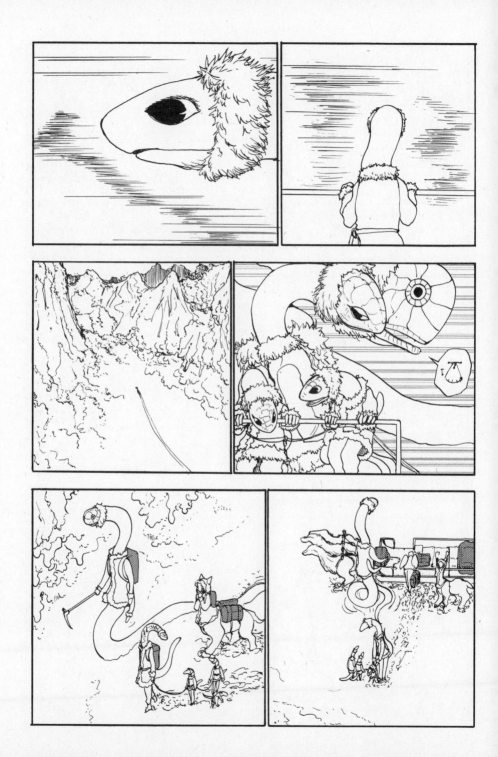

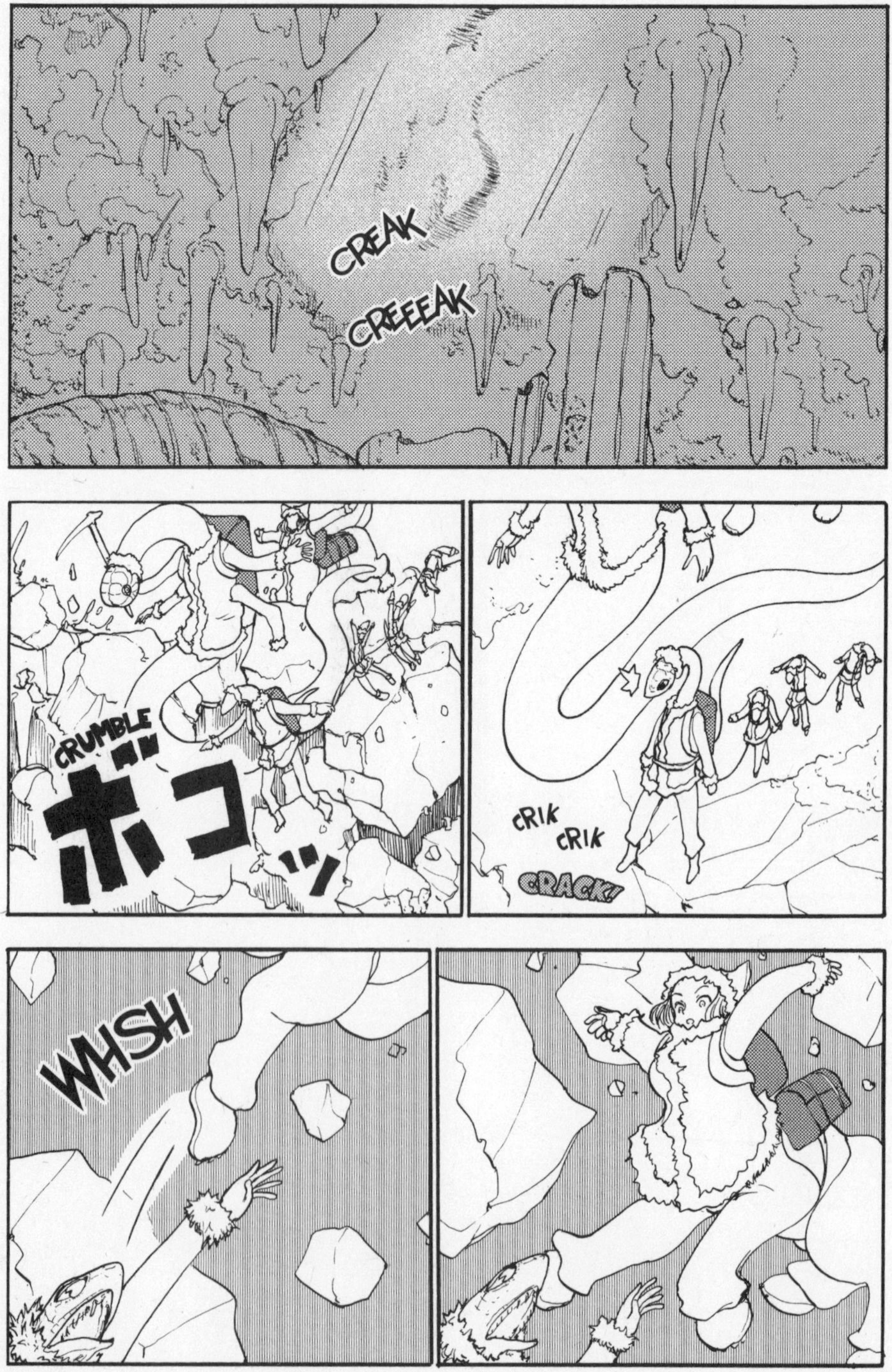
CREAK
CREEEAK
CRIK
CRIK
CRACK!
CRUMBLE
ボコッ
WHSH

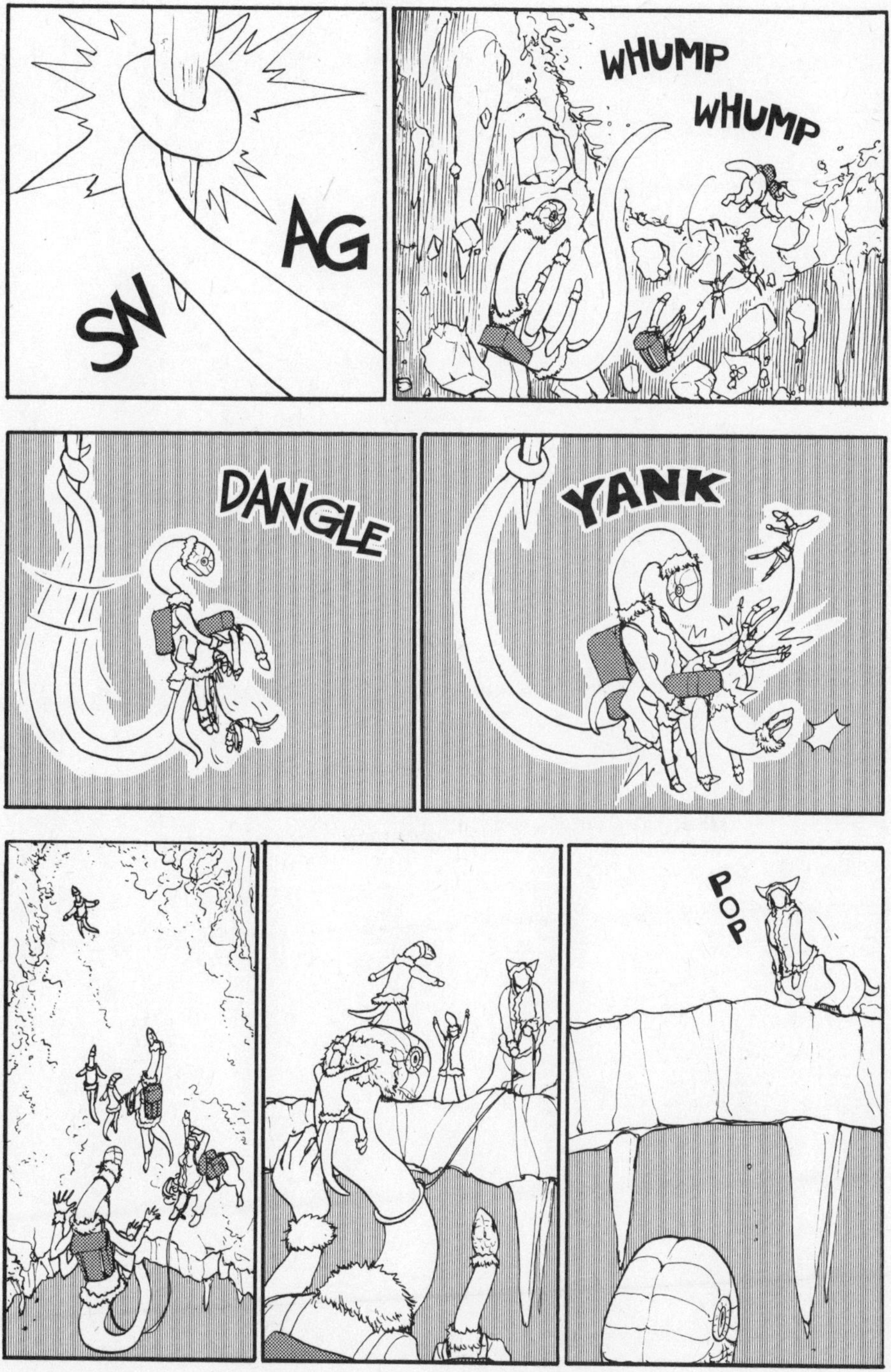

WHUMP
WHUMP
SN
AG
YANK
DANGLE
POP

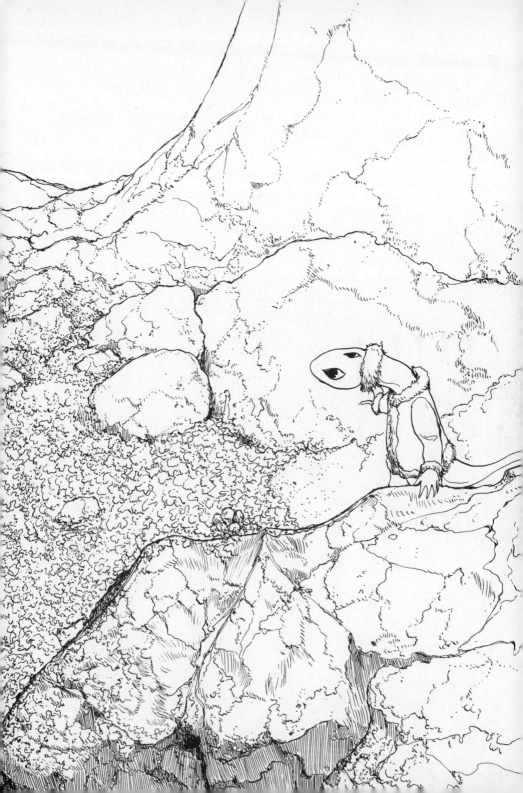

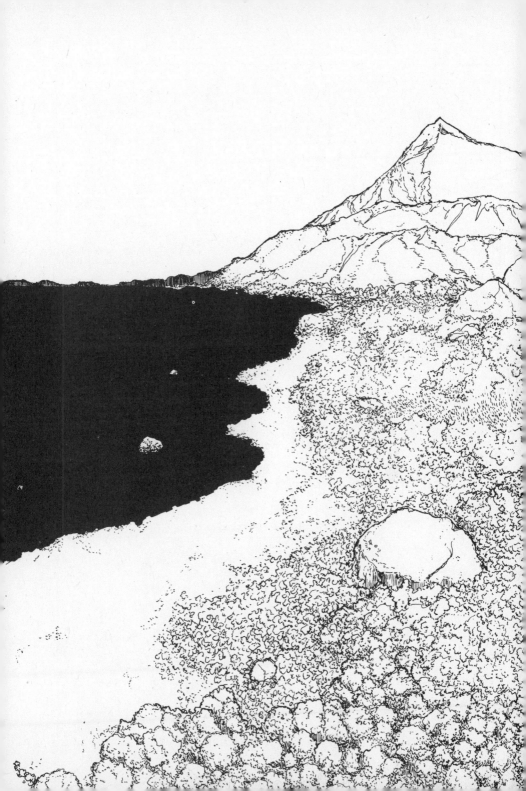

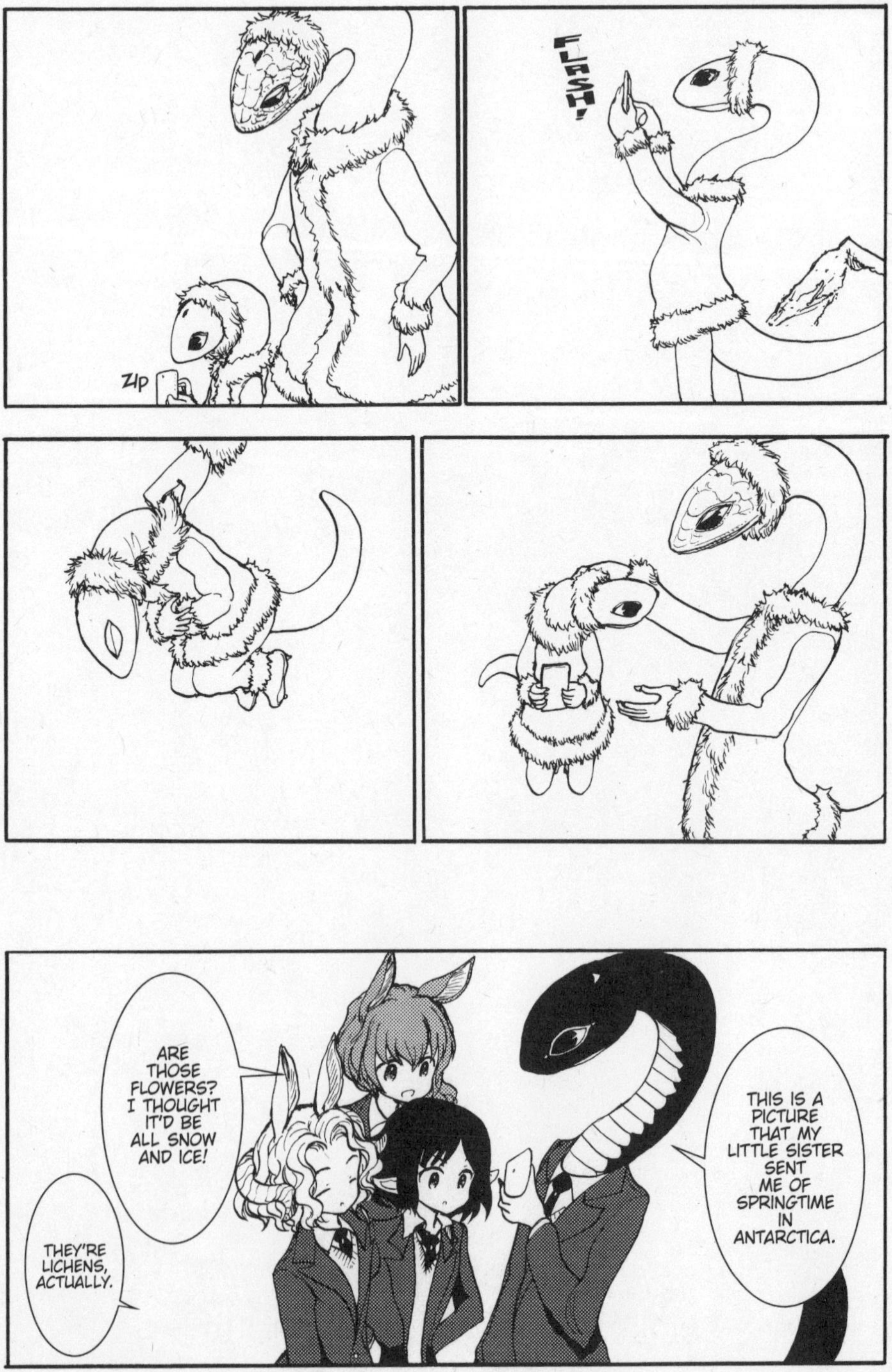
FLASH!
ZIP
THIS IS A PICTURE THAT MY LITTLE SISTER SENT ME OF SPRINGTIME IN ANTARCTICA.
ARE THOSE FLOWERS? I THOUGHT IT'D BE ALL SNOW AND ICE!
THEY'RE LICHENS, ACTUALLY.

A Centaur's Life

HISTORY OF ARCHITECTURE IN JAPAN AND OTHER COUNTRIES: <7> MAMMOTH-BONE HUT

THIS DWELLING WAS MADE FROM A CLUSTER OF MAMMOTH BONES THAT WERE LIKELY FASTENED TOGETHER WITH LEATHER CORDS AND COVERED WITH ANIMAL HIDES. FEW NATURAL SHELTERS, SUCH AS CAVES, EXISTED IN THE COLD STEPPE REGIONS WHERE MAMMOTHS USED TO ROAM, AND DIGGING IN FROZEN GROUND IS VERY DIFFICULT EVEN WITH MODERN METAL TOOLS. STRUCTURES LIKE THIS WERE NECESSARY TO WEATHER THE COLD. GAINING THE ABILITY TO CREATE THEM WOULD LIKELY HAVE EXPANDED NOT ONLY THE GEOGRAPHIC RANGE OF HUMANITY, BUT ALSO THE POSSIBILITY OF THEIR SURVIVAL AS A SPECIES. THIS DWELLING WAS NOT EASILY PORTABLE, WHICH SUGGESTS THAT HUMANS MAY HAVE SETTLED DOWN IN ONE PLACE, BUT IT COULD ALSO HAVE BEEN USED SEASONALLY, LIKE A MODERN-DAY HUNTING LODGE.

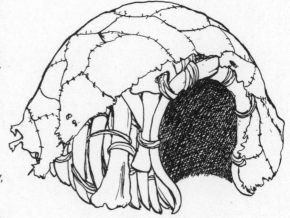

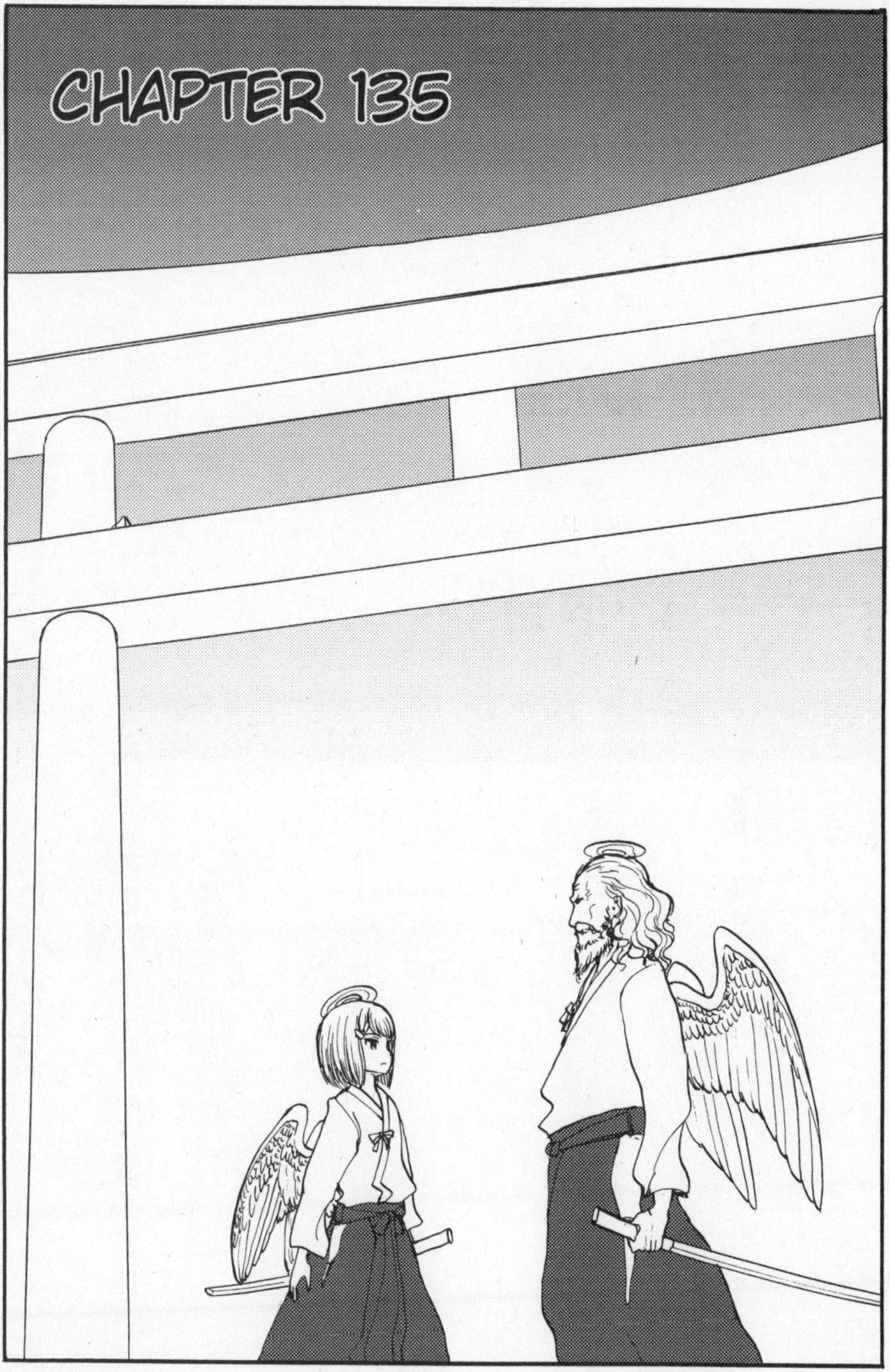
CHAPTER 135

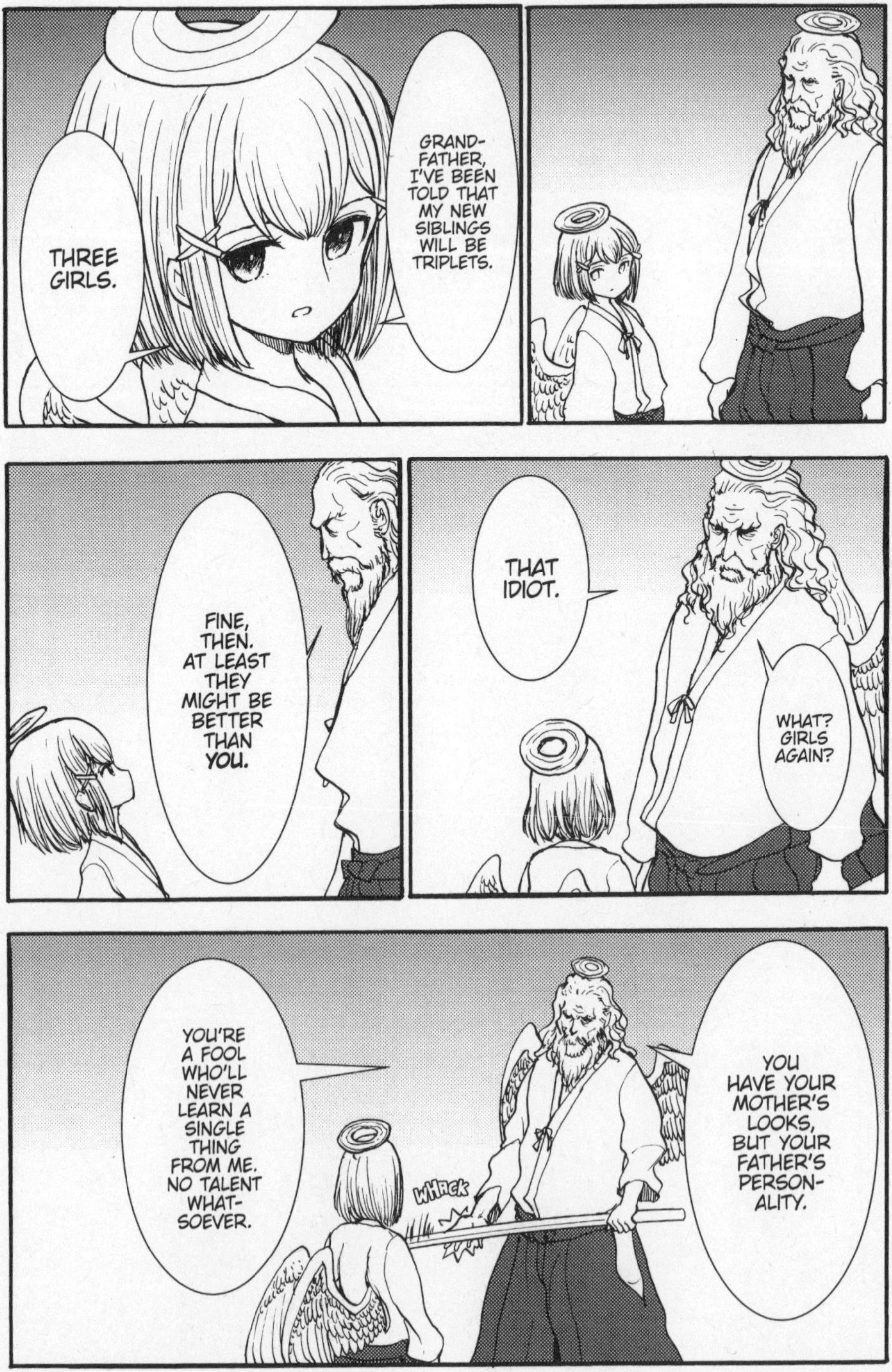
GRAND-FATHER, I'VE BEEN TOLD THAT MY NEW SIBLINGS WILL BE TRIPLETS.
THREE GIRLS.
WHAT? GIRLS AGAIN?
THAT IDIOT.
FINE, THEN. AT LEAST THEY MIGHT BE BETTER THAN YOU.
YOU HAVE YOUR MOTHER'S LOOKS, BUT YOUR FATHER'S PERSON-ALITY.
WHACK
YOU'RE A FOOL WHO'LL NEVER LEARN A SINGLE THING FROM ME. NO TALENT WHAT-SOEVER.

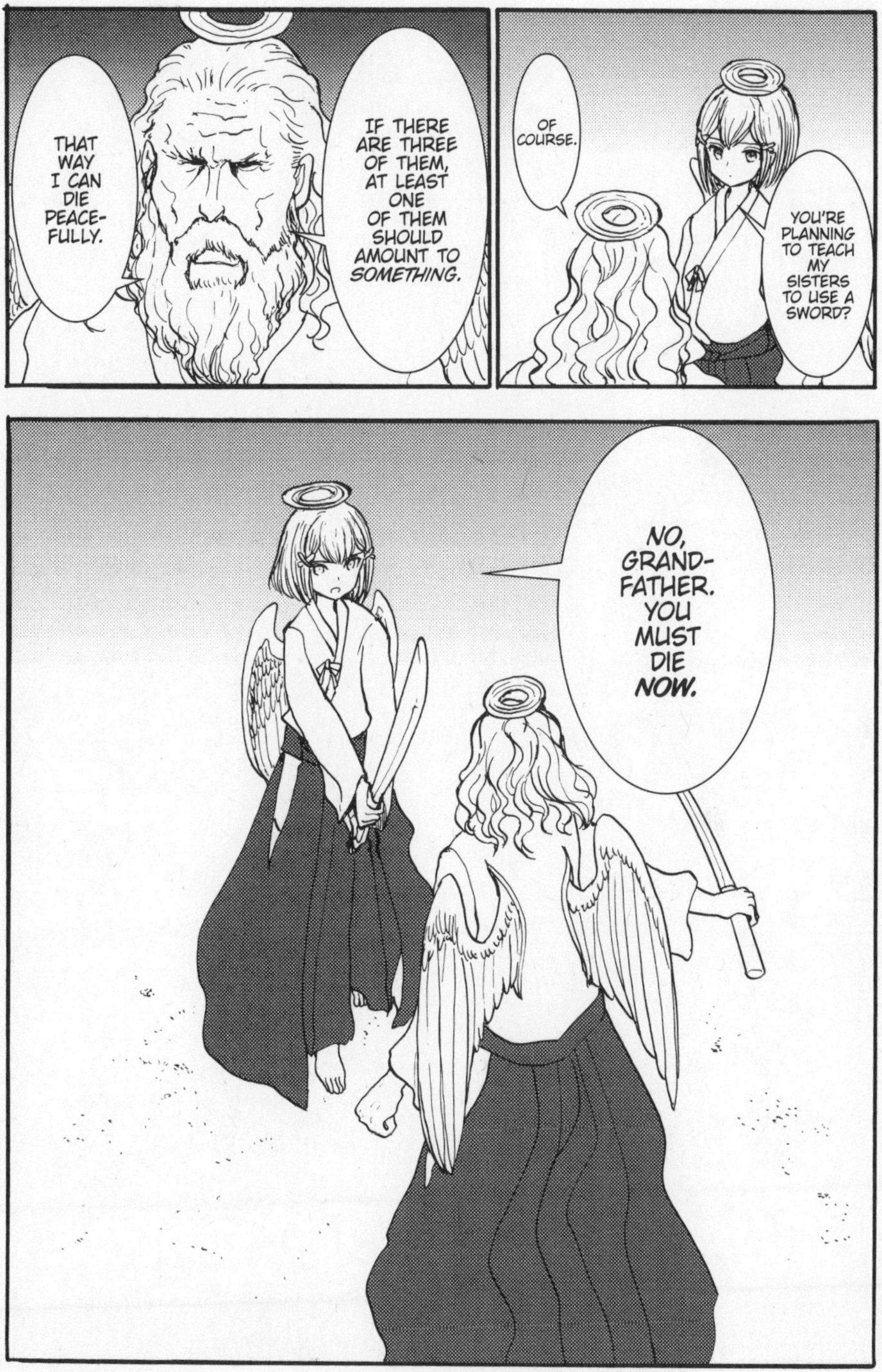
YOU'RE PLANNING TO TEACH MY SISTERS TO USE A SWORD?
OF COURSE.
IF THERE ARE THREE OF THEM, AT LEAST ONE OF THEM SHOULD AMOUNT TO *SOMETHING*.
THAT WAY I CAN DIE PEACE-FULLY.
NO, GRAND-FATHER. YOU MUST DIE *NOW*.

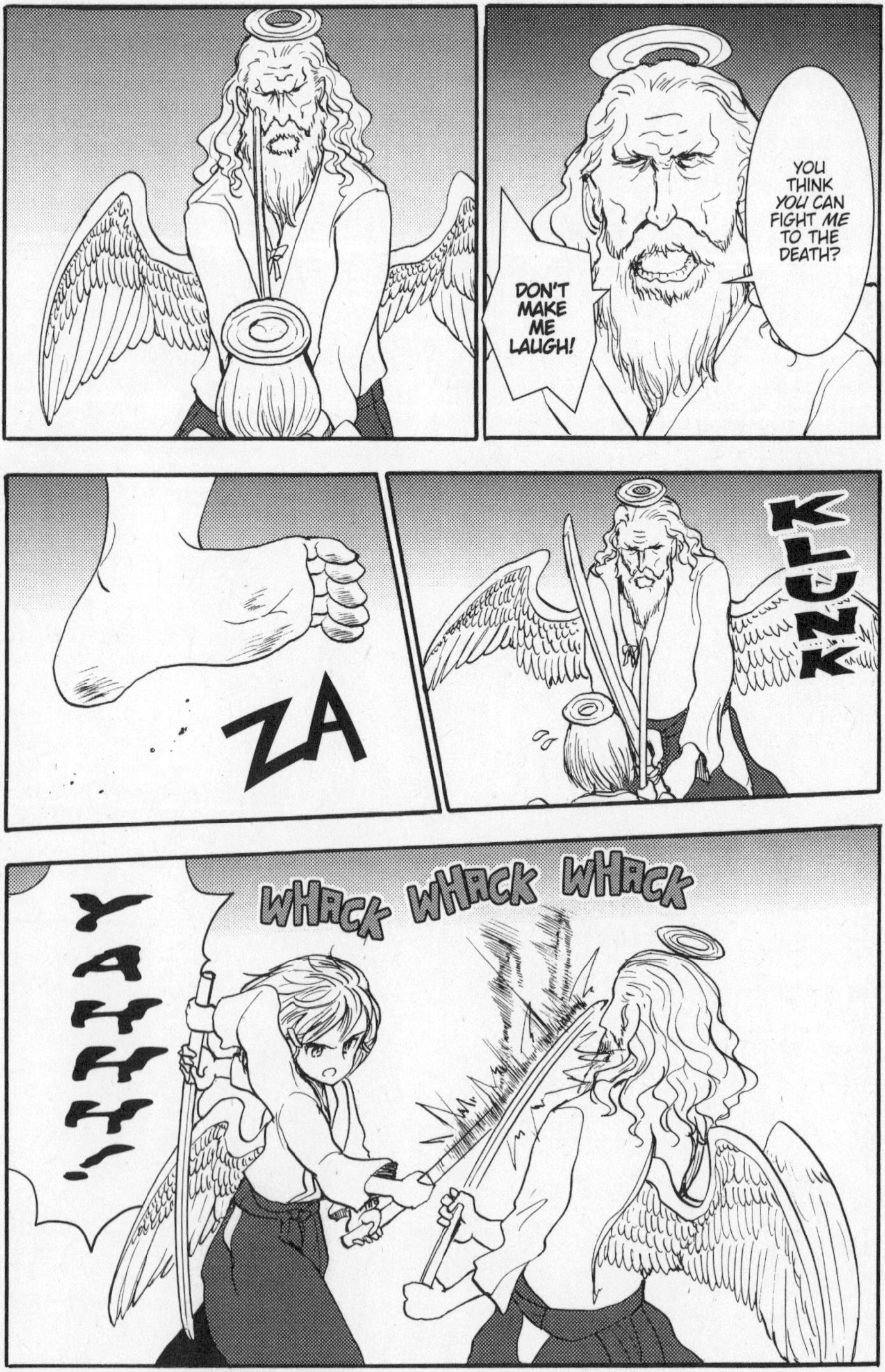
YOU THINK *YOU* CAN FIGHT *ME* TO THE DEATH?
DON'T MAKE ME LAUGH!
KLUNK
ZA
WHACK WHACK WHACK
YAHHH!

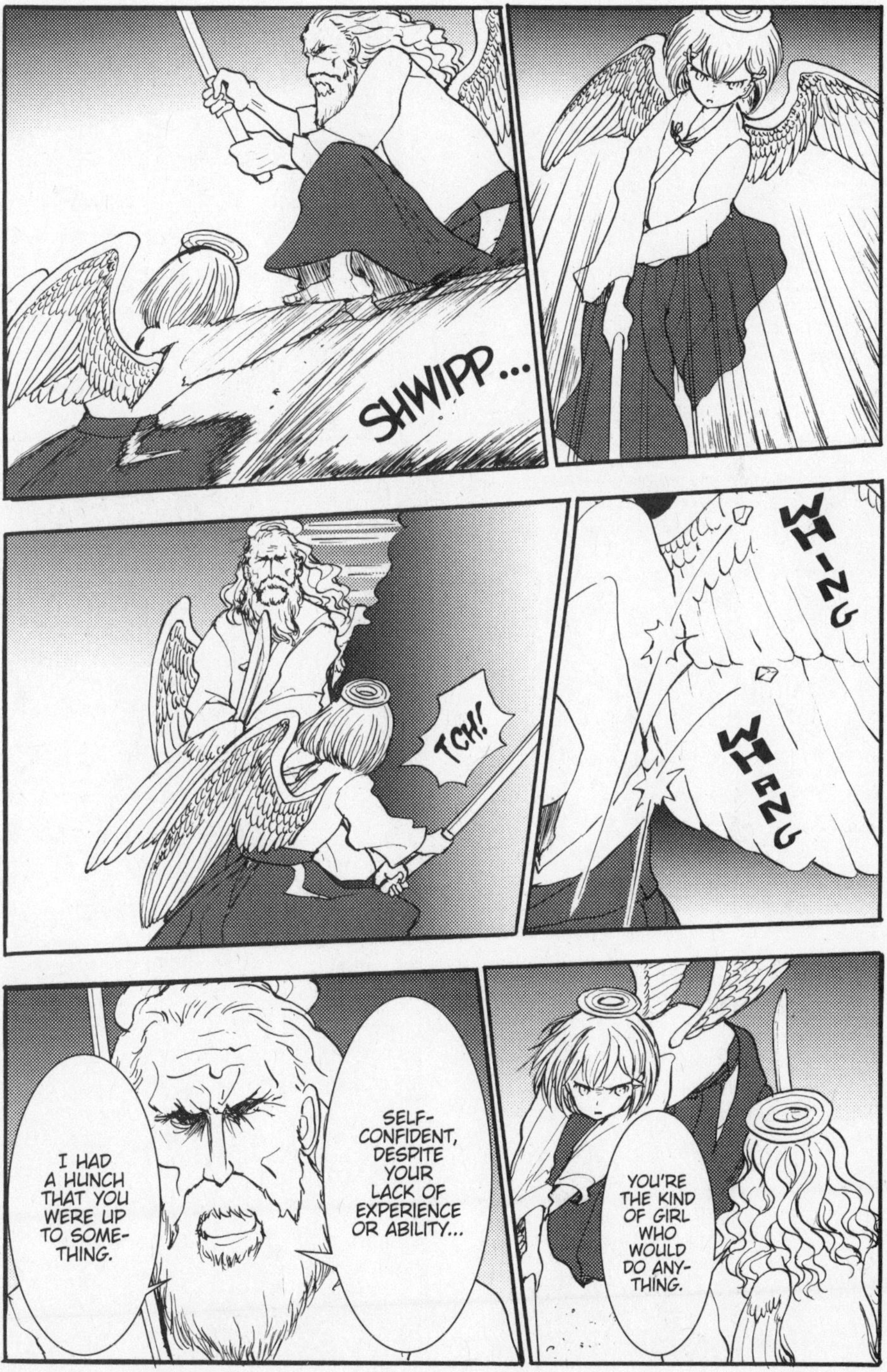
SHWIPP...
WHING
WHANG
TCH!
YOU'RE THE KIND OF GIRL WHO WOULD DO ANYTHING.
SELF-CONFIDENT, DESPITE YOUR LACK OF EXPERIENCE OR ABILITY...
I HAD A HUNCH THAT YOU WERE UP TO SOMETHING.

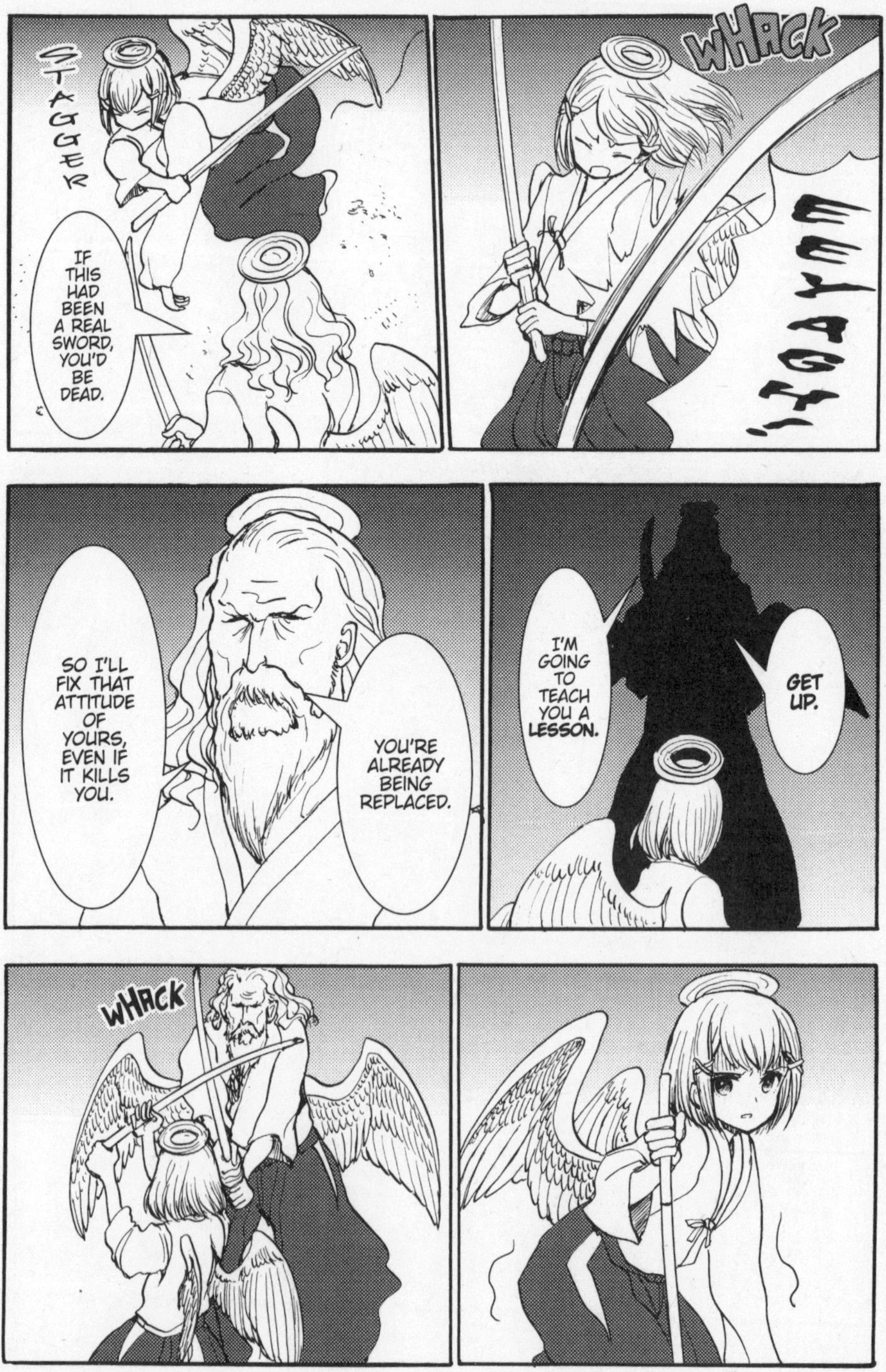
WHACK
EEYAGH!!
STAGGER
IF THIS HAD BEEN A REAL SWORD, YOU'D BE DEAD.
GET UP.
I'M GOING TO TEACH YOU A LESSON.
YOU'RE ALREADY BEING REPLACED.
SO I'LL FIX THAT ATTITUDE OF YOURS, EVEN IF IT KILLS YOU.
WHACK

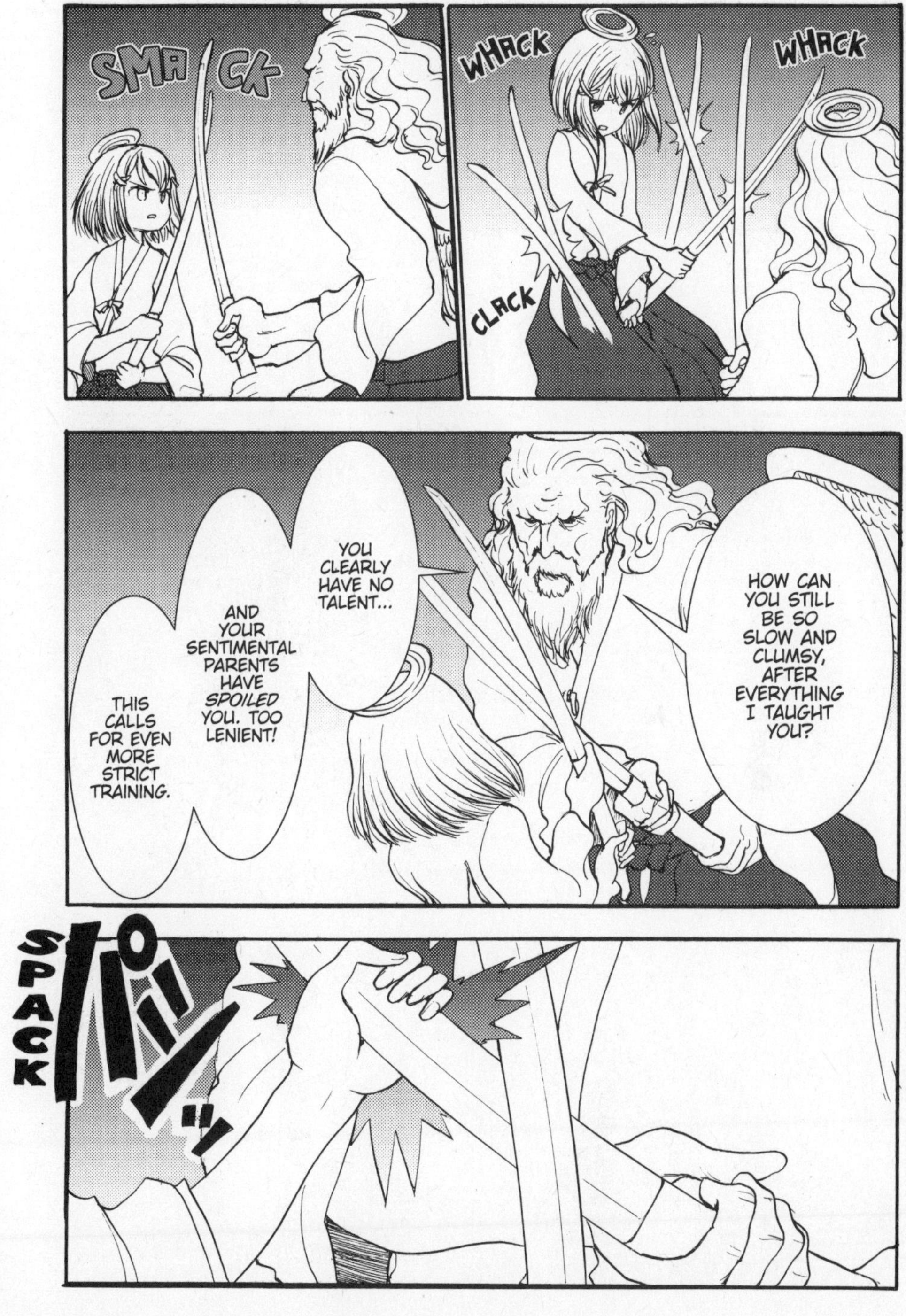
WHACK
WHACK
CLACK
SMACK
HOW CAN YOU STILL BE SO SLOW AND CLUMSY, AFTER EVERYTHING I TAUGHT YOU?
YOU CLEARLY HAVE NO TALENT...
AND YOUR SENTIMENTAL PARENTS HAVE *SPOILED* YOU. TOO LENIENT!
THIS CALLS FOR EVEN MORE STRICT TRAINING.
SPACK

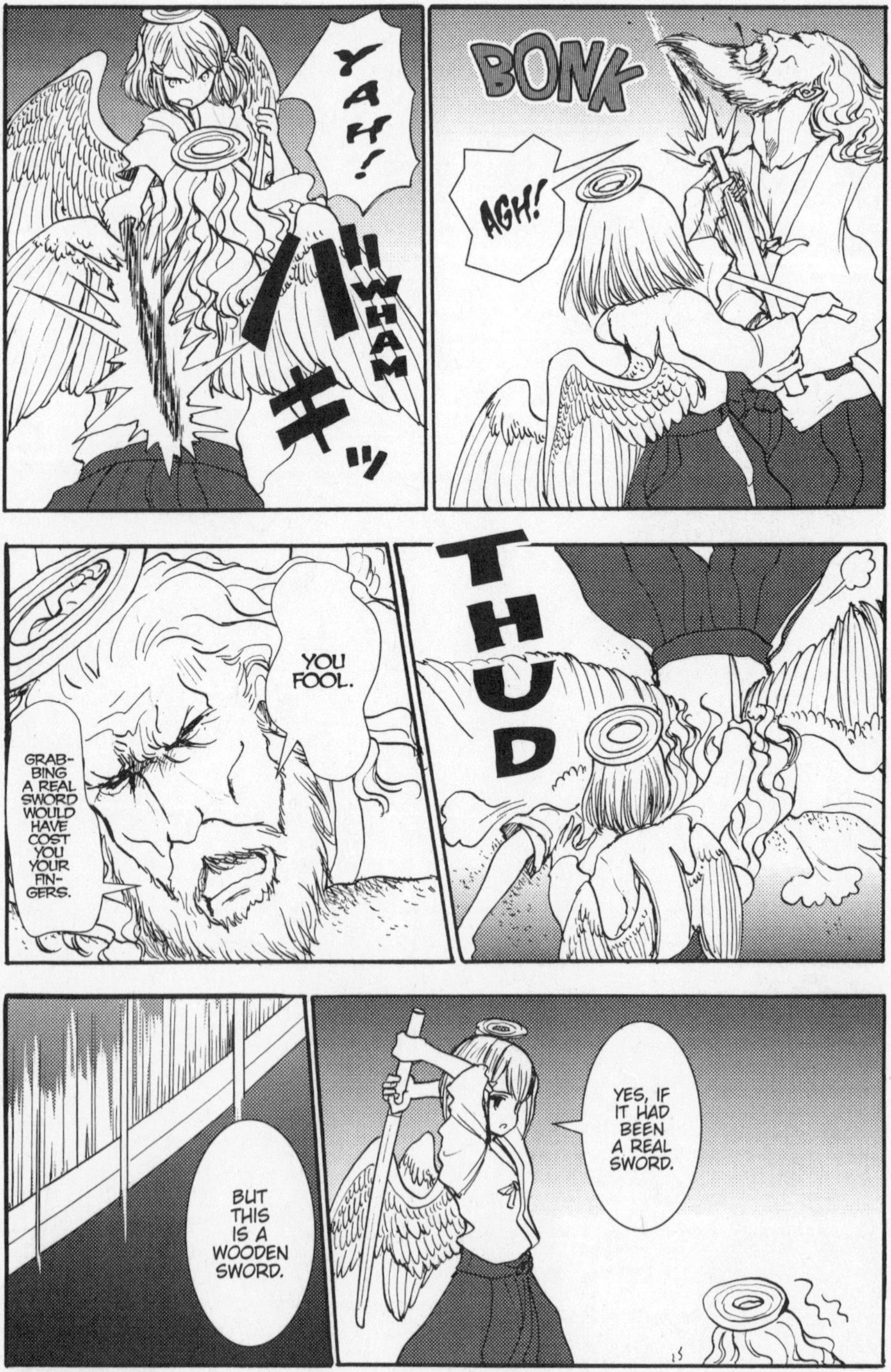
BONK
AGH!
YAH!
WHAM
バキッ
THUD
YOU FOOL.
GRABBING A REAL SWORD WOULD HAVE COST YOU YOUR FINGERS.
YES, IF IT HAD BEEN A REAL SWORD.
BUT THIS IS A WOODEN SWORD.

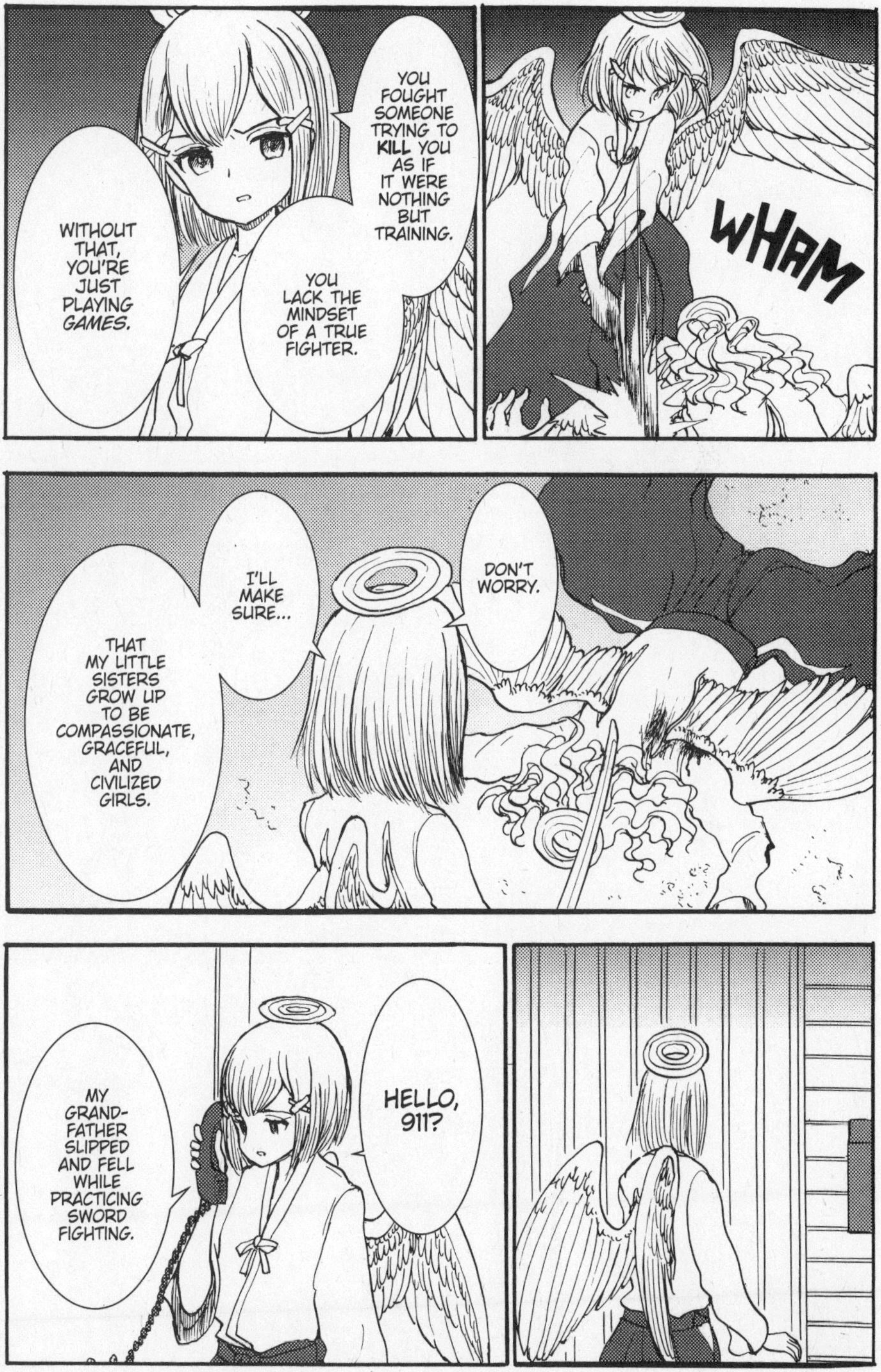
WHAM
YOU FOUGHT SOMEONE TRYING TO **KILL** YOU AS IF IT WERE NOTHING BUT TRAINING.
YOU LACK THE MINDSET OF A TRUE FIGHTER.
WITHOUT THAT, YOU'RE JUST PLAYING *GAMES.*
DON'T WORRY.
I'LL MAKE SURE...
THAT MY LITTLE SISTERS GROW UP TO BE COMPASSIONATE, GRACEFUL, AND CIVILIZED GIRLS.
HELLO, 911?
MY GRAND-FATHER SLIPPED AND FELL WHILE PRACTICING SWORD FIGHTING.

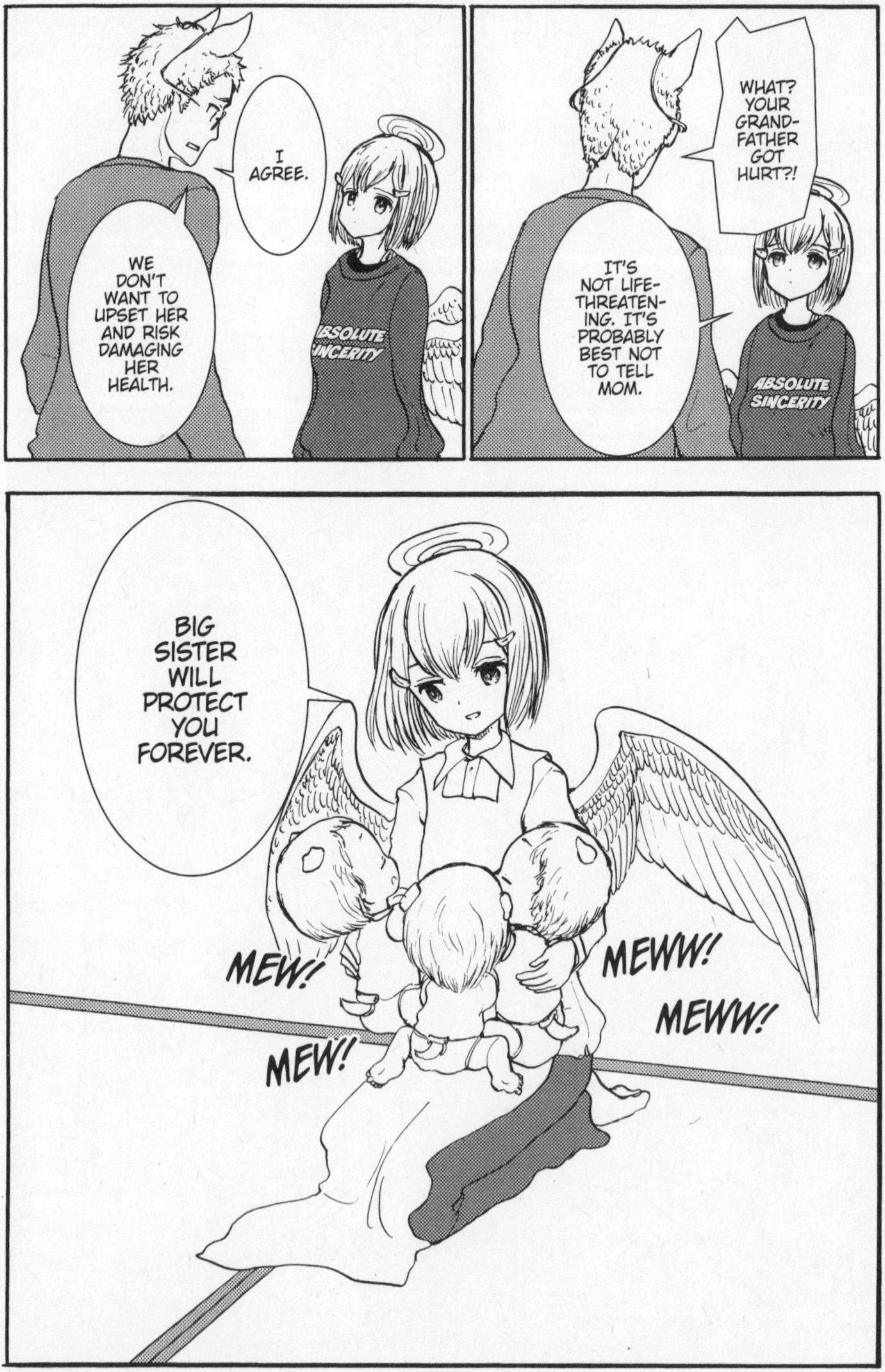
WHAT? YOUR GRANDFATHER GOT HURT?!
IT'S NOT LIFE-THREATENING. IT'S PROBABLY BEST NOT TO TELL MOM.
ABSOLUTE SINCERITY
I AGREE.
ABSOLUTE SINCERITY
WE DON'T WANT TO UPSET HER AND RISK DAMAGING HER HEALTH.
BIG SISTER WILL PROTECT YOU FOREVER.
MEWW!
MEW!
MEWW!
MEW!

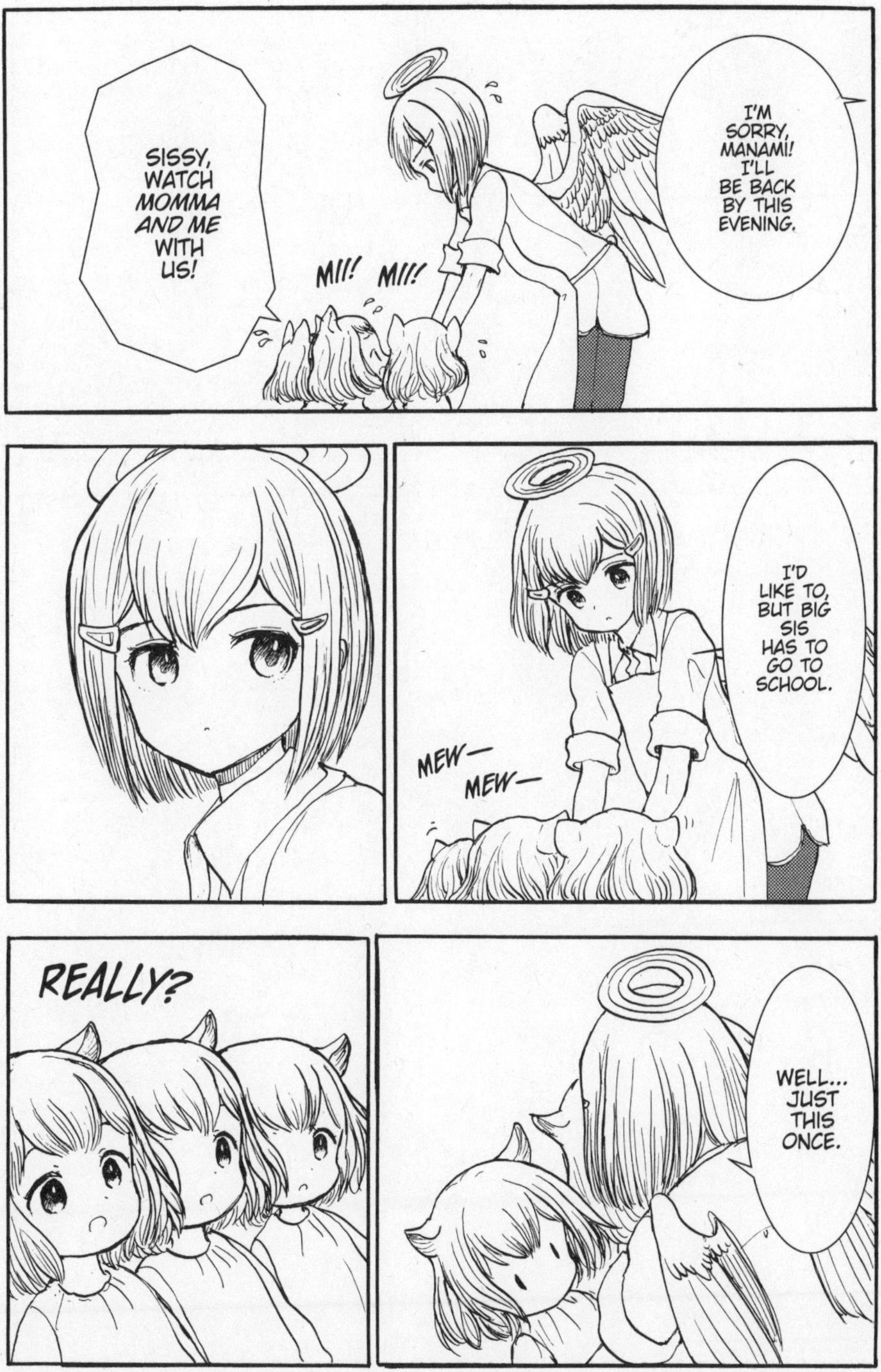
I'M SORRY, MANAMI! I'LL BE BACK BY THIS EVENING.
SISSY, WATCH MOMMA AND ME WITH US!
MII! MII!
I'D LIKE TO, BUT BIG SIS HAS TO GO TO SCHOOL.
MEW— MEW—
WELL... JUST THIS ONCE.
REALLY?

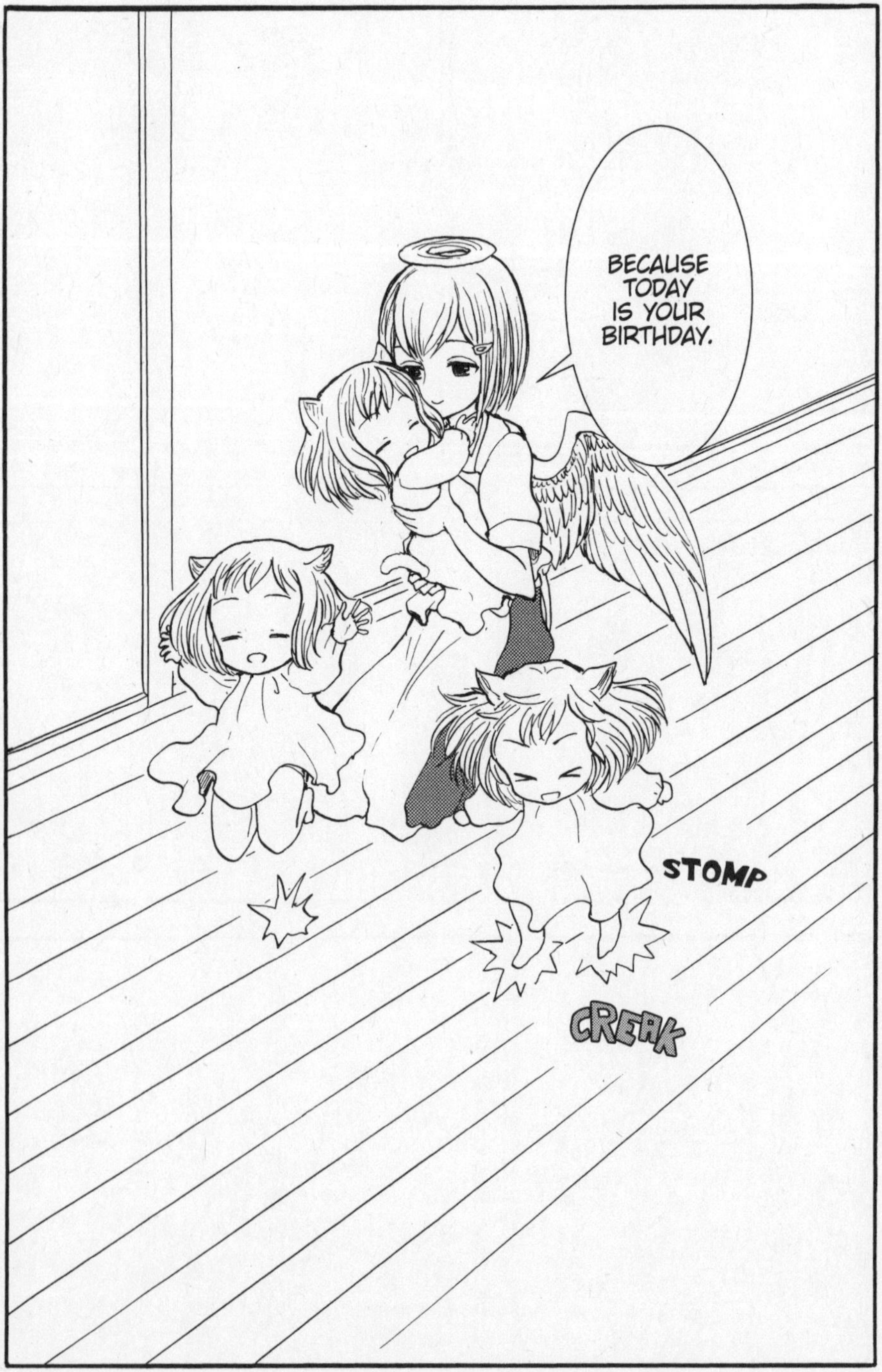
BECAUSE TODAY IS YOUR BIRTHDAY.
STOMP
CREAK

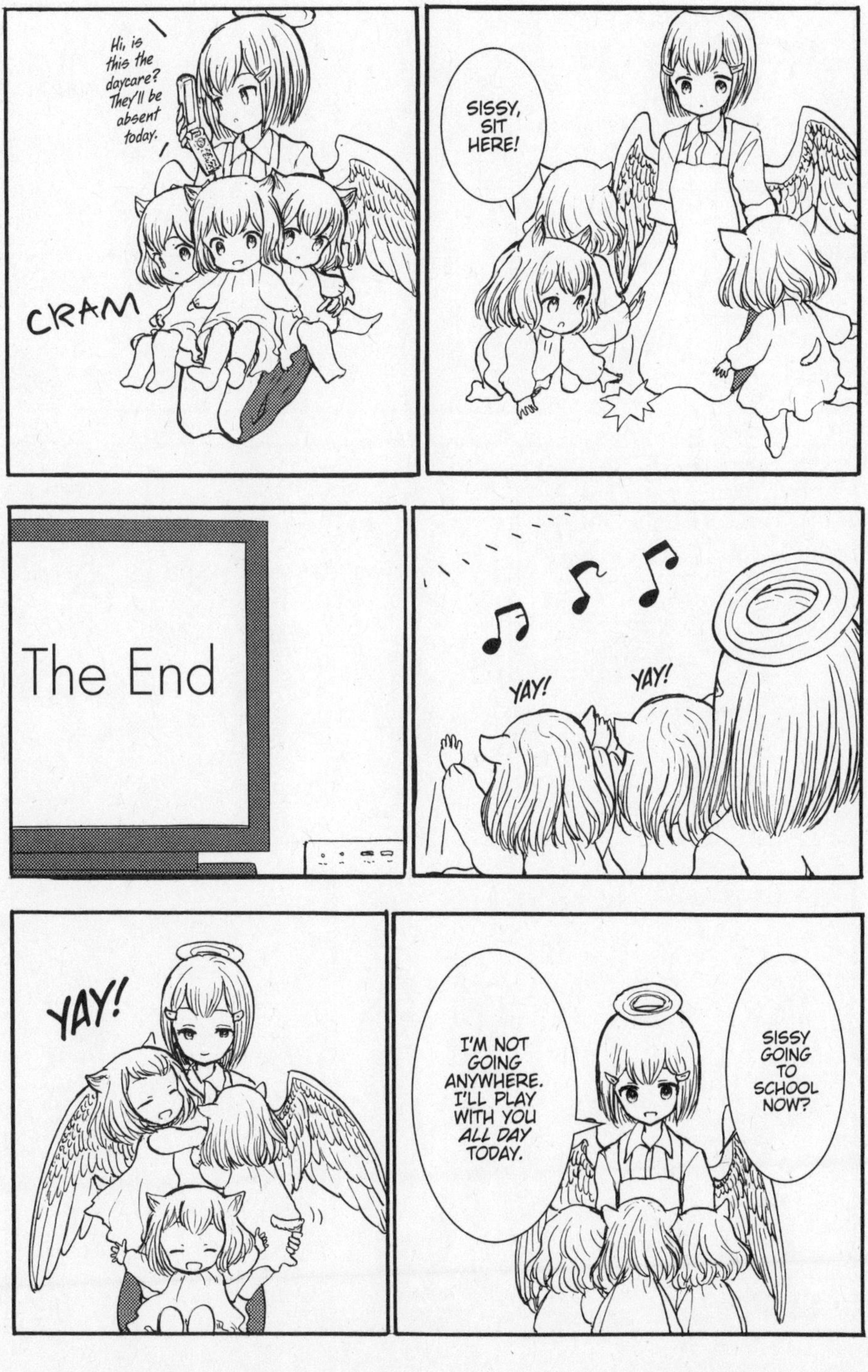
SISSY, SIT HERE!
Hi, is this the daycare? They'll be absent today.
CRAM
YAY!
YAY!
The End
SISSY GOING TO SCHOOL NOW?
I'M NOT GOING ANYWHERE. I'LL PLAY WITH YOU ALL DAY TODAY.
YAY!

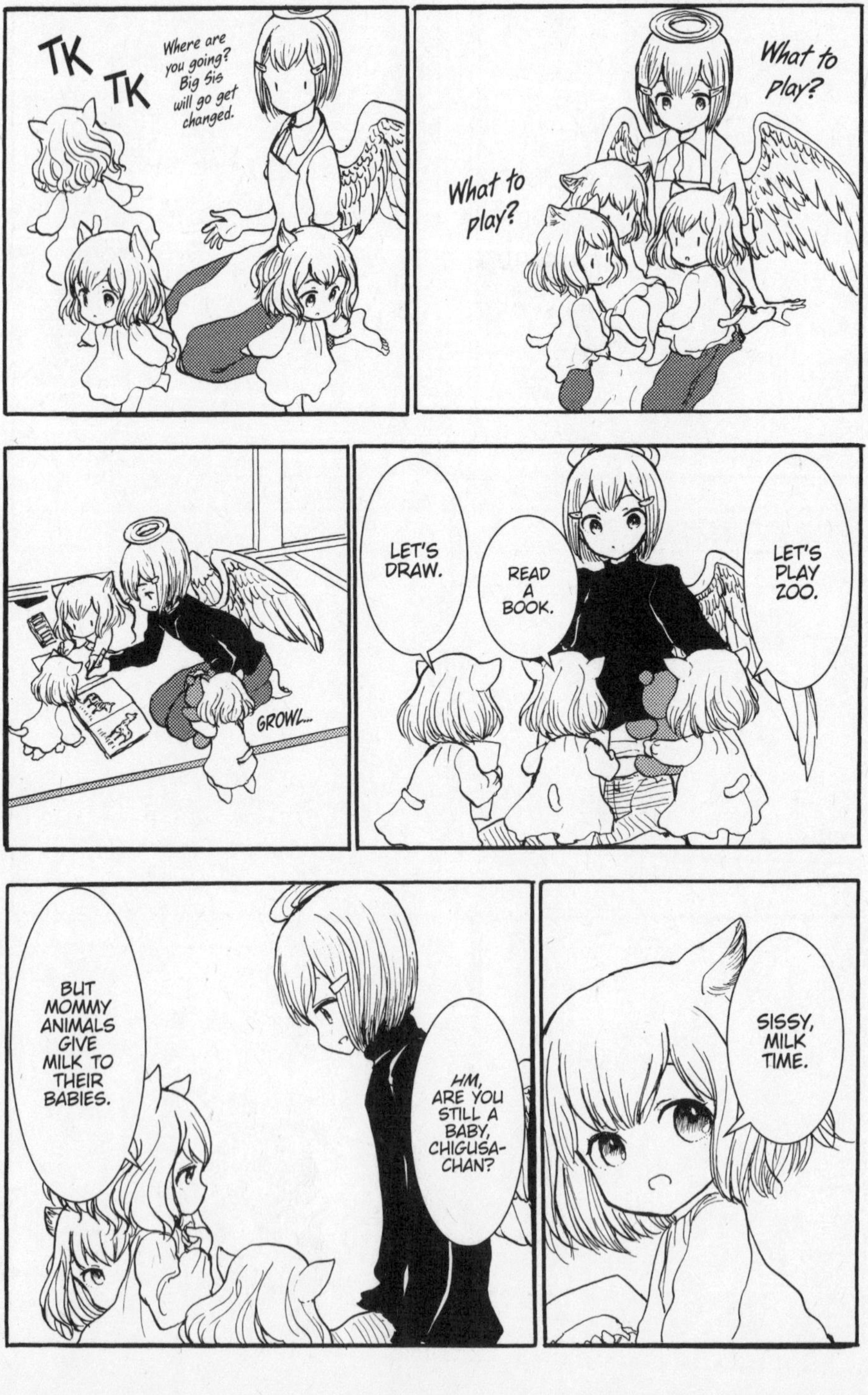
What to play?
What to play?
TK
TK
Where are you going? Big Sis will go get changed.
LET'S PLAY ZOO.
READ A BOOK.
LET'S DRAW.
GROWL...
SISSY, MILK TIME.
HM, ARE YOU STILL A BABY, CHIGUSA-CHAN?
BUT MOMMY ANIMALS GIVE MILK TO THEIR BABIES.

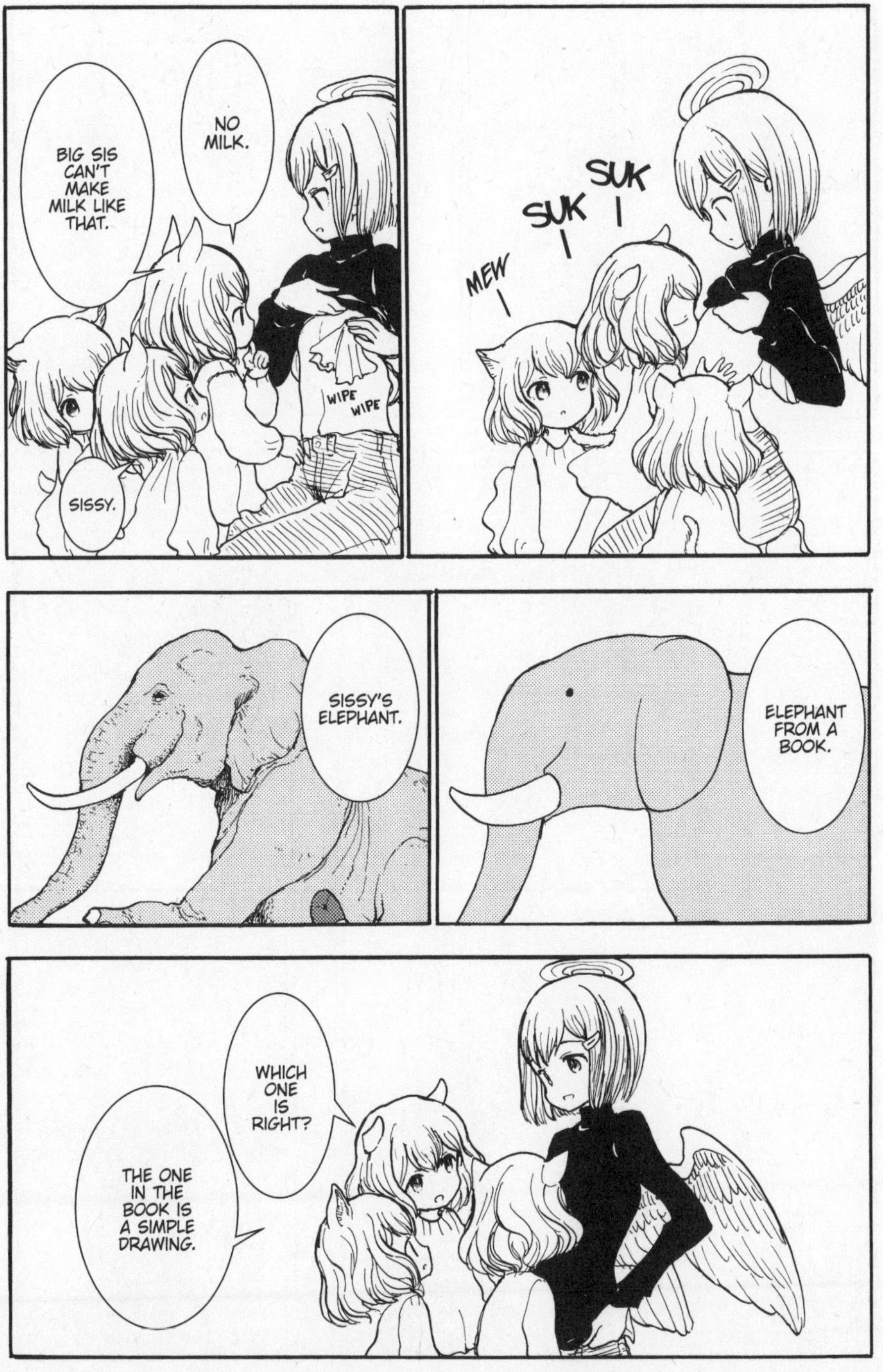
SUK
SUK
MEW
NO MILK.
BIG SIS CAN'T MAKE MILK LIKE THAT.
WIPE WIPE
SISSY.
ELEPHANT FROM A BOOK.
SISSY'S ELEPHANT.
WHICH ONE IS RIGHT?
THE ONE IN THE BOOK IS A SIMPLE DRAWING.

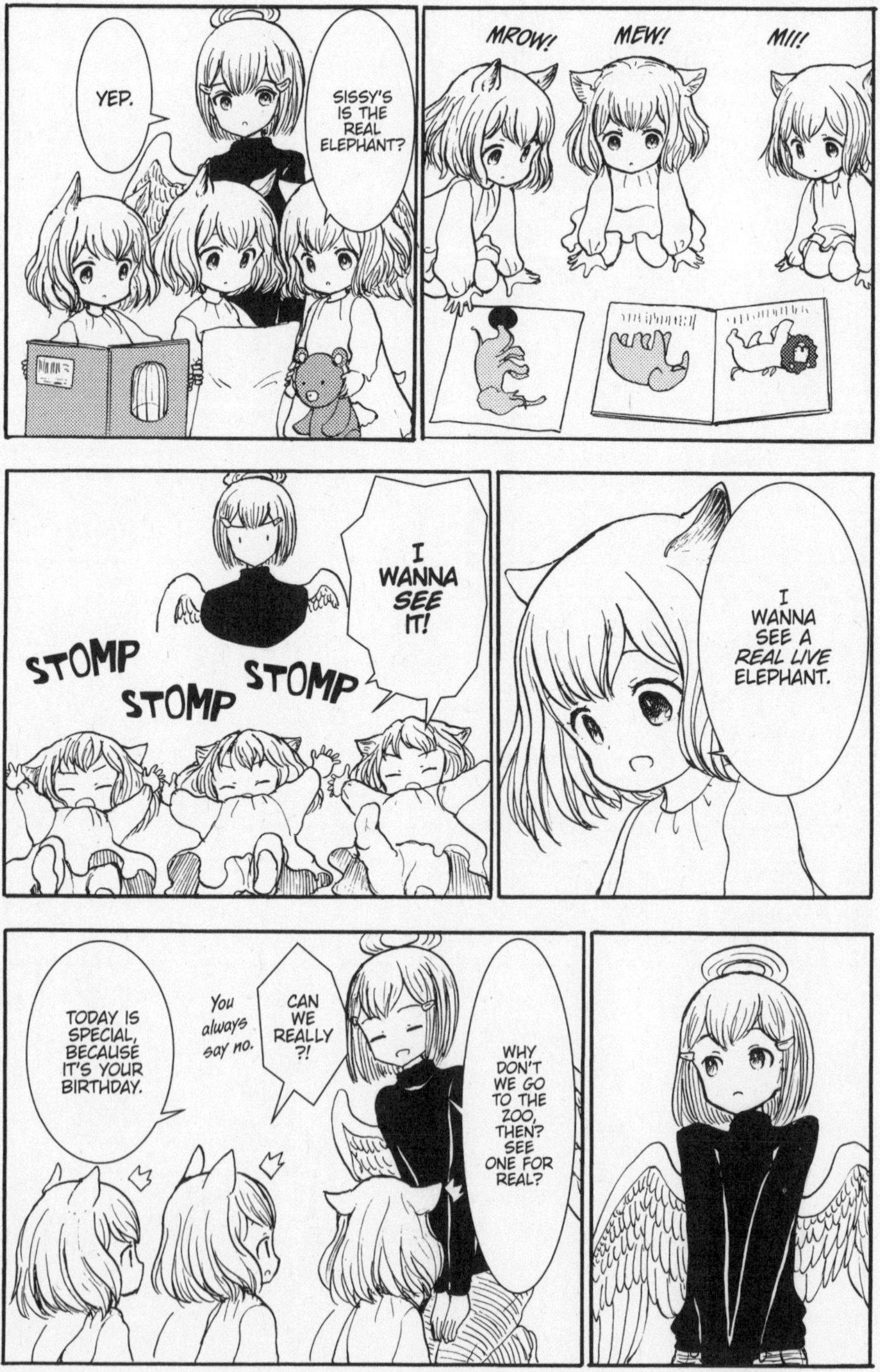
MII!
MEW!
MROW!
SISSY'S IS THE REAL ELEPHANT?
YEP.
I WANNA SEE A REAL LIVE ELEPHANT.
I WANNA SEE IT!
STOMP
STOMP
STOMP
WHY DON'T WE GO TO THE ZOO, THEN? SEE ONE FOR REAL?
CAN WE REALLY?!
You always say no.
TODAY IS SPECIAL, BECAUSE IT'S YOUR BIRTHDAY.

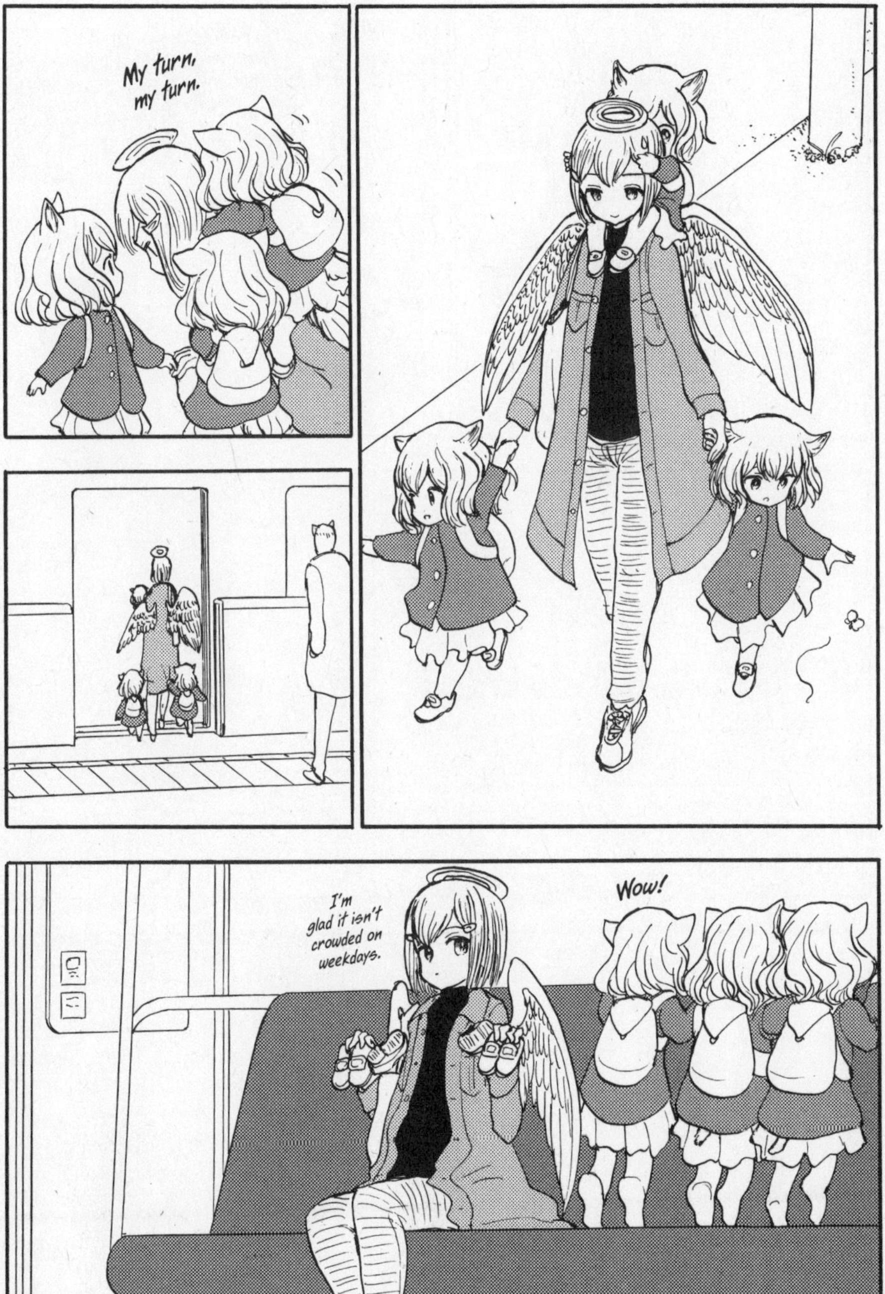
My turn, my turn.
Wow!
I'm glad it isn't crowded on weekdays.

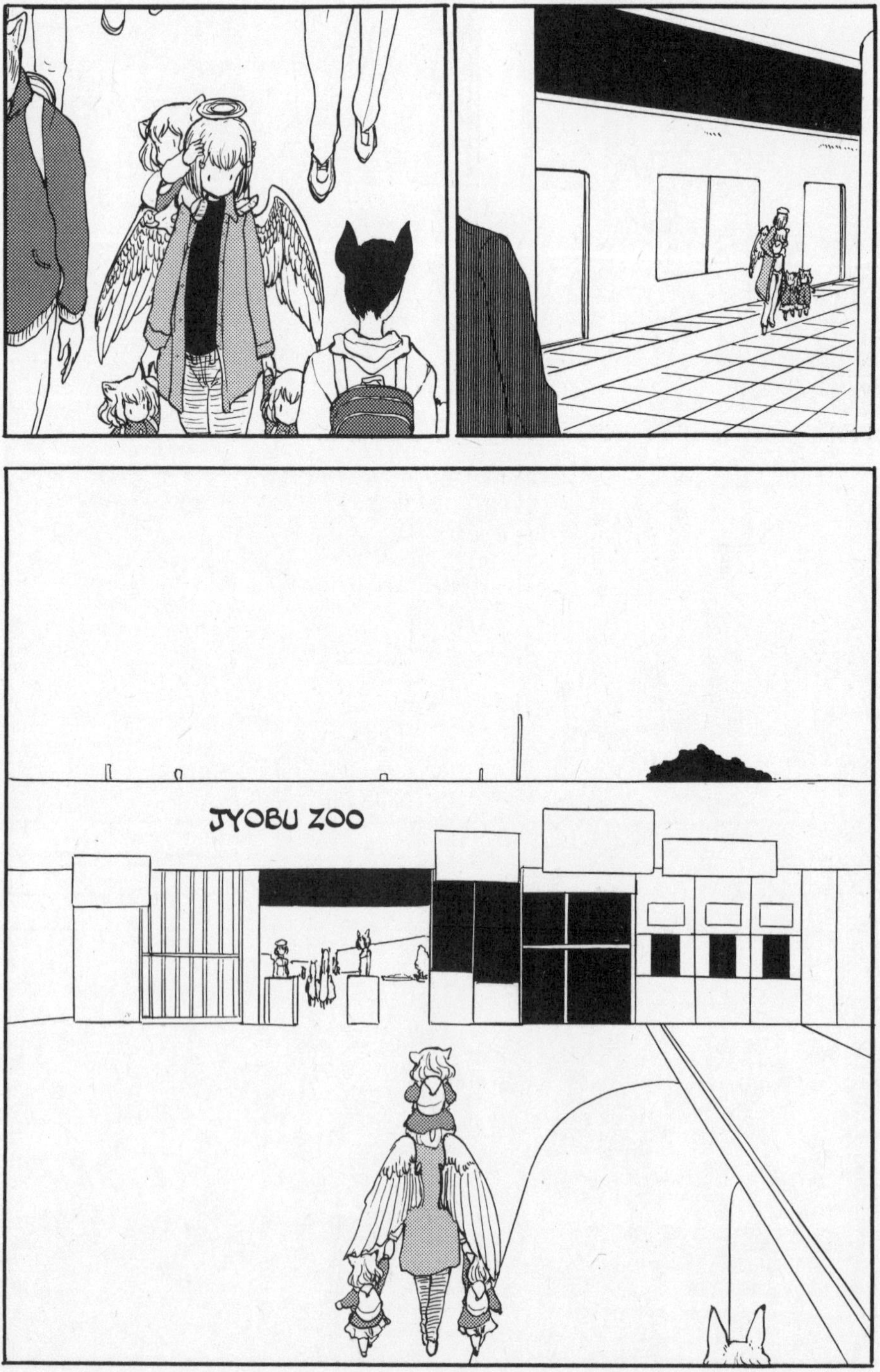
JYOBU ZOO

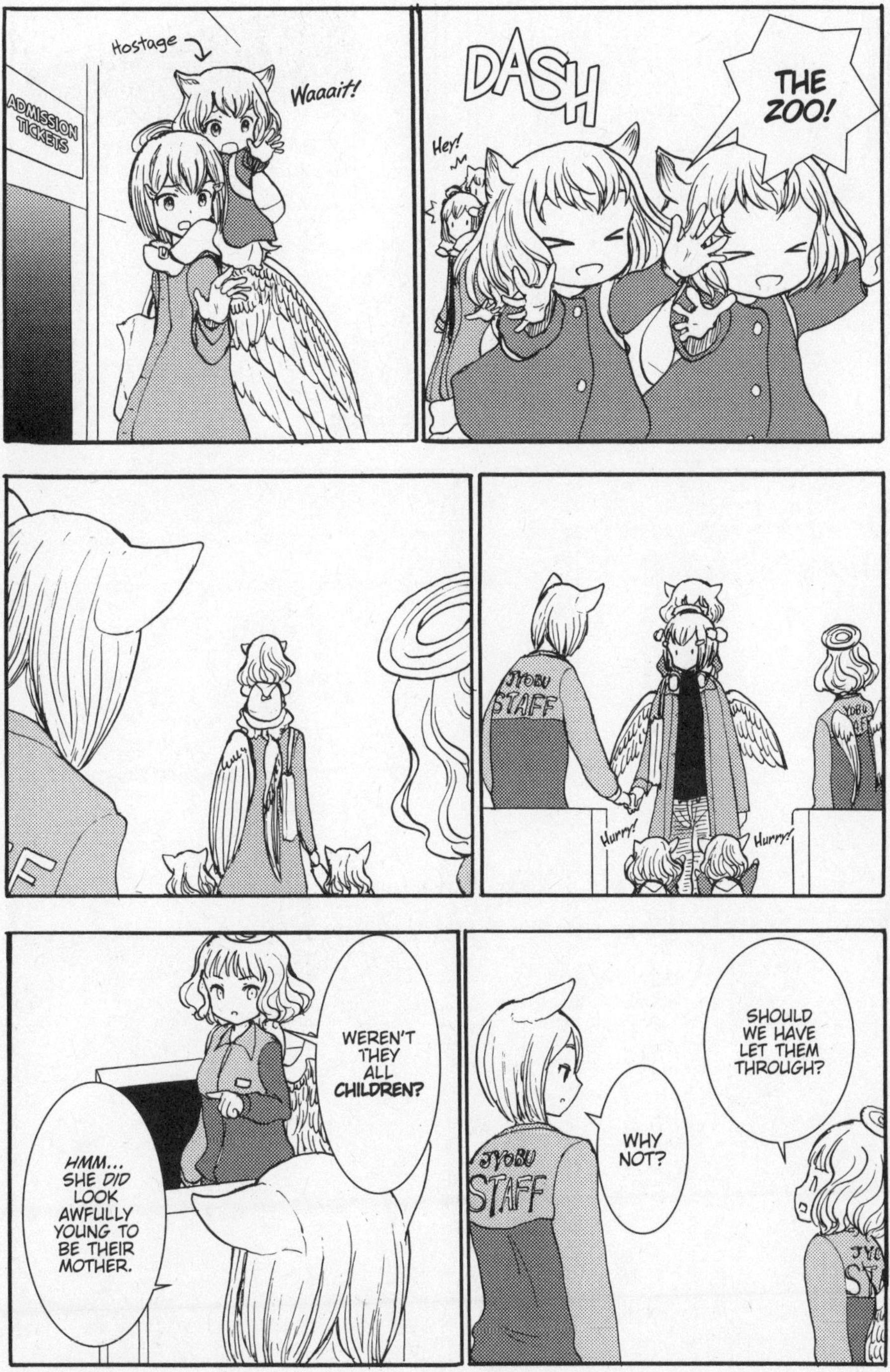
THE ZOO!
DASH
Hey!
Hostage
Waaait!
ADMISSION TICKETS
JYOBU STAFF
Hurry!
Hurry!
SHOULD WE HAVE LET THEM THROUGH?
WHY NOT?
JYOBU STAFF
WEREN'T THEY ALL CHILDREN?
HMM... SHE DID LOOK AWFULLY YOUNG TO BE THEIR MOTHER.

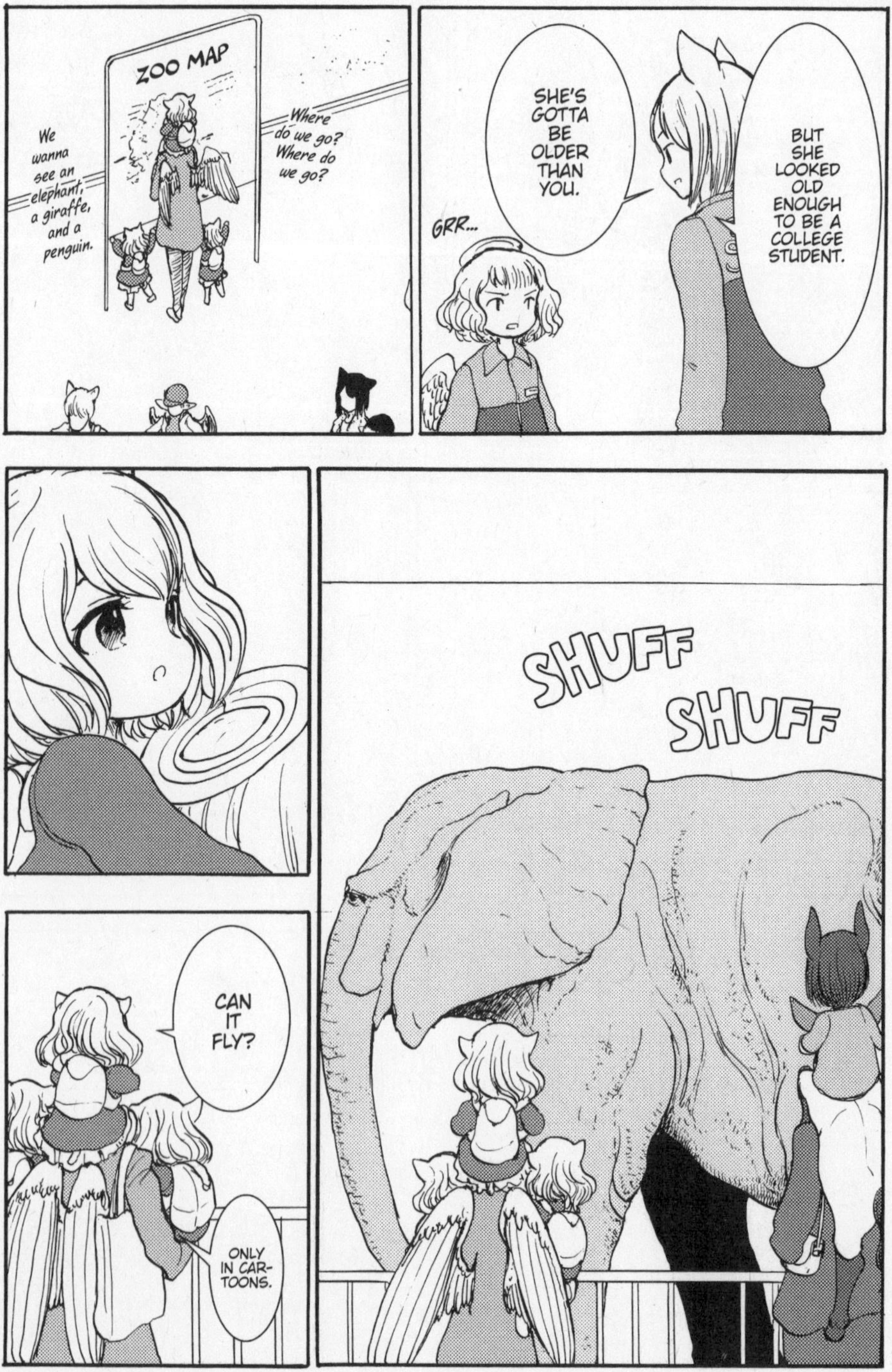
BUT SHE LOOKED OLD ENOUGH TO BE A COLLEGE STUDENT.
SHE'S GOTTA BE OLDER THAN YOU.
GRR...
ZOO MAP
Where do we go? Where do we go?
We wanna see an elephant, a giraffe, and a penguin.
SHUFF
SHUFF
CAN IT FLY?
ONLY IN CAR-TOONS.

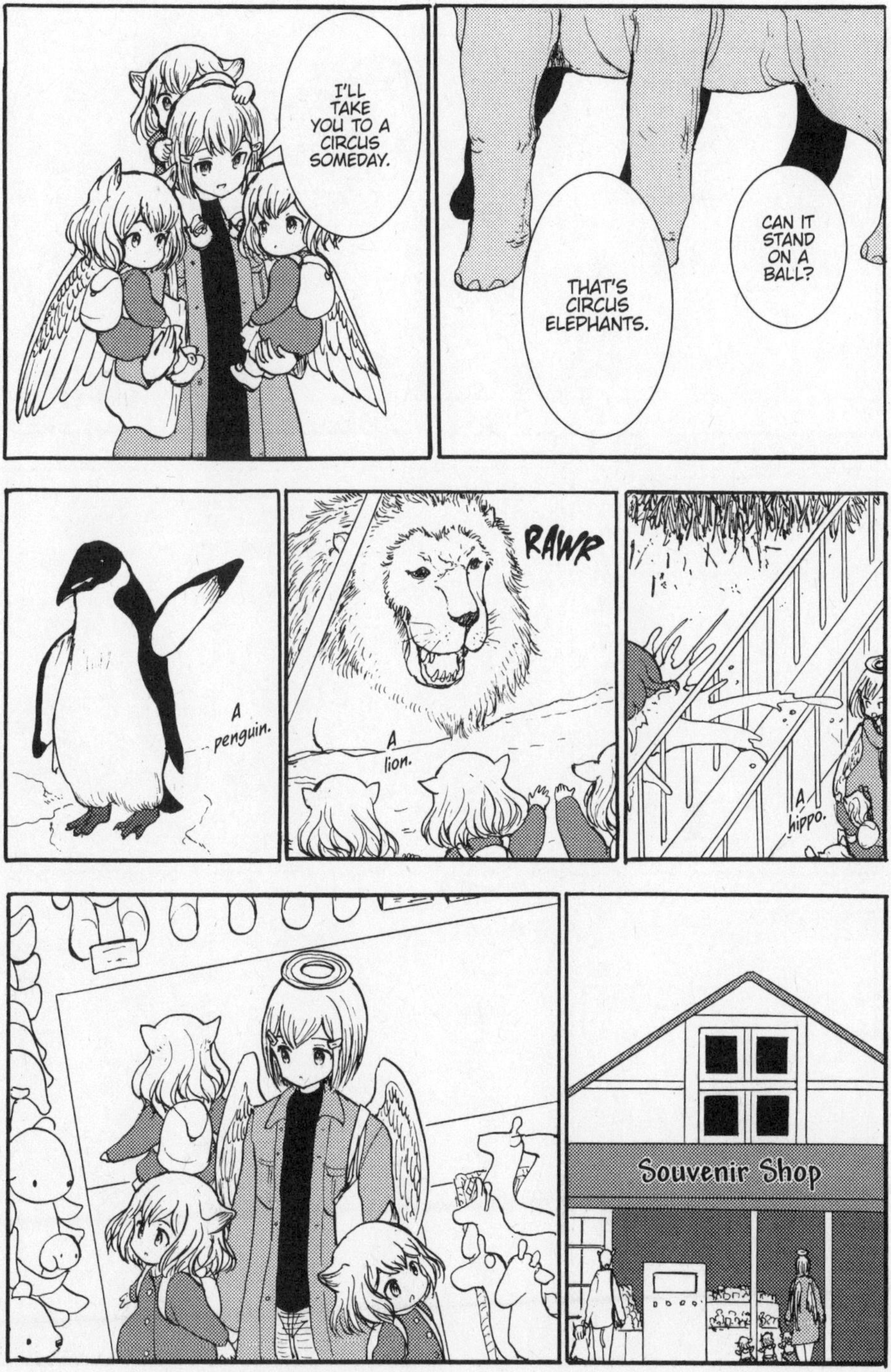
CAN IT STAND ON A BALL?
THAT'S CIRCUS ELEPHANTS.
I'LL TAKE YOU TO A CIRCUS SOMEDAY.
A hippo.
RAWR
A lion.
A penguin.
Souvenir Shop

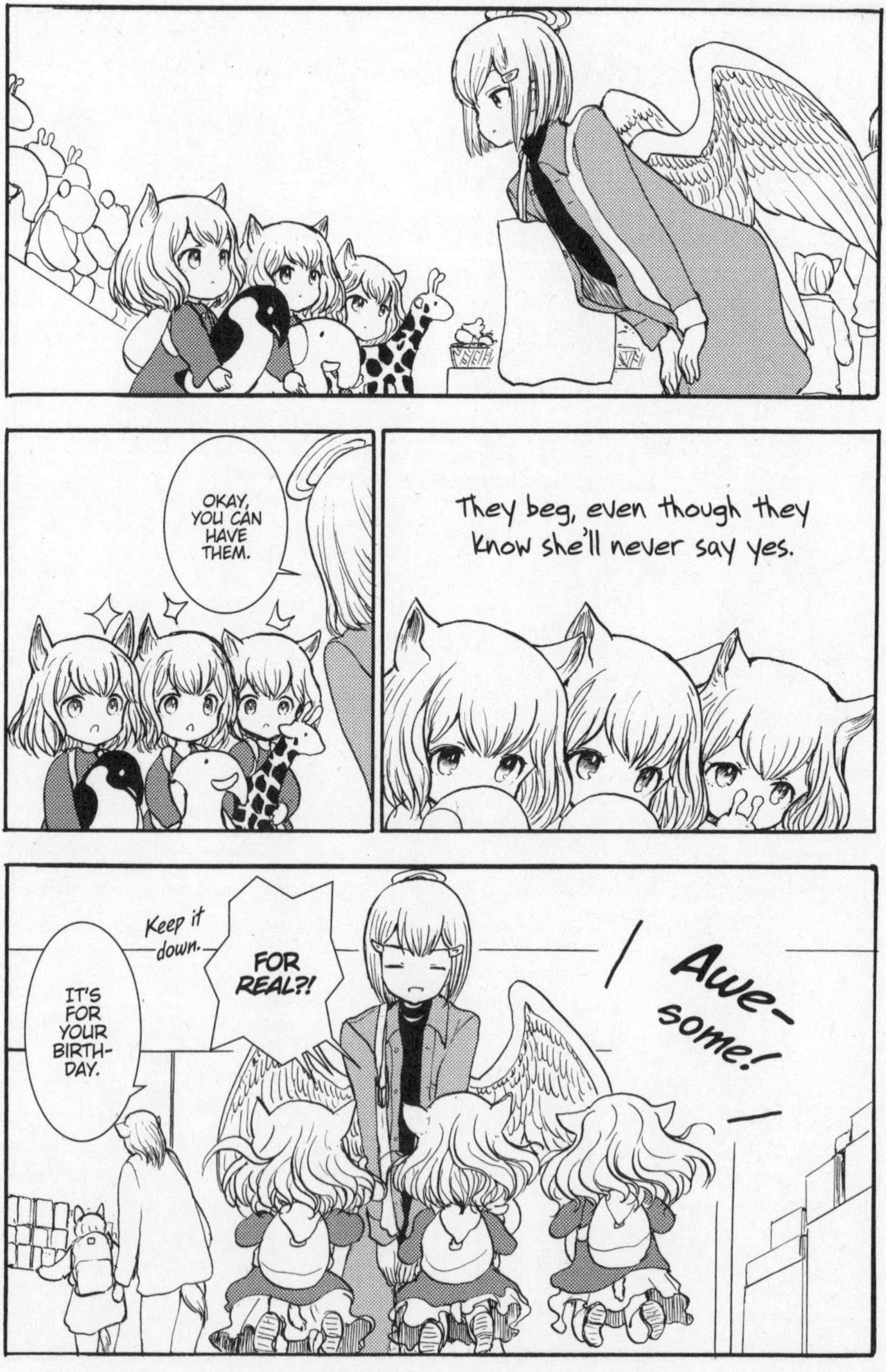
They beg, even though they know she'll never say yes.
OKAY, YOU CAN HAVE THEM.
Awe-some!
FOR REAL?!
Keep it down.
IT'S FOR YOUR BIRTH-DAY.

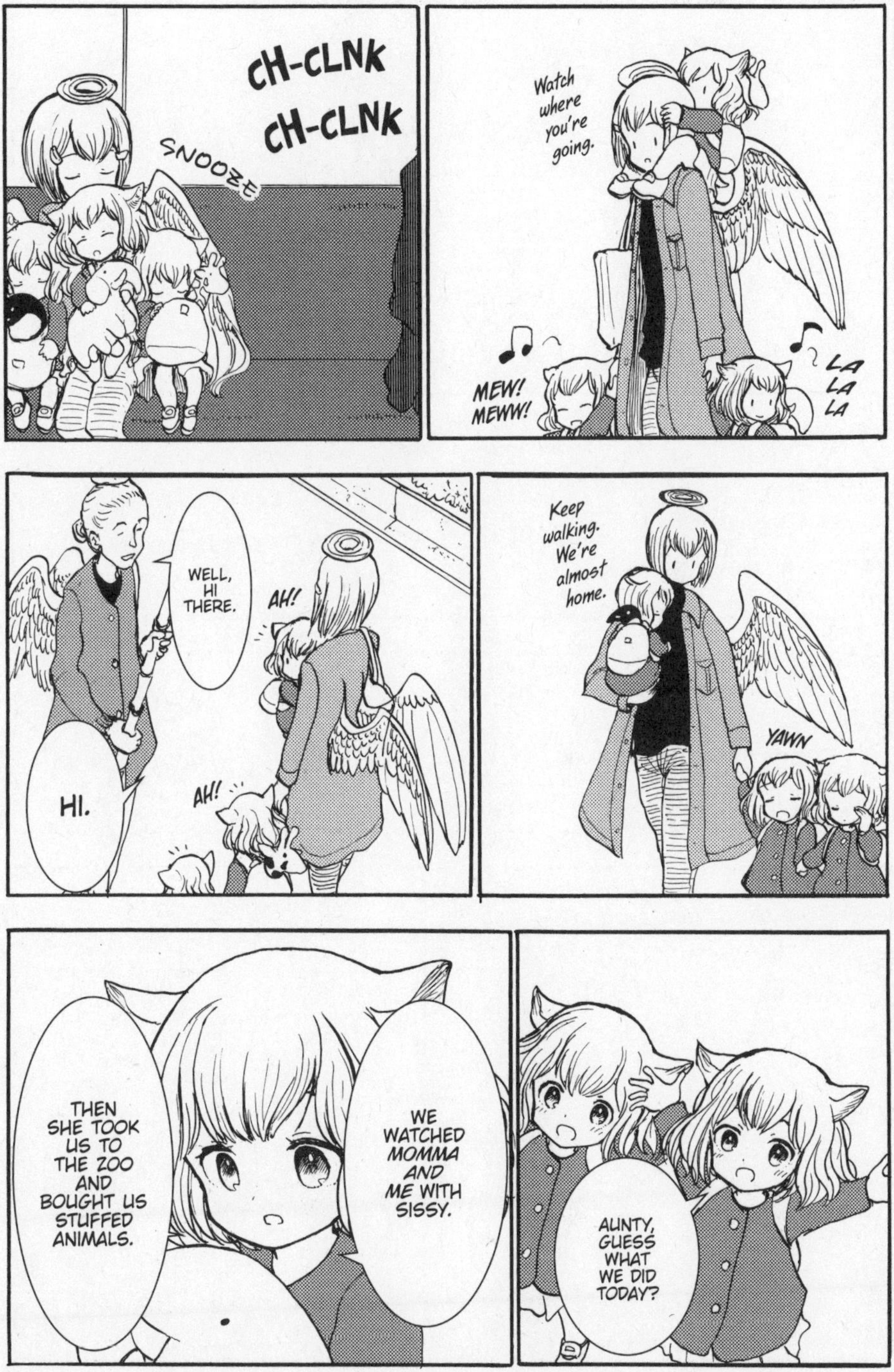
Watch where you're going.
LA LA LA
MEW! MEWW!
CH-CLNK
CH-CLNK
SNOOZE
Keep walking. We're almost home.
YAWN
WELL, HI THERE.
AH!
AH!
HI.
AUNTY, GUESS WHAT WE DID TODAY?
WE WATCHED MOMMA AND ME WITH SISSY.
THEN SHE TOOK US TO THE ZOO AND BOUGHT US STUFFED ANIMALS.

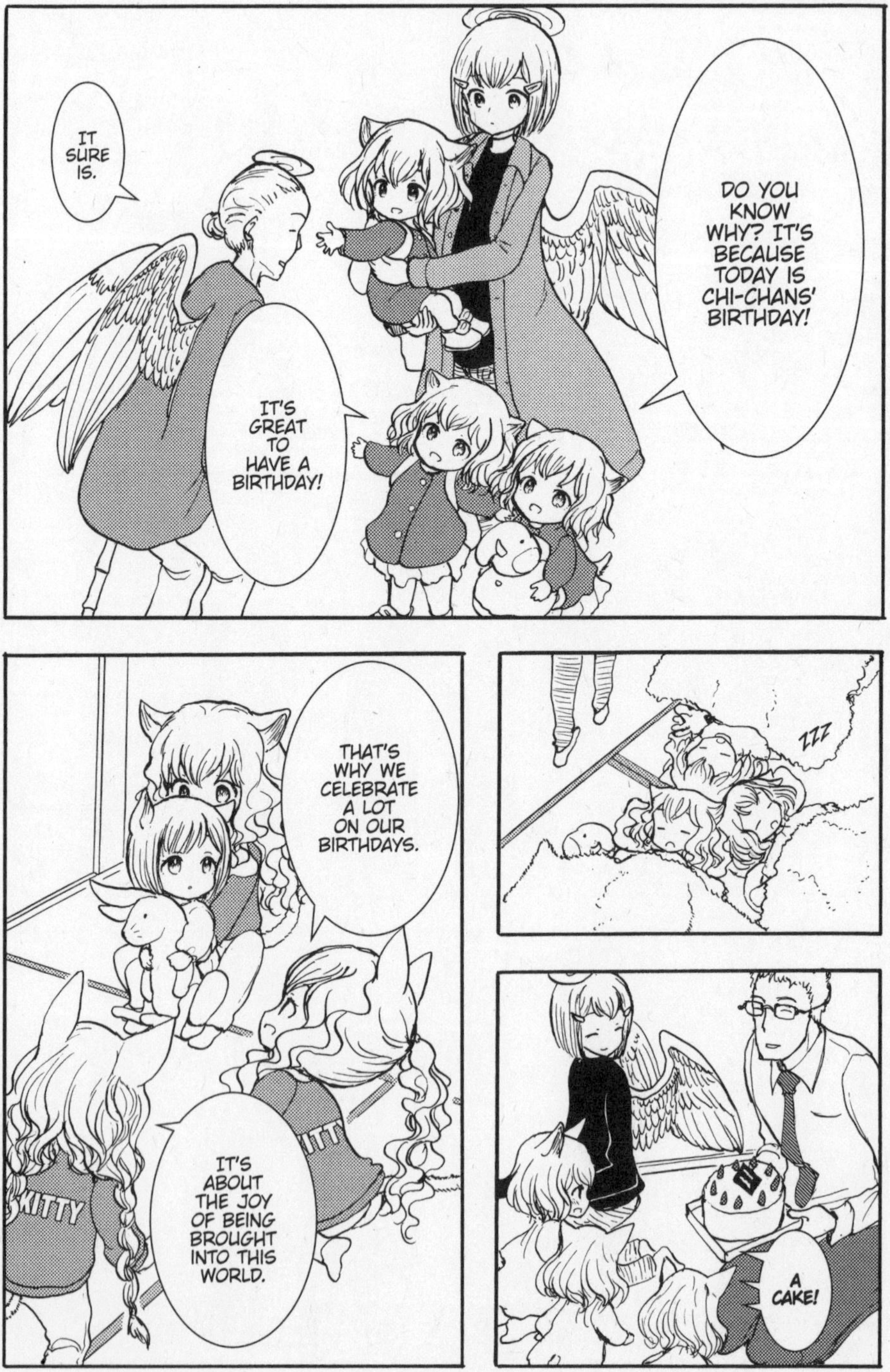
DO YOU KNOW WHY? IT'S BECAUSE TODAY IS CHI-CHANS' BIRTHDAY!
IT SURE IS.
IT'S GREAT TO HAVE A BIRTHDAY!
ZZZ
A CAKE!
THAT'S WHY WE CELEBRATE A LOT ON OUR BIRTHDAYS.
IT'S ABOUT THE JOY OF BEING BROUGHT INTO THIS WORLD.
KITTY

A Centaur's Life

HISTORY OF ARCHITECTURE IN JAPAN AND OTHER COUNTRIES: < 8 > ANATOLIAN DWELLING FROM 10,000 YEARS AGO

AGRICULTURE AND ANIMAL HUSBANDRY ARE SAID TO HAVE BEGUN AROUND 10,000 BC IN ANATOLIA. THIS STRUCTURE CONSISTS OF HOUSES MADE OF REEDS PLASTERED WITH MUD, WHICH ARE INTERCONNECTED WITH WALLS. THE ENTRANCES TO THESE HOUSES FACE INWARD. THE PURPOSE OF THIS MAY HAVE BEEN TO FENCE IN LIVESTOCK, AS WELL AS TO PROVIDE DEFENSE. PEOPLE ALSO SHARED THEIR LIVING SPACE WITH LIVESTOCK. THE DISCOVERY OF STONE TOOLS INDICATES THAT THE PEOPLE WHO LIVED IN THESE DWELLINGS SUBSISTED AT LEAST PARTIALLY BY FARMING AND BY RAISING LIVESTOCK.

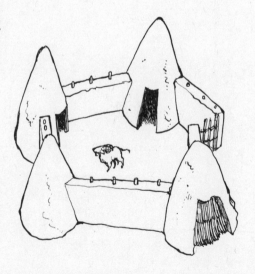

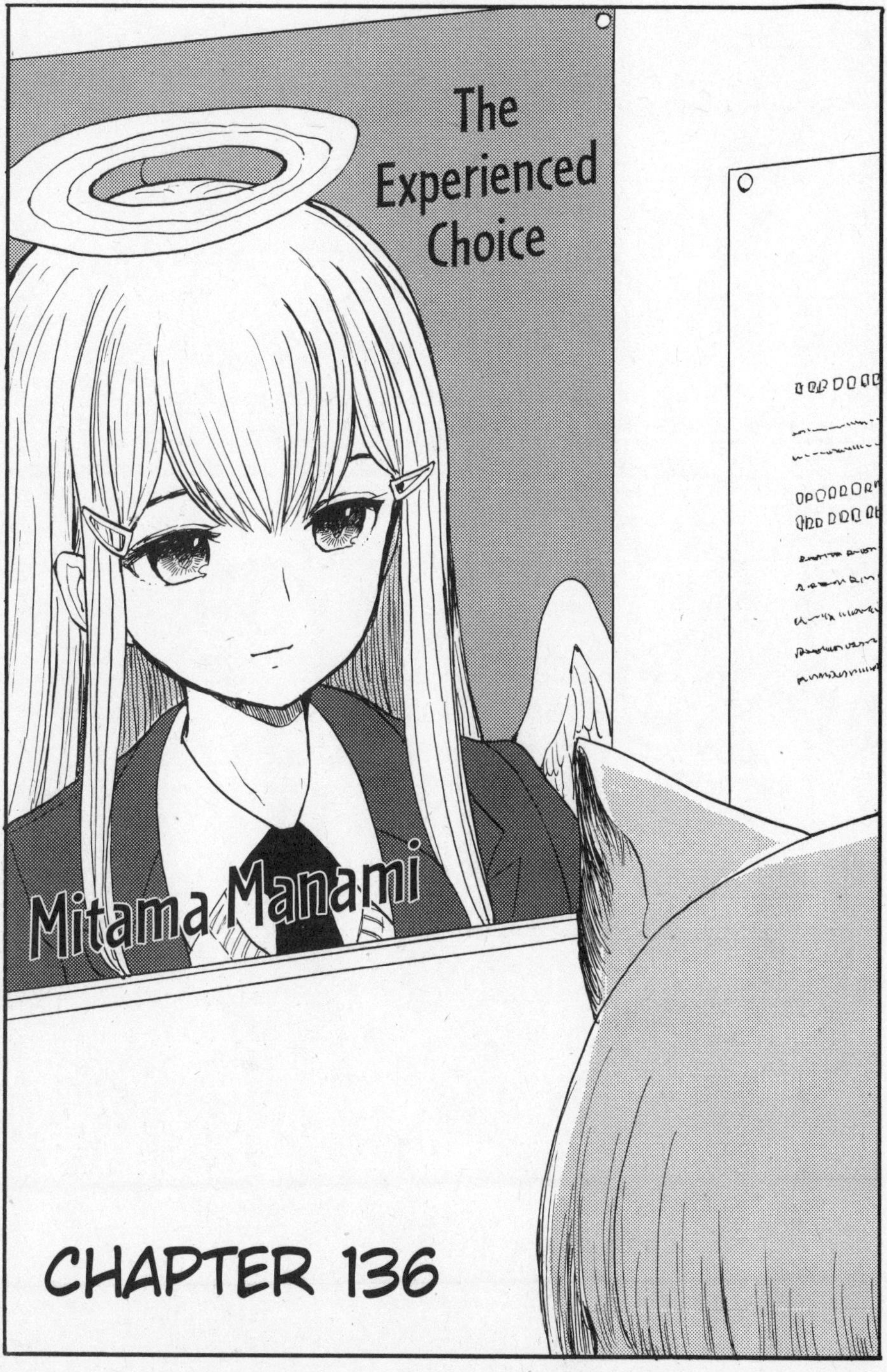
The Experienced Choice
Mitama Manami
CHAPTER 136

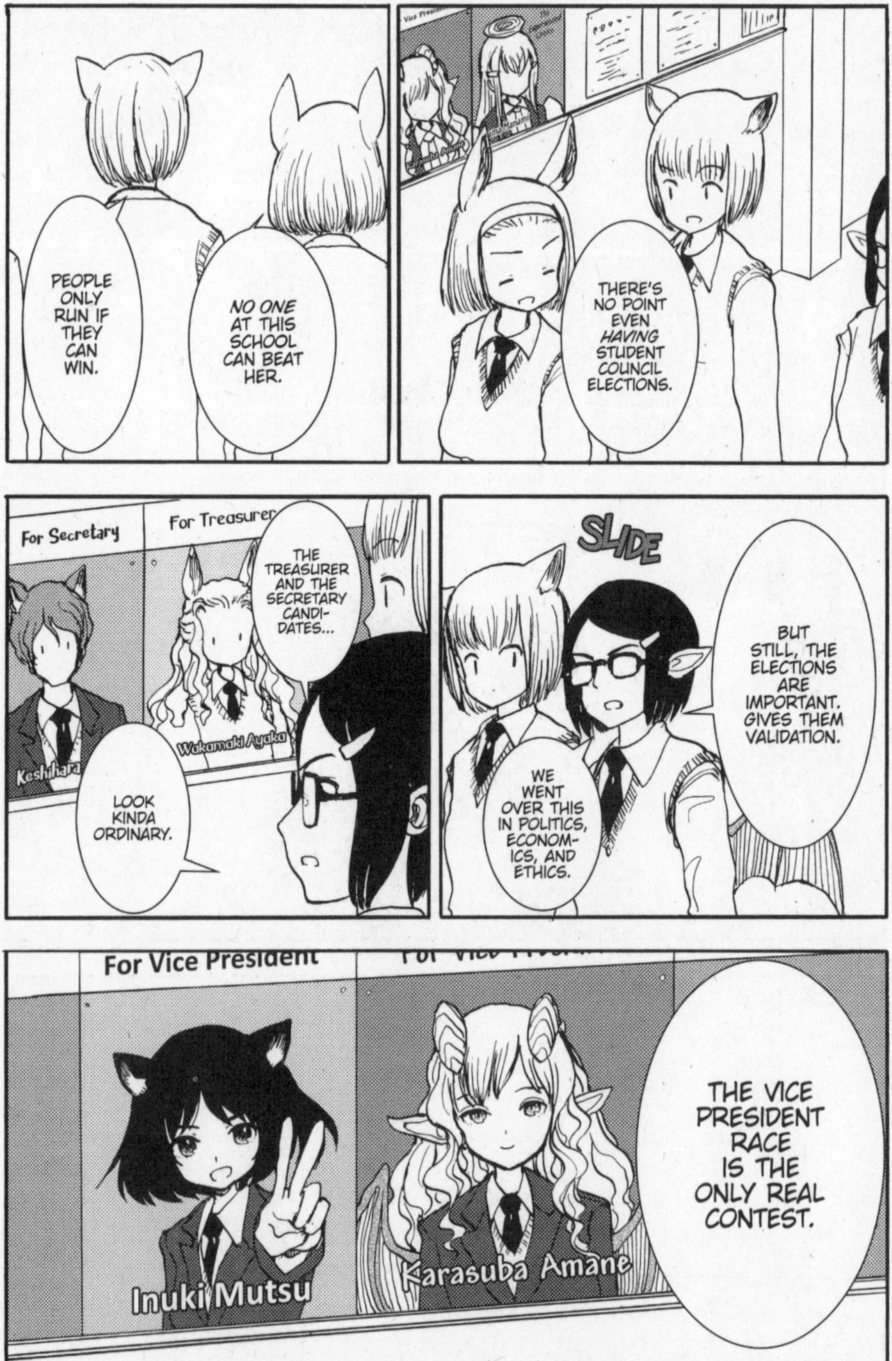
THERE'S NO POINT EVEN *HAVING* STUDENT COUNCIL ELECTIONS.
NO ONE AT THIS SCHOOL CAN BEAT HER.
PEOPLE ONLY RUN IF THEY CAN WIN.
SLIDE
BUT STILL, THE ELECTIONS ARE IMPORTANT. GIVES THEM VALIDATION.
WE WENT OVER THIS IN POLITICS, ECONOMICS, AND ETHICS.
THE TREASURER AND THE SECRETARY CANDIDATES...
For Treasurer
For Secretary
Wakamaki Ayaka
Keshihara
LOOK KINDA ORDINARY.
THE VICE PRESIDENT RACE IS THE ONLY REAL CONTEST.
For Vice President
Karasuba Amane
Inuki Mutsu

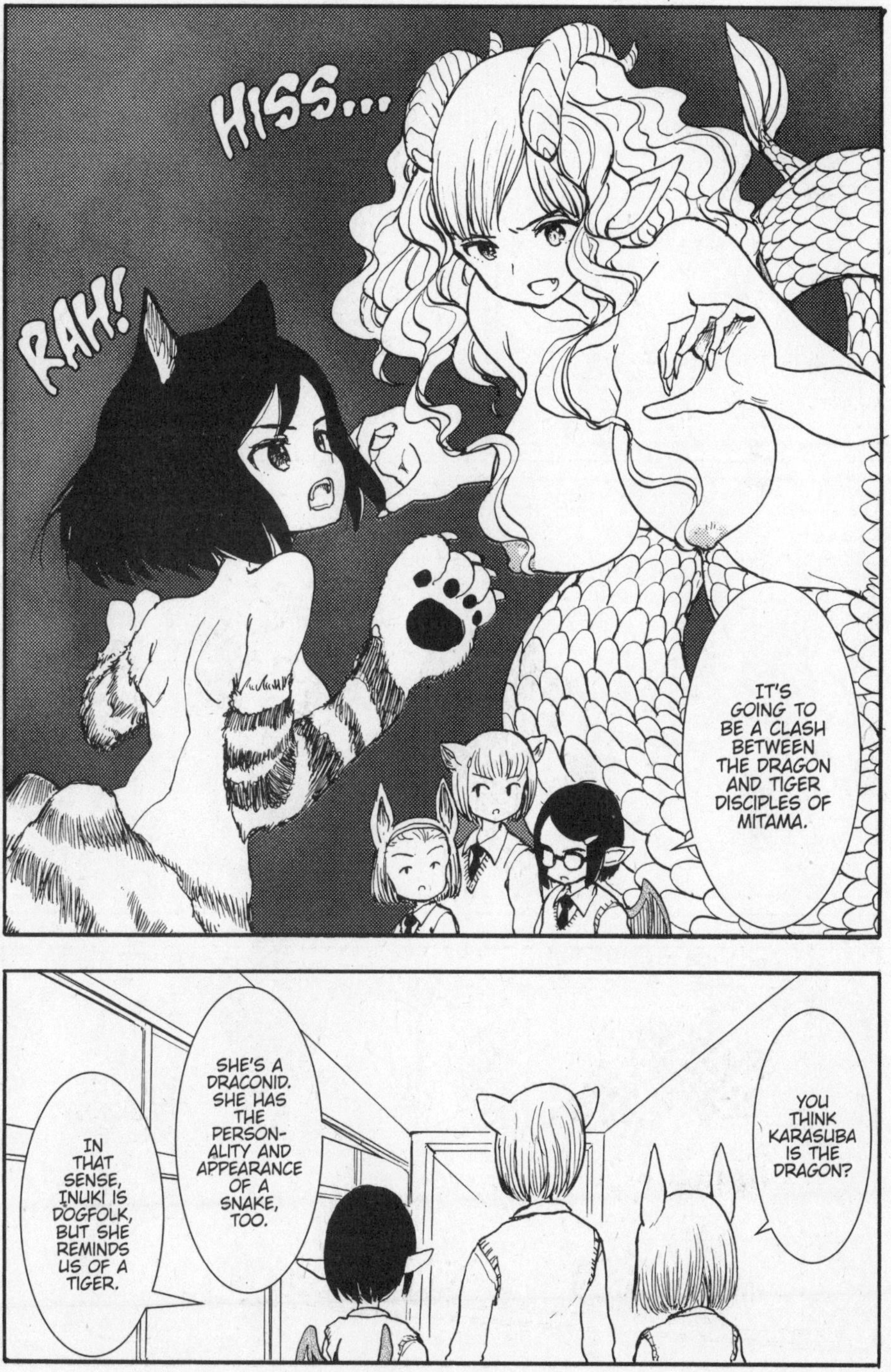
HISS...
RAH!
IT'S GOING TO BE A CLASH BETWEEN THE DRAGON AND TIGER DISCIPLES OF MITAMA.
YOU THINK KARASUBA IS THE DRAGON?
SHE'S A DRACONID. SHE HAS THE PERSON-ALITY AND APPEARANCE OF A SNAKE, TOO.
IN THAT SENSE, INUKI IS DOGFOLK, BUT SHE REMINDS US OF A TIGER.

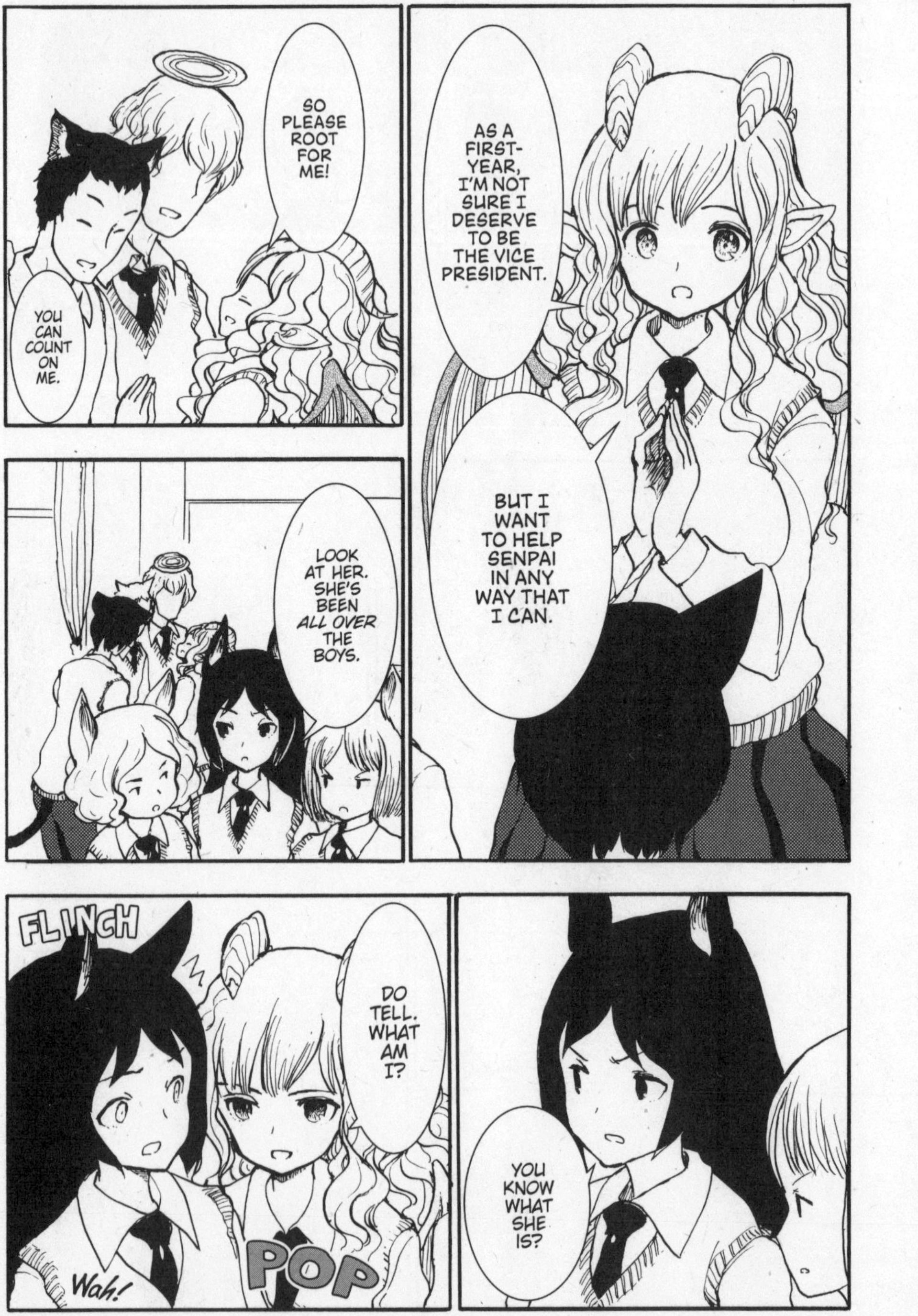
AS A FIRST-YEAR, I'M NOT SURE I DESERVE TO BE THE VICE PRESIDENT.
BUT I WANT TO HELP SENPAI IN ANY WAY THAT I CAN.
SO PLEASE ROOT FOR ME!
YOU CAN COUNT ON ME.
LOOK AT HER. SHE'S BEEN *ALL OVER* THE BOYS.
YOU KNOW WHAT SHE IS?
DO TELL. WHAT AM I?
FLINCH
POP
Wah!

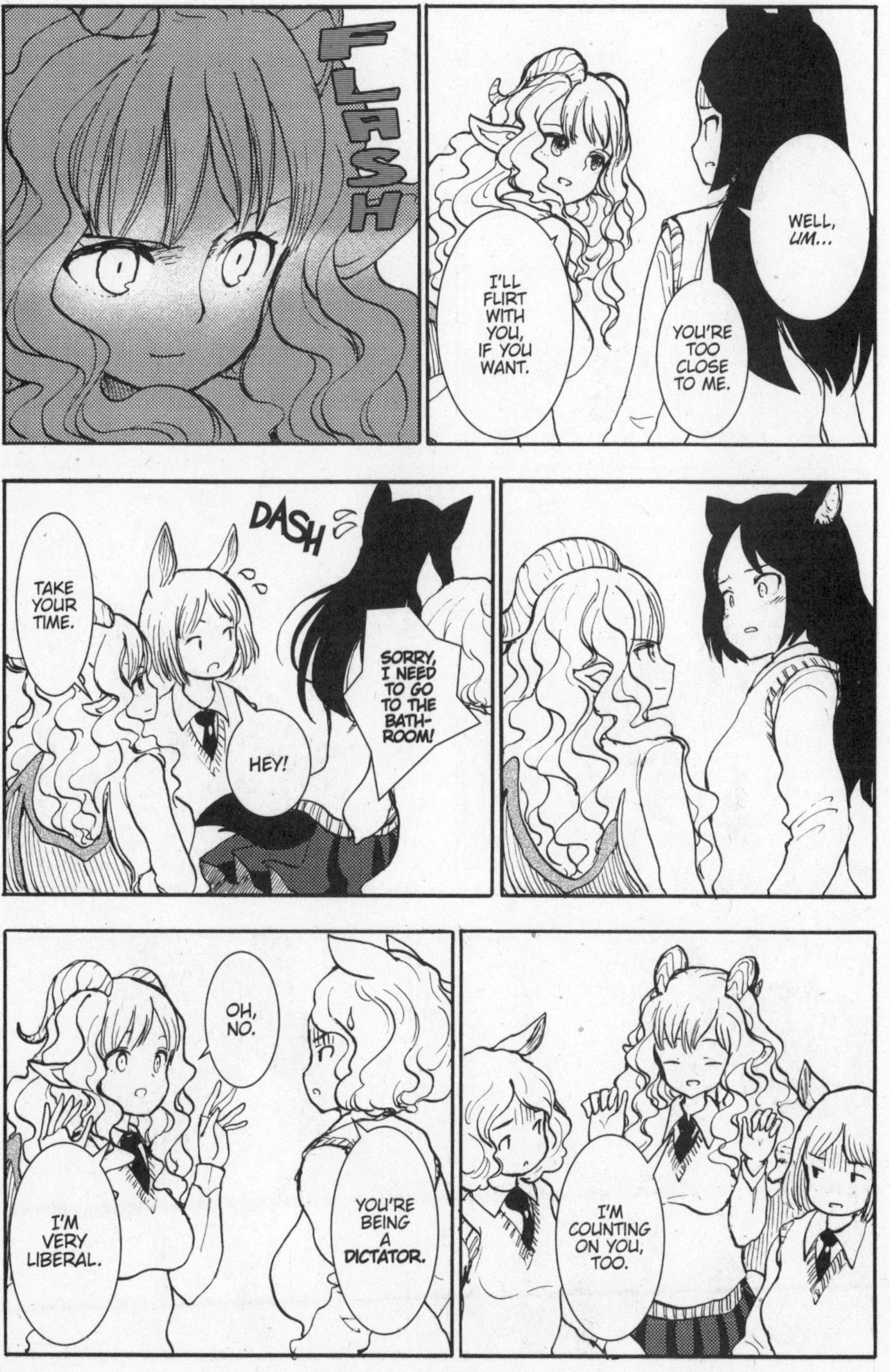
WELL, UM...
YOU'RE TOO CLOSE TO ME.
I'LL FLIRT WITH YOU, IF YOU WANT.
FLASH
DASH
SORRY, I NEED TO GO TO THE BATHROOM!
HEY!
TAKE YOUR TIME.
I'M COUNTING ON YOU, TOO.
OH, NO.
YOU'RE BEING A DICTATOR.
I'M VERY LIBERAL.

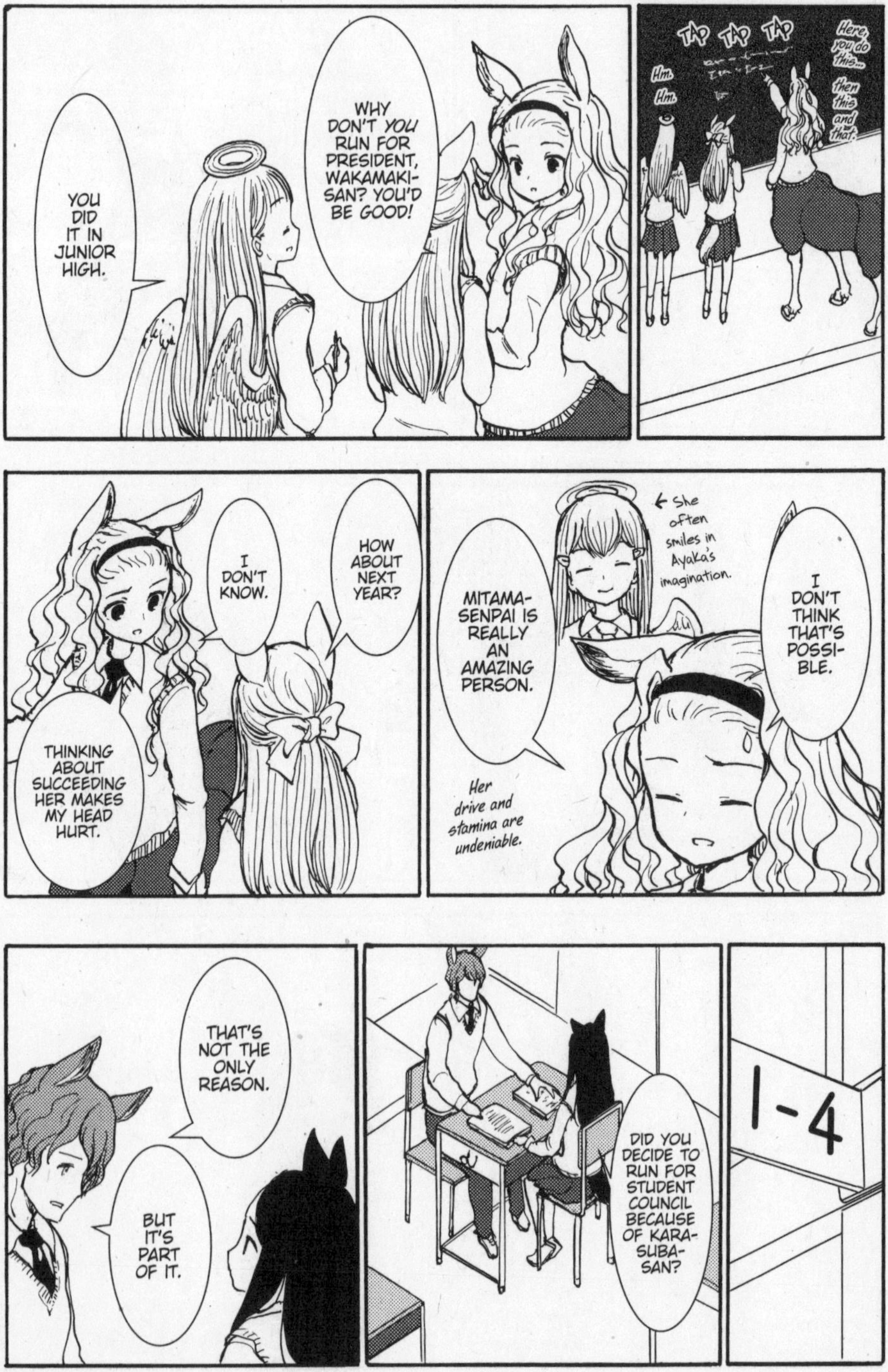
TAP TAP TAP
Here, you do this... then this and that.
Hm. Hm.
WHY DON'T YOU RUN FOR PRESIDENT, WAKAMAKI-SAN? YOU'D BE GOOD!
YOU DID IT IN JUNIOR HIGH.
I DON'T THINK THAT'S POSSIBLE.
← She often smiles in Ayaka's imagination.
MITAMA-SENPAI IS REALLY AN AMAZING PERSON.
Her drive and stamina are undeniable.
HOW ABOUT NEXT YEAR?
I DON'T KNOW.
THINKING ABOUT SUCCEEDING HER MAKES MY HEAD HURT.
1-4
DID YOU DECIDE TO RUN FOR STUDENT COUNCIL BECAUSE OF KARASUBA-SAN?
THAT'S NOT THE ONLY REASON.
BUT IT'S PART OF IT.

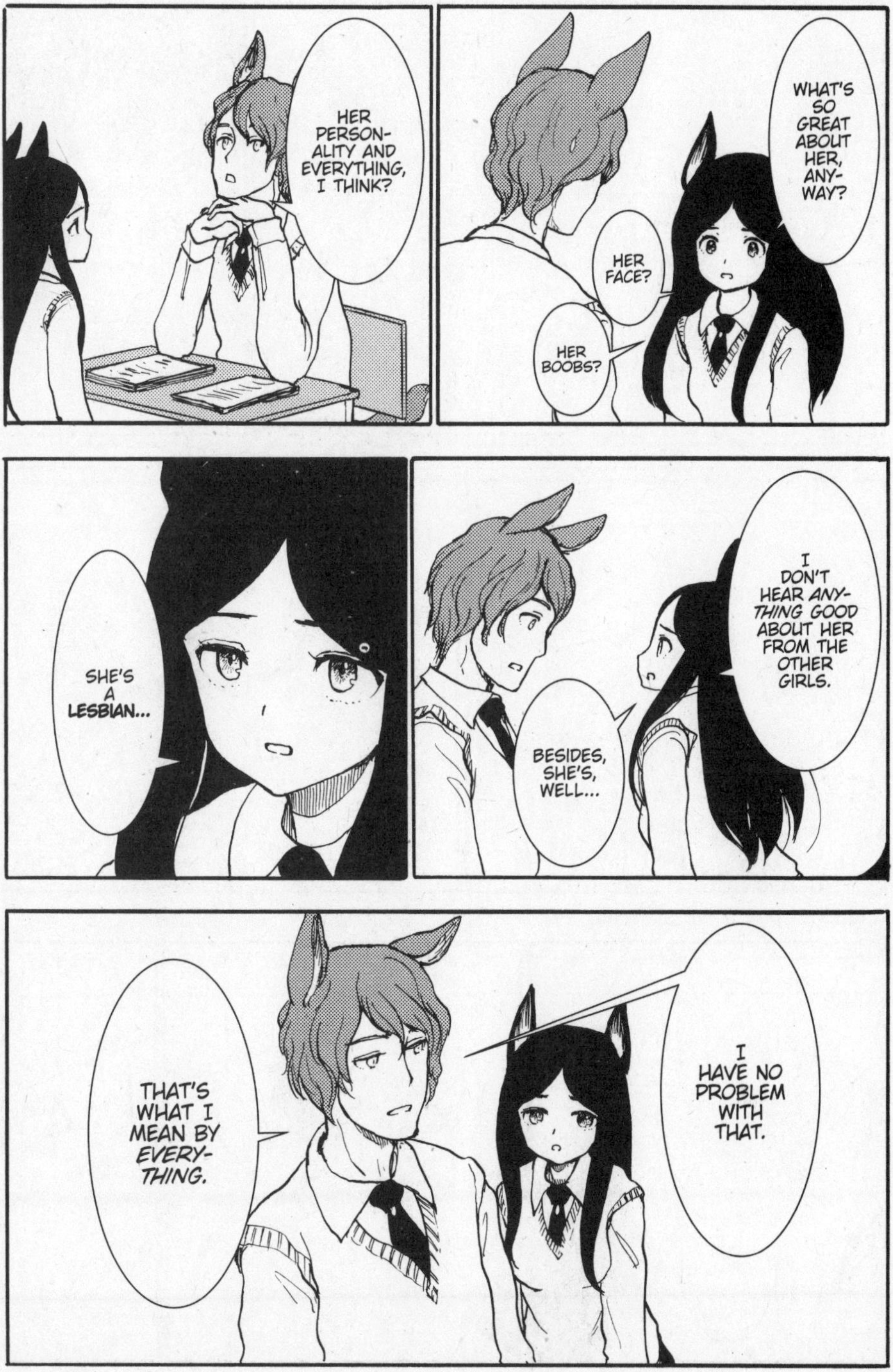
WHAT'S SO GREAT ABOUT HER, ANYWAY?
HER FACE?
HER BOOBS?
HER PERSONALITY AND EVERYTHING, I THINK?
I DON'T HEAR *ANYTHING* GOOD ABOUT HER FROM THE OTHER GIRLS.
BESIDES, SHE'S, WELL...
SHE'S A LESBIAN...
I HAVE NO PROBLEM WITH THAT.
THAT'S WHAT I MEAN BY *EVERYTHING*.

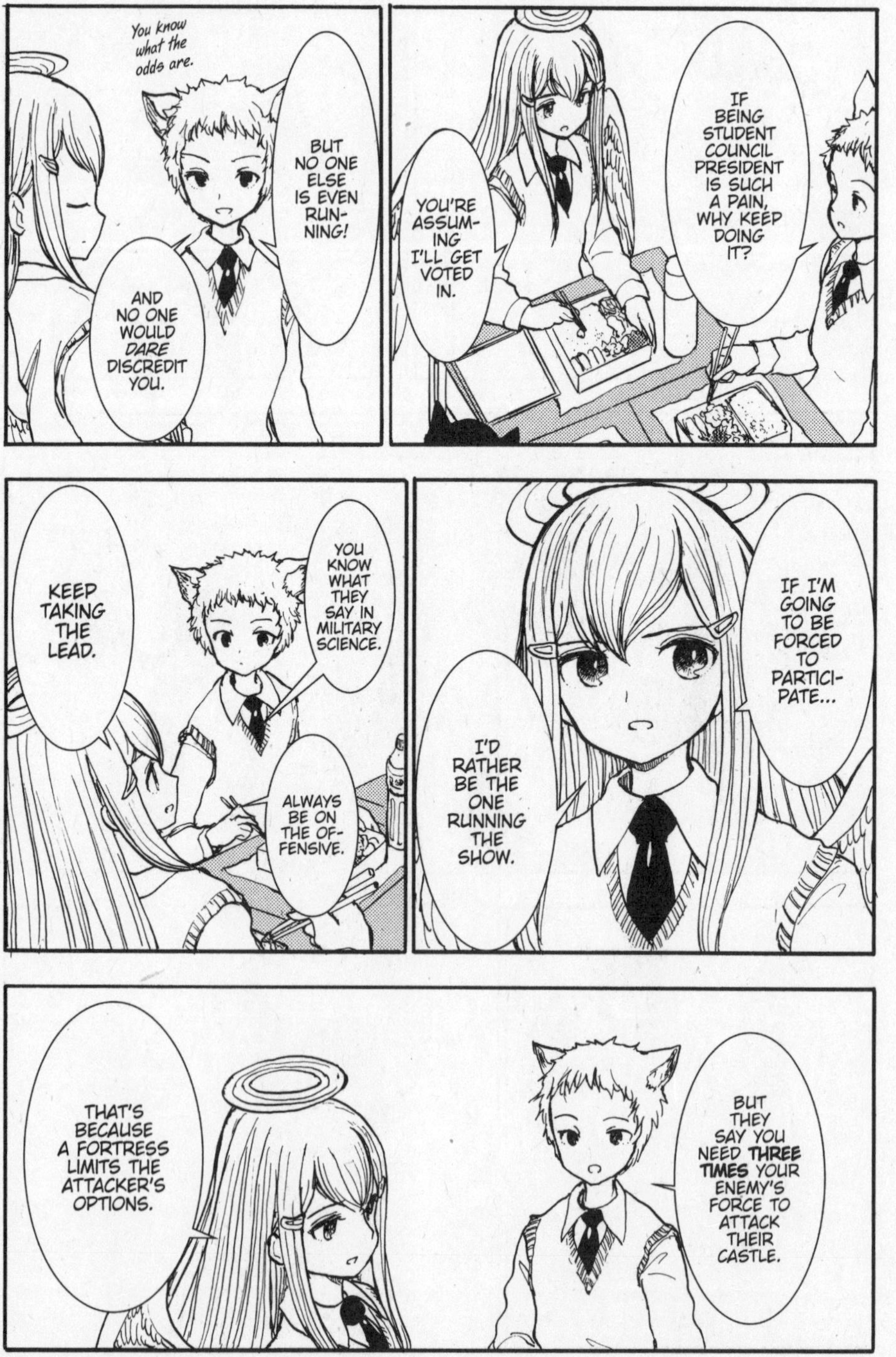
IF BEING STUDENT COUNCIL PRESIDENT IS SUCH A PAIN, WHY KEEP DOING IT?
YOU'RE ASSUMING I'LL GET VOTED IN.
BUT NO ONE ELSE IS EVEN RUNNING!
You know what the odds are.
AND NO ONE WOULD *DARE* DISCREDIT YOU.
IF I'M GOING TO BE FORCED TO PARTICIPATE...
I'D RATHER BE THE ONE RUNNING THE SHOW.
YOU KNOW WHAT THEY SAY IN MILITARY SCIENCE.
ALWAYS BE ON THE OFFENSIVE.
KEEP TAKING THE LEAD.
BUT THEY SAY YOU NEED **THREE TIMES** YOUR ENEMY'S FORCE TO ATTACK THEIR CASTLE.
THAT'S BECAUSE A FORTRESS LIMITS THE ATTACKER'S OPTIONS.

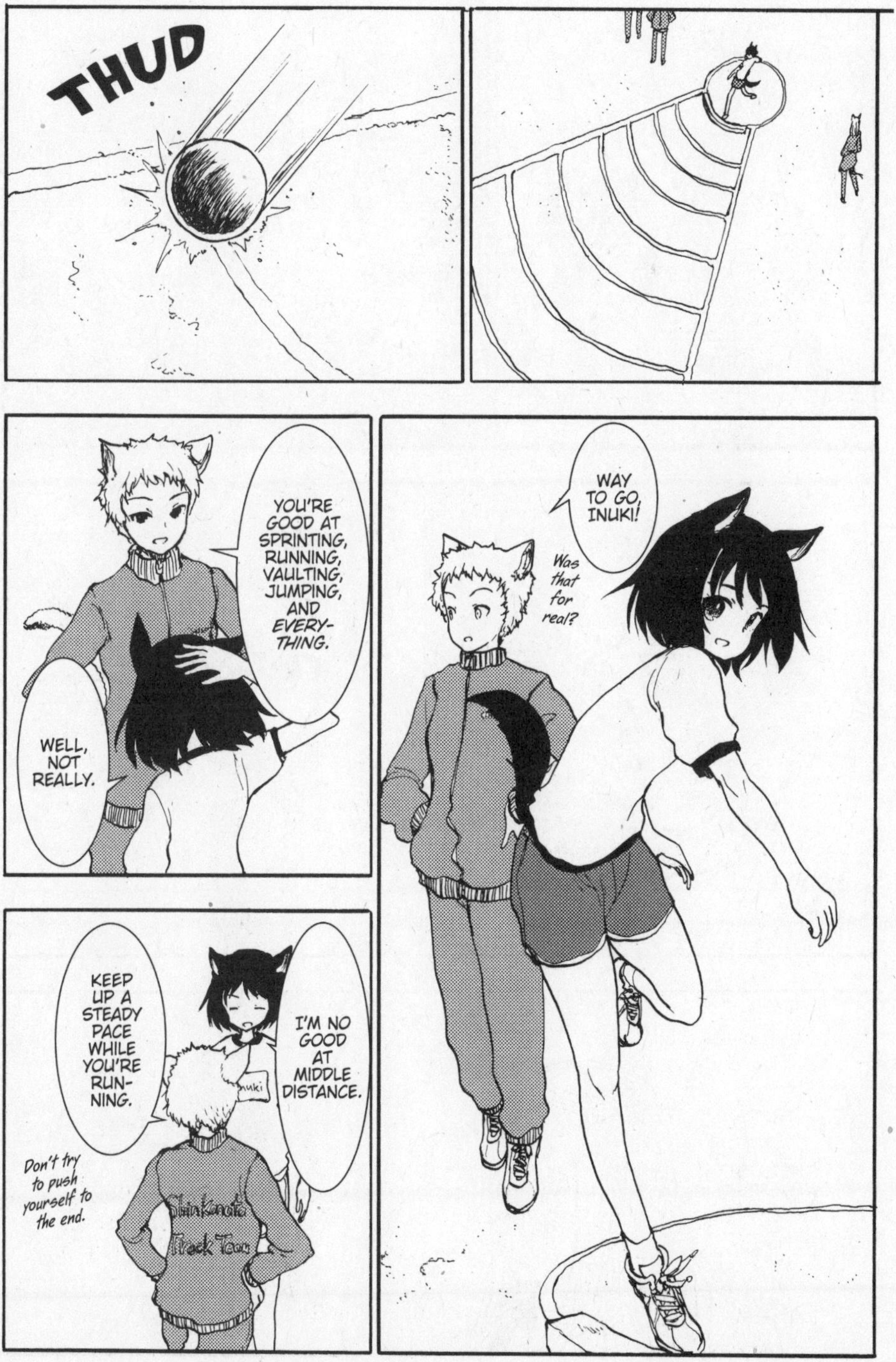
THUD
WAY TO GO, INUKI!
Was that for real?
YOU'RE GOOD AT SPRINTING, RUNNING, VAULTING, JUMPING, AND EVERY-THING.
WELL, NOT REALLY.
I'M NO GOOD AT MIDDLE DISTANCE.
KEEP UP A STEADY PACE WHILE YOU'RE RUN-NING.
Don't try to push yourself to the end.

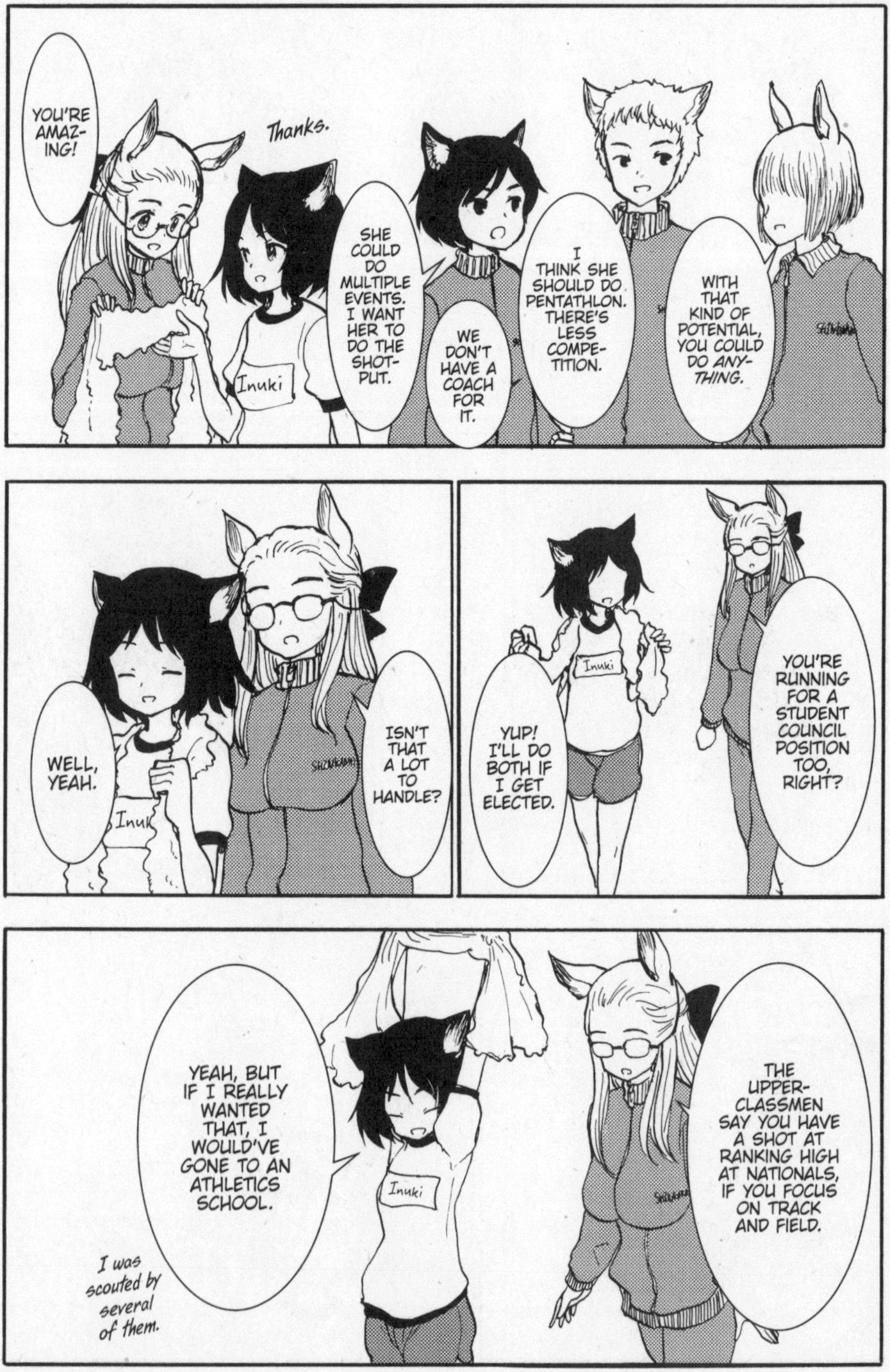
WITH THAT KIND OF POTENTIAL, YOU COULD DO *ANYTHING*.
I THINK SHE SHOULD DO PENTATHLON. THERE'S LESS COMPETITION.
SHE COULD DO MULTIPLE EVENTS. I WANT HER TO DO THE SHOT-PUT.
WE DON'T HAVE A COACH FOR IT.
Thanks.
YOU'RE AMAZ-ING!
YOU'RE RUNNING FOR A STUDENT COUNCIL POSITION TOO, RIGHT?
YUP! I'LL DO BOTH IF I GET ELECTED.
ISN'T THAT A LOT TO HANDLE?
WELL, YEAH.
THE UPPER-CLASSMEN SAY YOU HAVE A SHOT AT RANKING HIGH AT NATIONALS, IF YOU FOCUS ON TRACK AND FIELD.
YEAH, BUT IF I REALLY WANTED THAT, I WOULD'VE GONE TO AN ATHLETICS SCHOOL.
I was scouted by several of them.

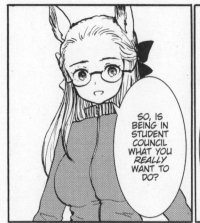

I LIKE WORKING OUT AND RUNNING.
I LIKE GETTING MEDALS, JUST LIKE EVERYONE ELSE.
BUT I DON'T INTEND TO GO PRO AND MAKE A LIVING OUT OF IT.
SO, IS BEING IN STUDENT COUNCIL WHAT YOU *REALLY* WANT TO DO?
THERE'S SOMEONE THERE THAT I LOOK UP TO.
KARA-SUBA-SAN?
NO WAY IN **HELL.**
I'D SAY SHE'S MORE LIKE MY **RIVAL.**
I'm better than you.
SHE'S IMPRESSIVE, I'LL ADMIT...
BUT I DON'T ADMIRE HER THAT WAY.
SHE'S POPULAR WITH GUYS BECAUSE SHE'S ALL GOOD LOOKS AND BOOBS.
CAN YOU WIN?
IT'S NOT A **PAGEANT,** YOU KNOW.

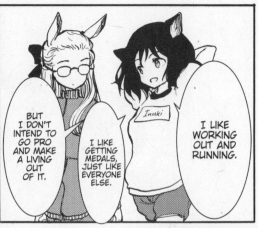

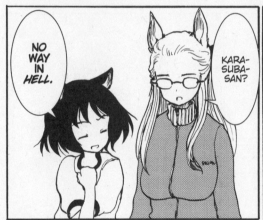

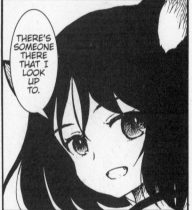

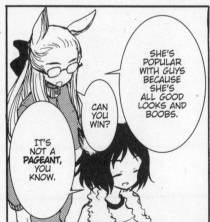

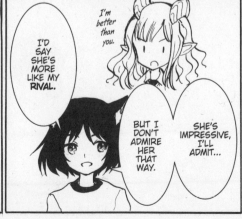

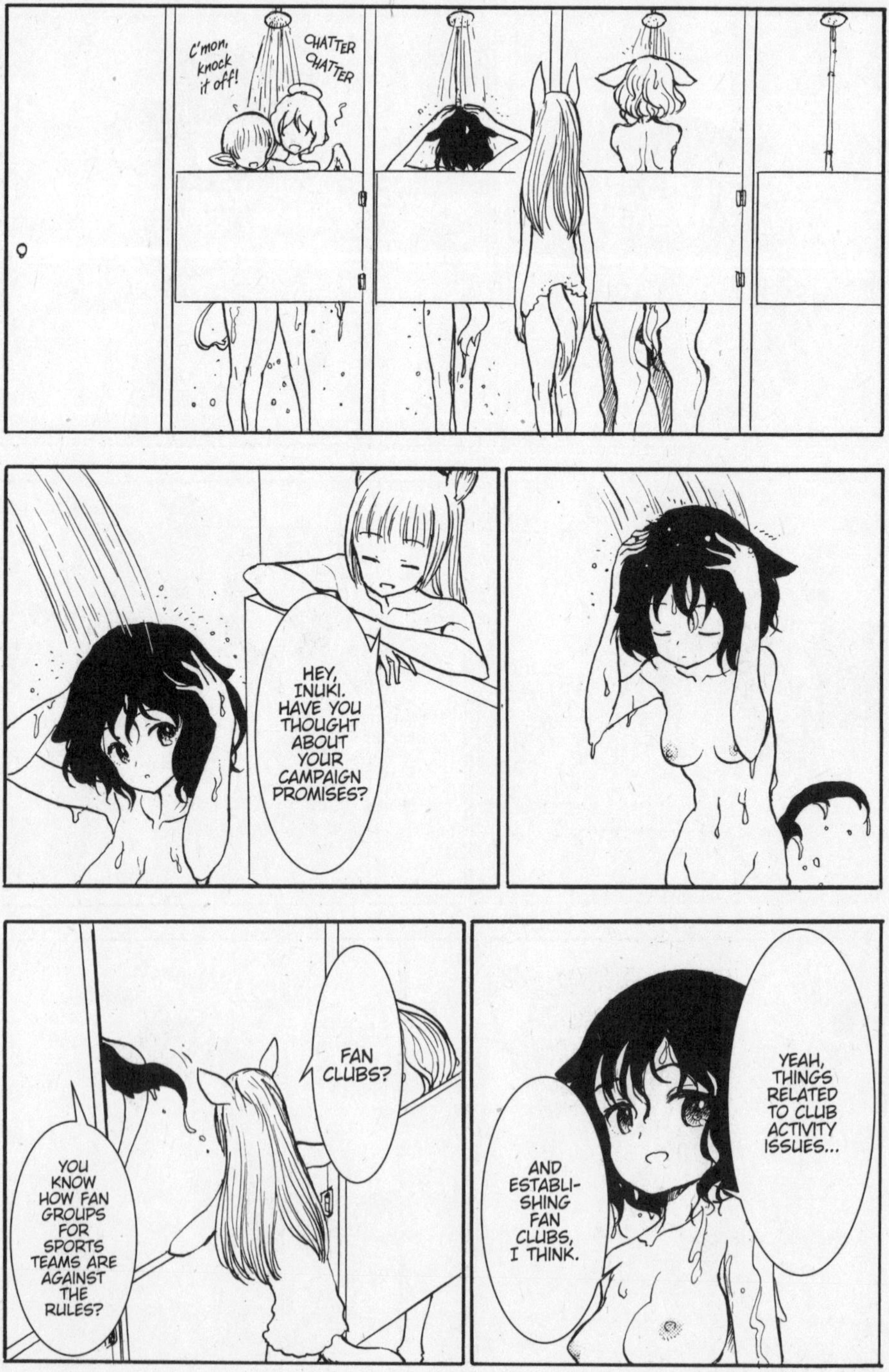
CHATTER CHATTER
C'mon, knock it off!
HEY, INUKI. HAVE YOU THOUGHT ABOUT YOUR CAMPAIGN PROMISES?
YEAH, THINGS RELATED TO CLUB ACTIVITY ISSUES...
AND ESTABLI-SHING FAN CLUBS, I THINK.
FAN CLUBS?
YOU KNOW HOW FAN GROUPS FOR SPORTS TEAMS ARE AGAINST THE RULES?

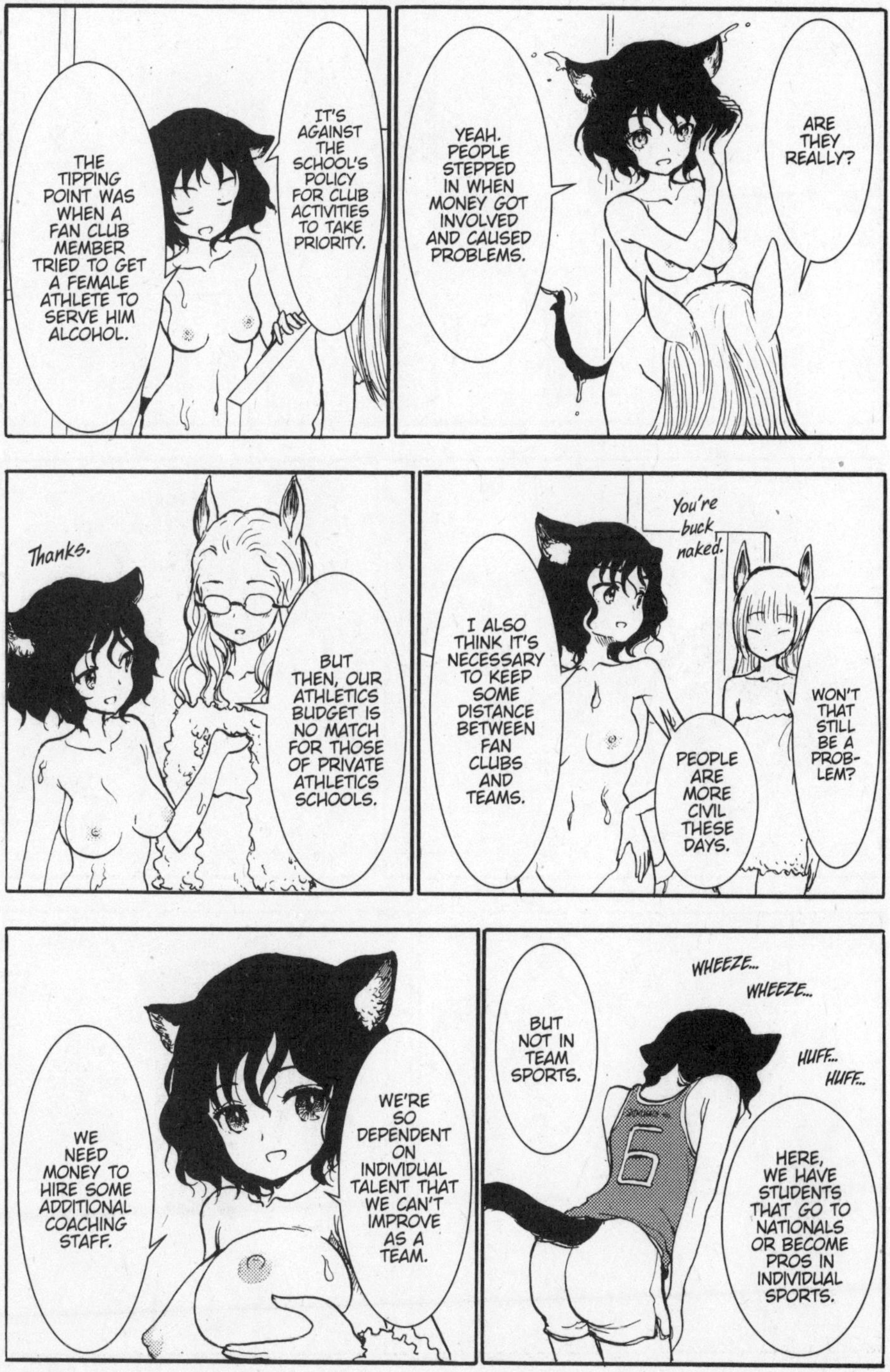
ARE THEY REALLY?
YEAH. PEOPLE STEPPED IN WHEN MONEY GOT INVOLVED AND CAUSED PROBLEMS.
IT'S AGAINST THE SCHOOL'S POLICY FOR CLUB ACTIVITIES TO TAKE PRIORITY.
THE TIPPING POINT WAS WHEN A FAN CLUB MEMBER TRIED TO GET A FEMALE ATHLETE TO SERVE HIM ALCOHOL.
You're buck naked.
WON'T THAT STILL BE A PROB-LEM?
PEOPLE ARE MORE CIVIL THESE DAYS.
I ALSO THINK IT'S NECESSARY TO KEEP SOME DISTANCE BETWEEN FAN CLUBS AND TEAMS.
BUT THEN, OUR ATHLETICS BUDGET IS NO MATCH FOR THOSE OF PRIVATE ATHLETICS SCHOOLS.
Thanks.
WHEEZE...
WHEEZE...
HUFF...
HUFF...
HERE, WE HAVE STUDENTS THAT GO TO NATIONALS OR BECOME PROS IN INDIVIDUAL SPORTS.
BUT NOT IN TEAM SPORTS.
WE'RE SO DEPENDENT ON INDIVIDUAL TALENT THAT WE CAN'T IMPROVE AS A TEAM.
WE NEED MONEY TO HIRE SOME ADDITIONAL COACHING STAFF.

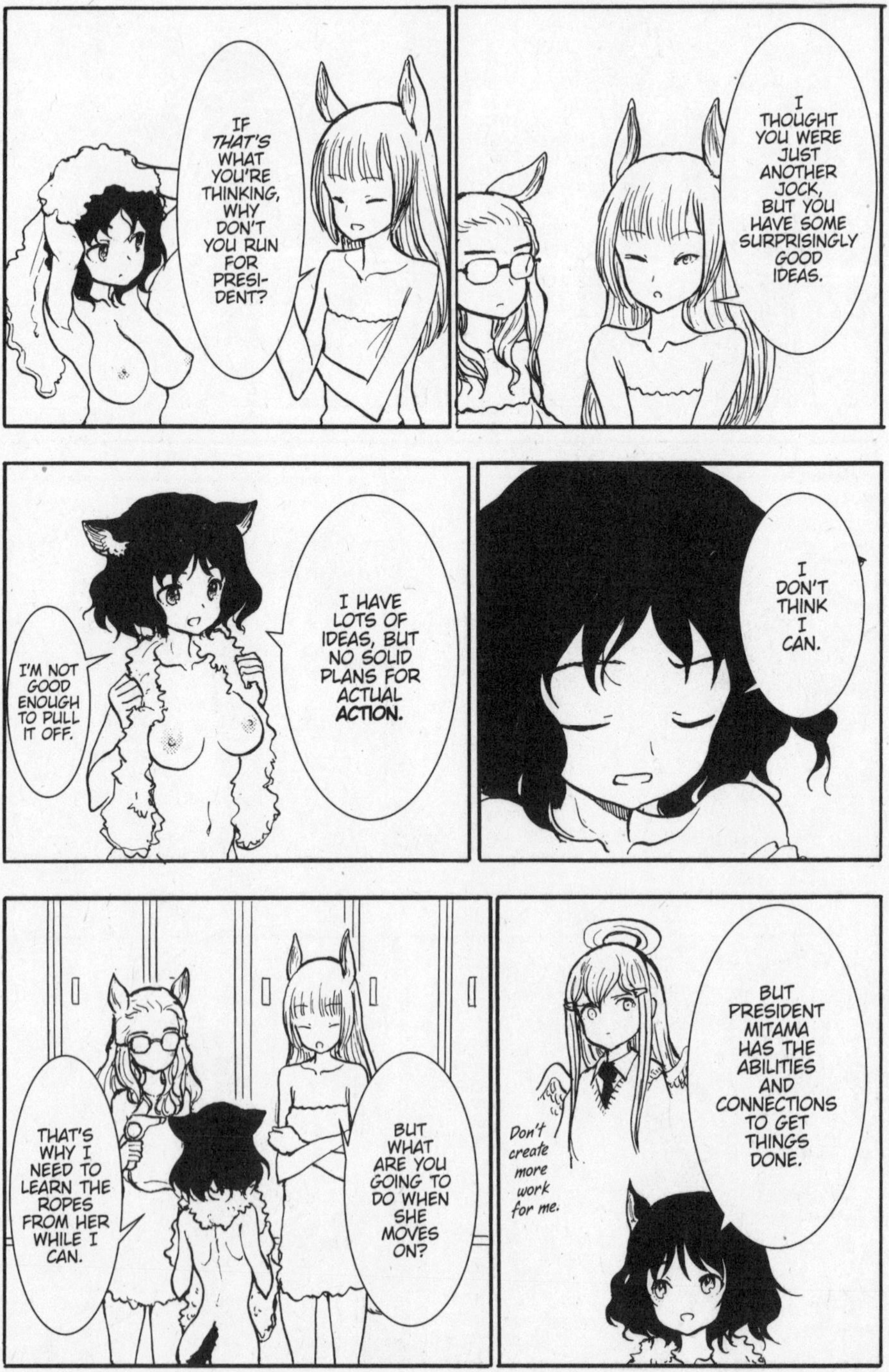
I THOUGHT YOU WERE JUST ANOTHER JOCK, BUT YOU HAVE SOME SURPRISINGLY GOOD IDEAS.
IF *THAT'S* WHAT YOU'RE THINKING, WHY DON'T YOU RUN FOR PRESI-DENT?
I DON'T THINK I CAN.
I HAVE LOTS OF IDEAS, BUT NO SOLID PLANS FOR ACTUAL **ACTION.**
I'M NOT GOOD ENOUGH TO PULL IT OFF.
BUT PRESIDENT MITAMA HAS THE ABILITIES AND CONNECTIONS TO GET THINGS DONE.
Don't create more work for me.
BUT WHAT ARE YOU GOING TO DO WHEN SHE MOVES ON?
THAT'S WHY I NEED TO LEARN THE ROPES FROM HER WHILE I CAN.

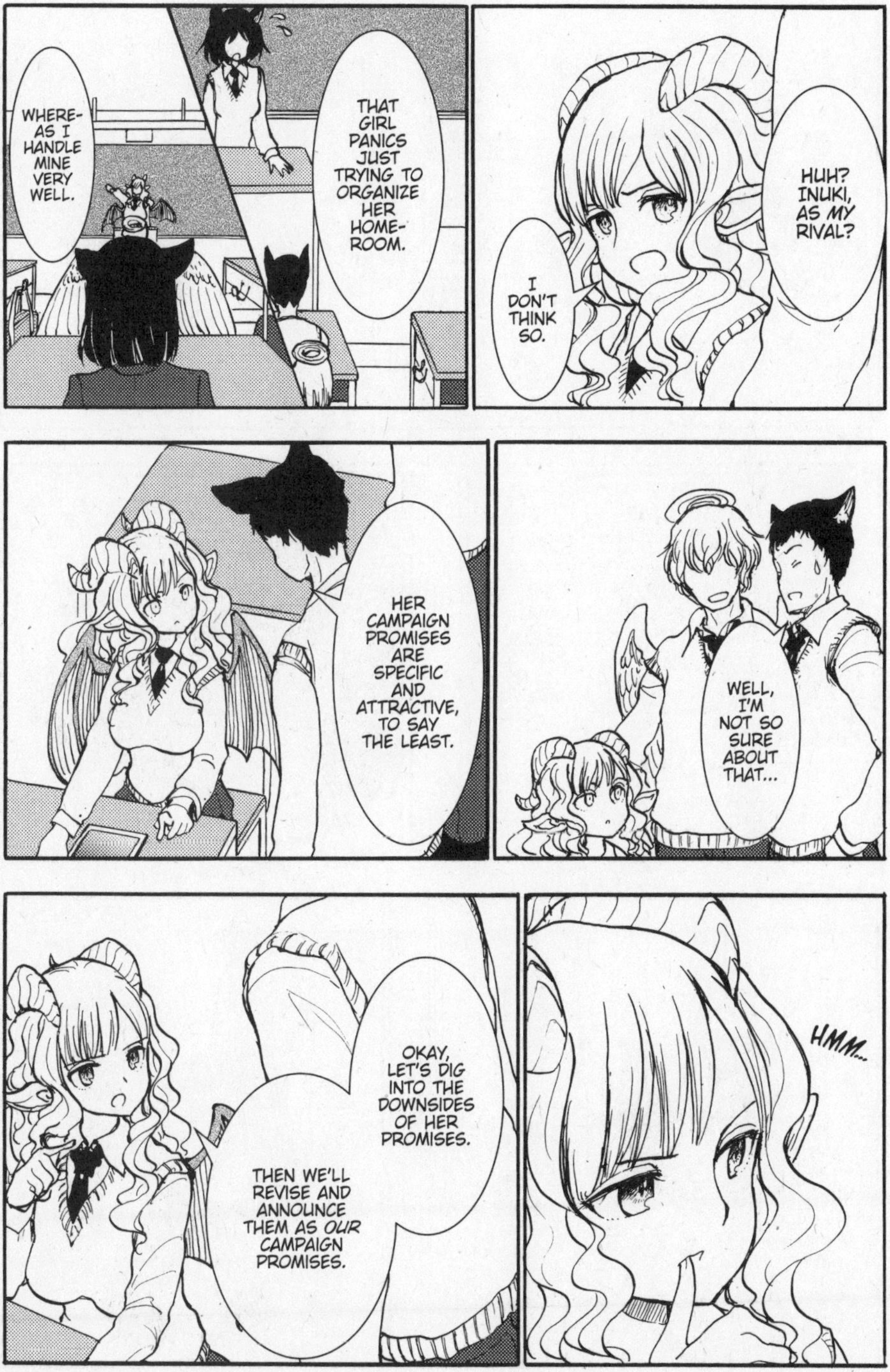
HUH? INUKI, AS MY RIVAL?
I DON'T THINK SO.
THAT GIRL PANICS JUST TRYING TO ORGANIZE HER HOME-ROOM.
WHERE-AS I HANDLE MINE VERY WELL.
WELL, I'M NOT SO SURE ABOUT THAT...
HER CAMPAIGN PROMISES ARE SPECIFIC AND ATTRACTIVE, TO SAY THE LEAST.
HMM...
OKAY, LET'S DIG INTO THE DOWNSIDES OF HER PROMISES.
THEN WE'LL REVISE AND ANNOUNCE THEM AS *OUR* CAMPAIGN PROMISES.

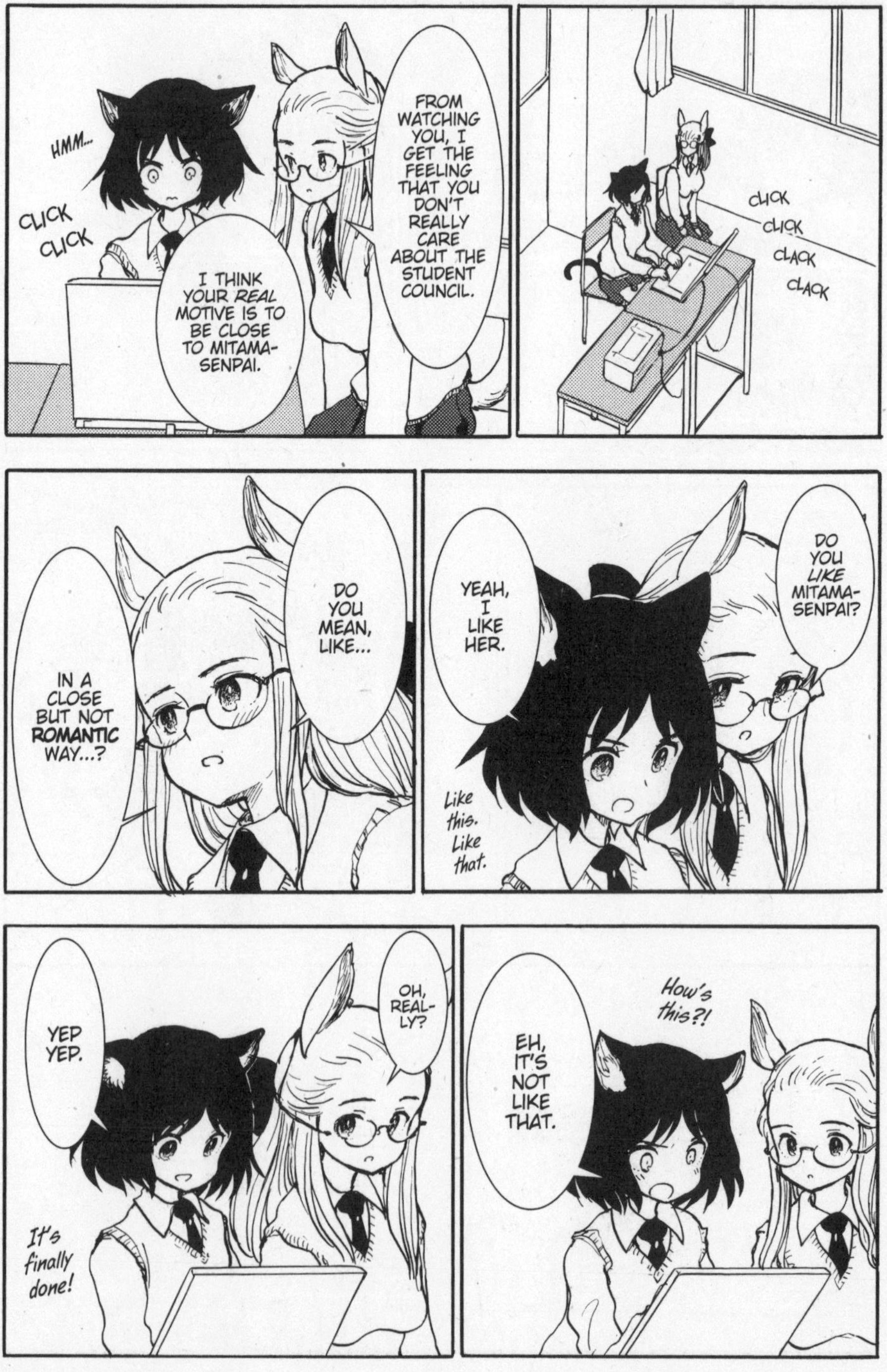
CLICK
CLICK
CLACK
CLACK
FROM WATCHING YOU, I GET THE FEELING THAT YOU DON'T REALLY CARE ABOUT THE STUDENT COUNCIL.
I THINK YOUR *REAL* MOTIVE IS TO BE CLOSE TO MITAMA-SENPAI.
HMM...
CLICK CLICK
DO YOU *LIKE* MITAMA-SENPAI?
YEAH, I LIKE HER.
Like this. Like that.
DO YOU MEAN, LIKE...
IN A CLOSE BUT NOT **ROMANTIC** WAY...?
How's this?!
EH, IT'S NOT LIKE THAT.
OH, REAL-LY?
YEP YEP.
It's finally done!

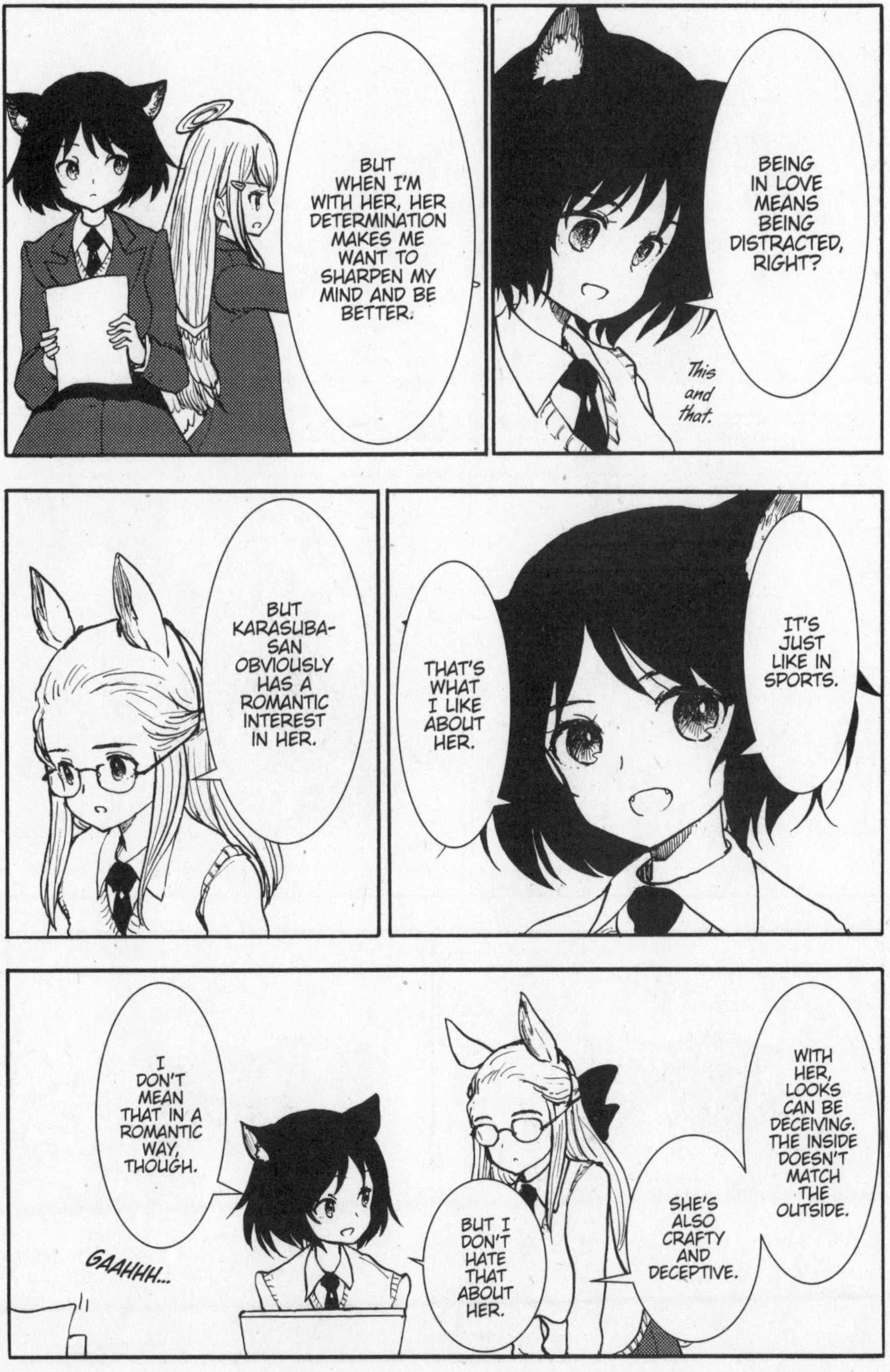
BEING IN LOVE MEANS BEING DISTRACTED, RIGHT?
This and that.
BUT WHEN I'M WITH HER, HER DETERMINATION MAKES ME WANT TO SHARPEN MY MIND AND BE BETTER.
IT'S JUST LIKE IN SPORTS.
THAT'S WHAT I LIKE ABOUT HER.
BUT KARASUBA-SAN OBVIOUSLY HAS A ROMANTIC INTEREST IN HER.
WITH HER, LOOKS CAN BE DECEIVING. THE INSIDE DOESN'T MATCH THE OUTSIDE.
SHE'S ALSO CRAFTY AND DECEPTIVE.
BUT I DON'T HATE THAT ABOUT HER.
I DON'T MEAN THAT IN A ROMANTIC WAY, THOUGH.
GAAHHH...

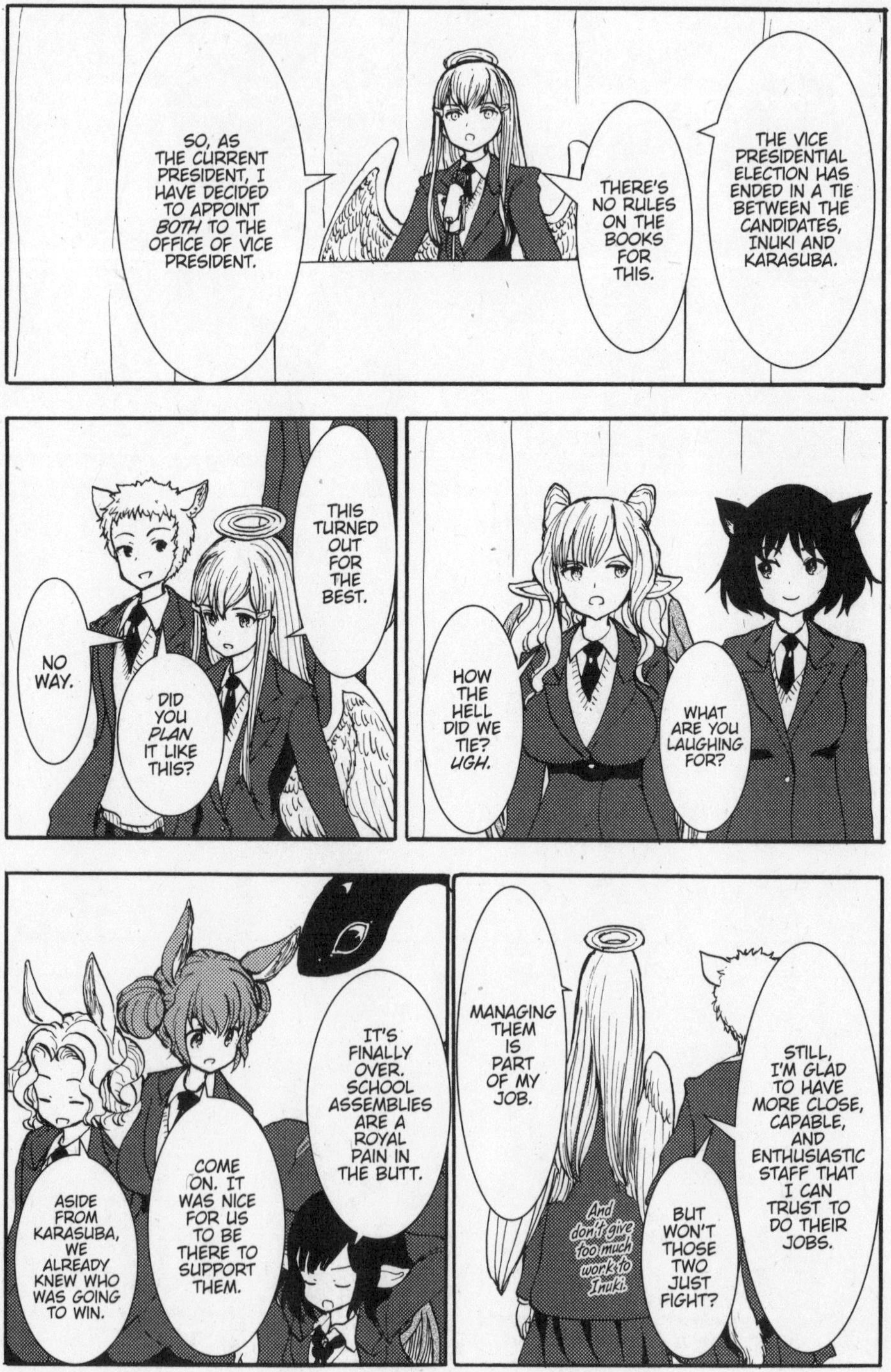
THE VICE PRESIDENTIAL ELECTION HAS ENDED IN A TIE BETWEEN THE CANDIDATES, INUKI AND KARASUBA.
THERE'S NO RULES ON THE BOOKS FOR THIS.
SO, AS THE CURRENT PRESIDENT, I HAVE DECIDED TO APPOINT *BOTH* TO THE OFFICE OF VICE PRESIDENT.
WHAT ARE YOU LAUGHING FOR?
HOW THE HELL DID WE TIE? *UGH.*
THIS TURNED OUT FOR THE BEST.
DID YOU *PLAN* IT LIKE THIS?
NO WAY.
STILL, I'M GLAD TO HAVE MORE CLOSE, CAPABLE, AND ENTHUSIASTIC STAFF THAT I CAN TRUST TO DO THEIR JOBS.
BUT WON'T THOSE TWO JUST FIGHT?
MANAGING THEM IS PART OF MY JOB.
And don't give too much work to Inuki.
IT'S FINALLY OVER. SCHOOL ASSEMBLIES ARE A ROYAL PAIN IN THE BUTT.
COME ON. IT WAS NICE FOR US TO BE THERE TO SUPPORT THEM.
ASIDE FROM KARASUBA, WE ALREADY KNEW WHO WAS GOING TO WIN.

A Centaur's Life

HISTORY OF ARCHITECTURE IN JAPAN AND OTHER COUNTRIES: < 9 > WESTERN CASTLES

IN THE ANCIENT EMPIRE, ALL PEOPLE--INCLUDING CENTAURS-- WERE ALLOWED TO BECOME CITIZENS AND COULD EVEN RISE TO EMPEROR STATUS. IN CONTRAST, THE WESTERN CIVILIZATION THAT TOOK ITS PLACE RECOGNIZED CENTAURS ONLY AS LIVESTOCK. MEDIEVAL CASTLES, WHICH SUFFERED ATTACKS BY BANDS OF NOMADIC CENTAURS, WERE MASSIVE BUT SIMPLE STRUCTURES OF STONE. THE TECHNOLOGIES OF ARCHES AND CONCRETE THAT WERE USED IN THE ARCHITECTURE OF THE ANCIENT EMPIRE WERE LOST, AND LARGE, THICK STONES WERE REQUIRED TO SUPPORT THE WEIGHT OF THE STRUCTURE. PASSAGES THAT LED TO THE CASTELLAN OR OTHER IMPORTANT AREAS WERE SO NARROW AND CRAMPED THAT IT WAS DIFFICULT FOR CENTAURS TO PASS THROUGH. DESPITE THEIR INVULNERABLE APPEARANCE, SUCH FORTRESSES WERE OFTEN INEFFECTIVE AGAINST THE ADVANCED SIEGE WEAPONRY USED BY THE NOMADS, WHO WERE LOOKED UPON AS BARBARIANS.

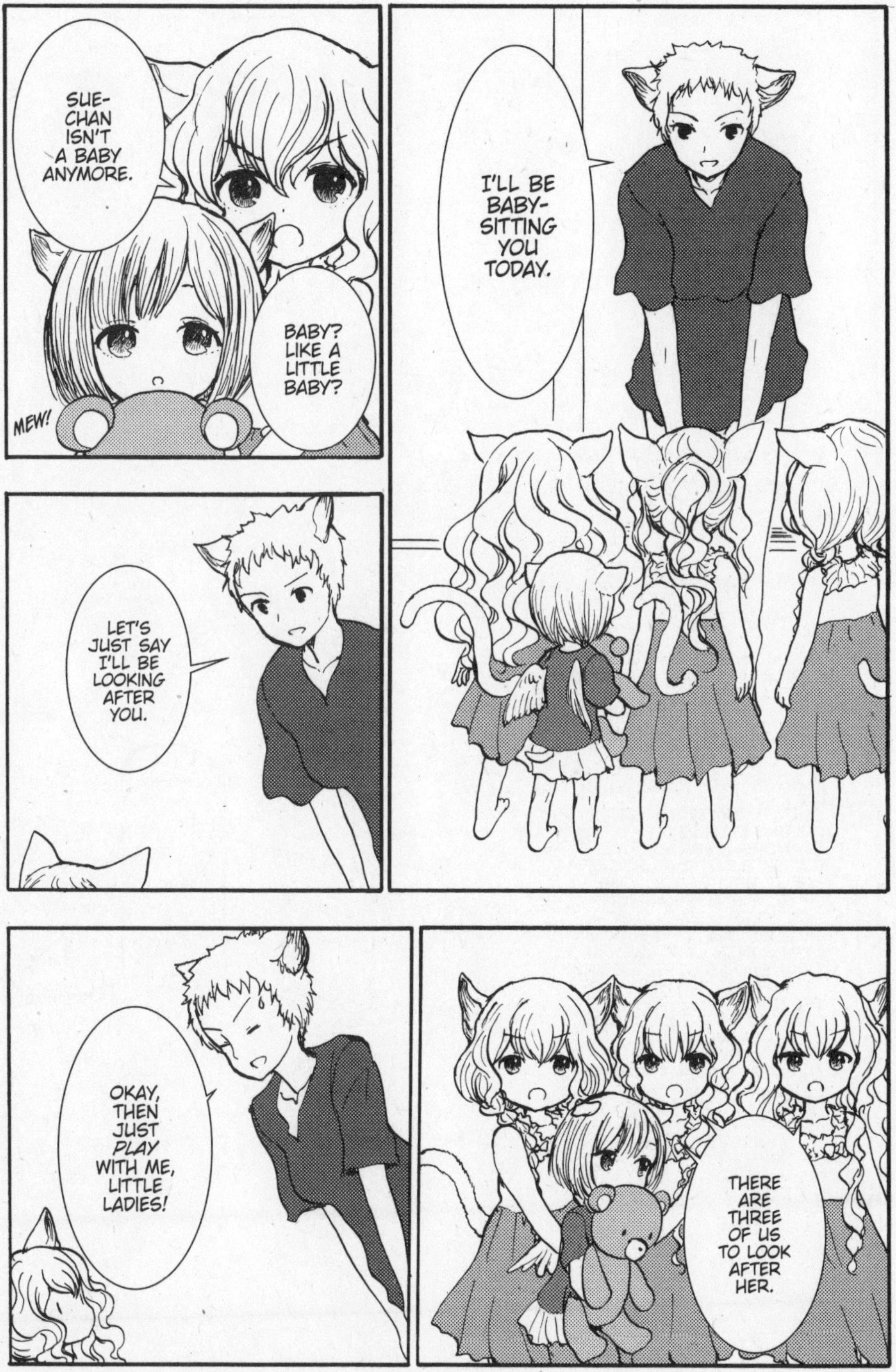
I'LL BE BABY-SITTING YOU TODAY.
BABY? LIKE A LITTLE BABY?
SUE-CHAN ISN'T A BABY ANYMORE.
MEW!
LET'S JUST SAY I'LL BE LOOKING AFTER YOU.
THERE ARE THREE OF US TO LOOK AFTER HER.
OKAY, THEN JUST *PLAY* WITH ME, LITTLE LADIES!

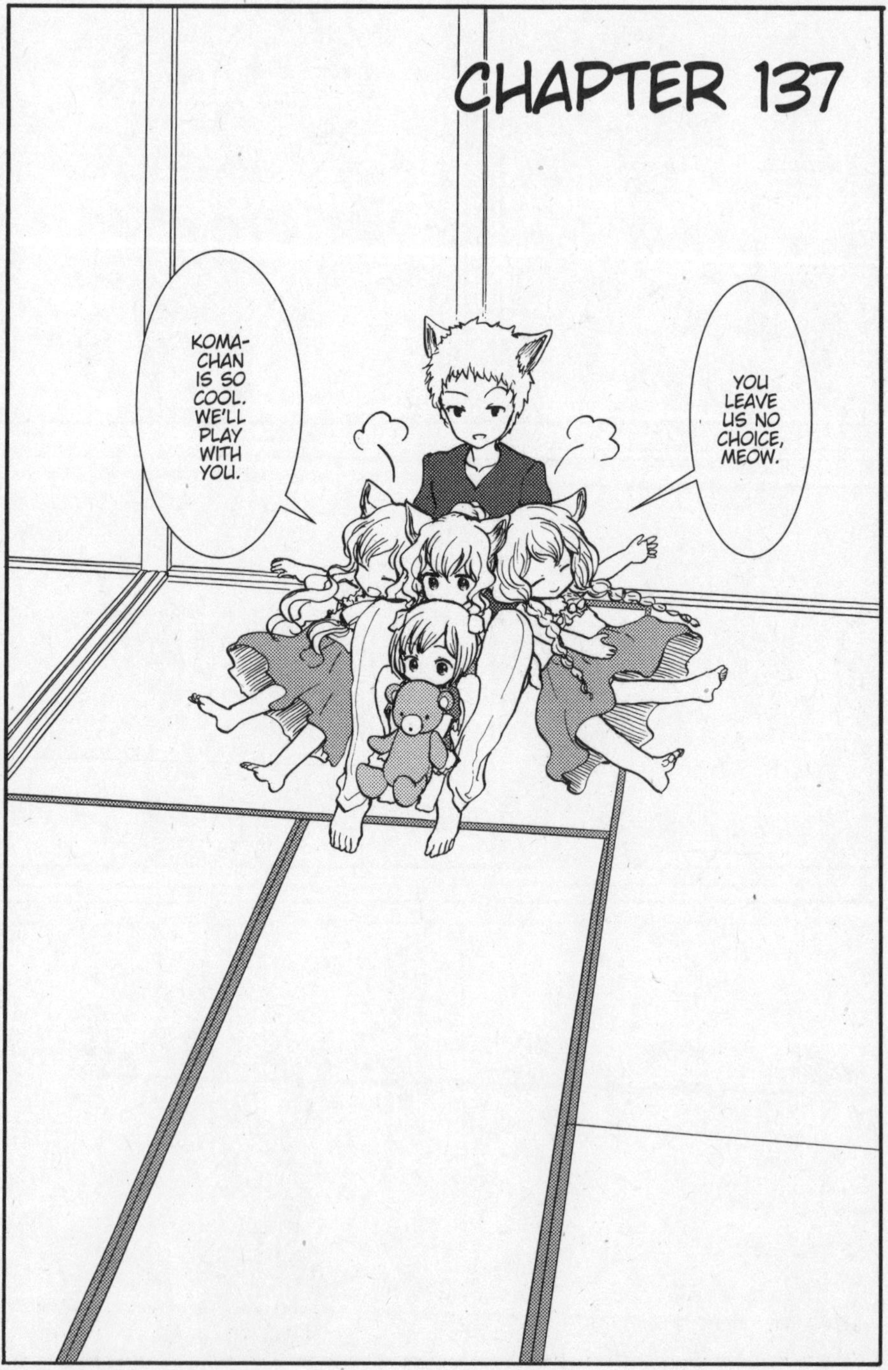
CHAPTER 137
YOU LEAVE US NO CHOICE, MEOW.
KOMA-CHAN IS SO COOL. WE'LL PLAY WITH YOU.

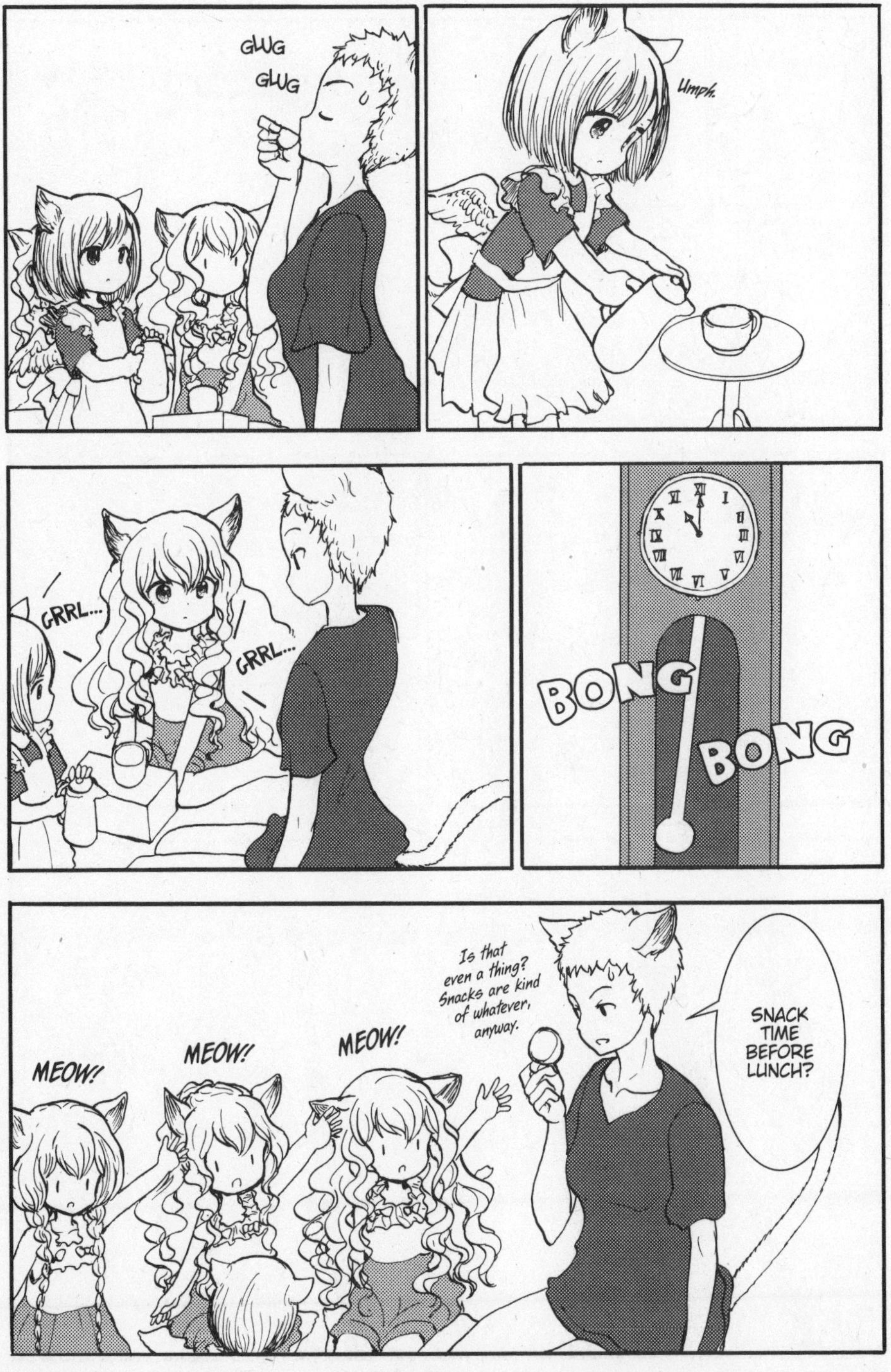
Umph.
GLUG
GLUG
BONG
BONG
GRRL...
GRRL...
SNACK TIME BEFORE LUNCH?
Is that even a thing? Snacks are kind of whatever, anyway.
MEOW!
MEOW!
MEOW!

WATCH THIS.

Don't give them too many snacks.

Don't spoil them too much, either.

Whatever.

She's so demanding when I'm doing her a favor.

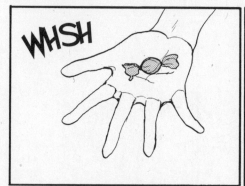

WHSH

CLENCH

WOW! A MAGIC TRICK!

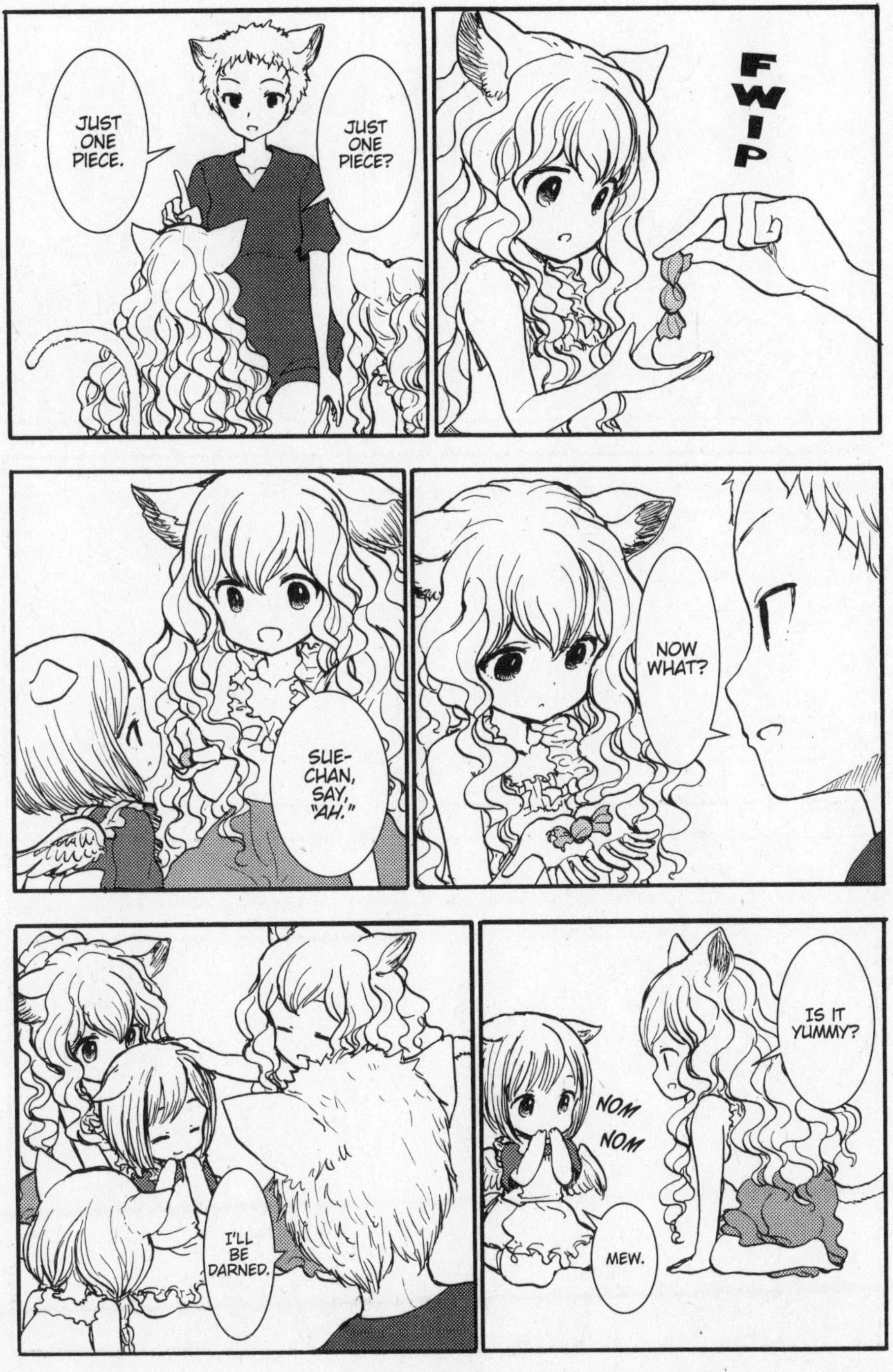
FWIP
JUST ONE PIECE?
JUST ONE PIECE.
NOW WHAT?
SUE-CHAN, SAY, "AH."
IS IT YUMMY?
NOM NOM
MEW.
I'LL BE DARNED.

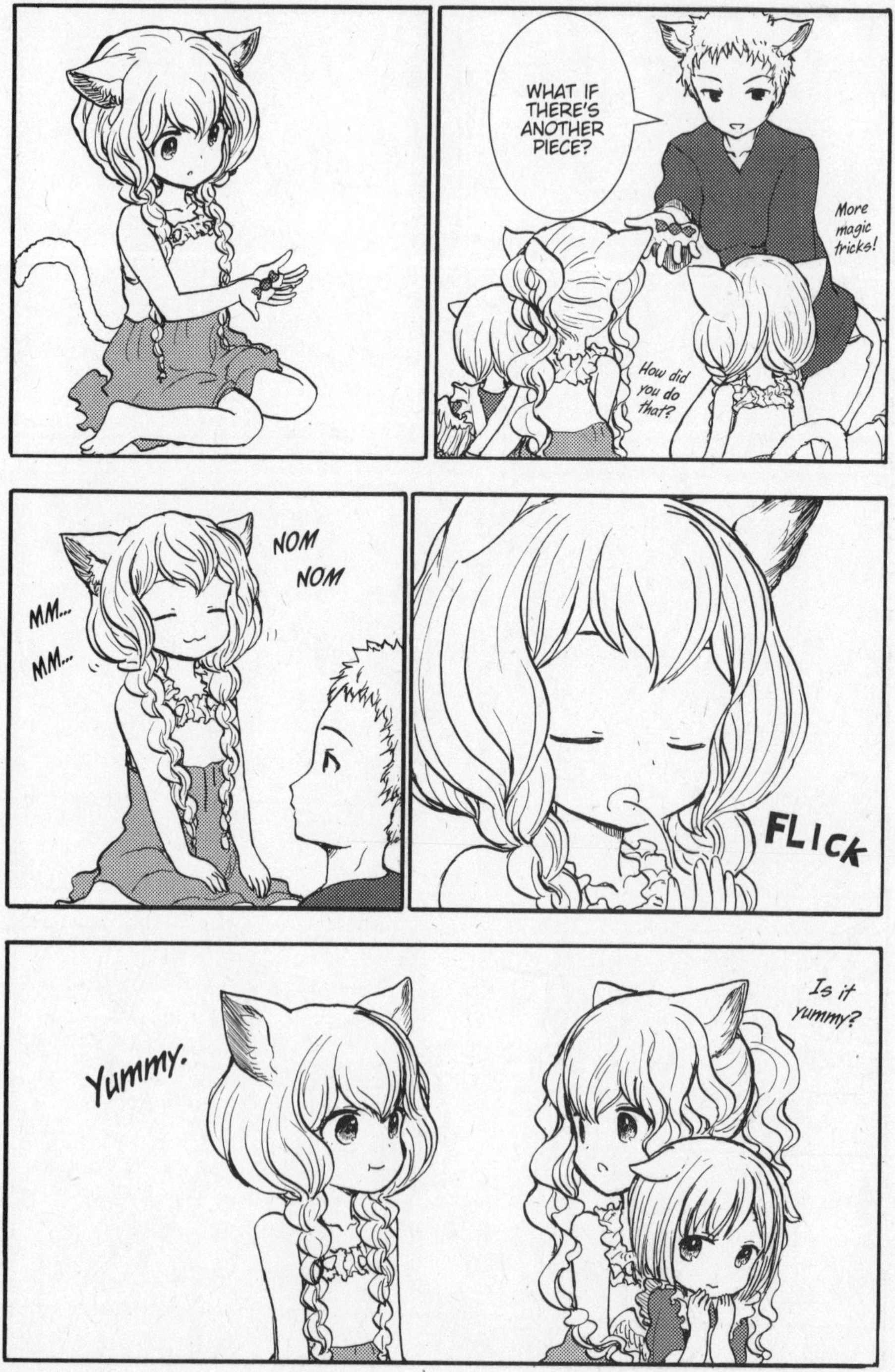
WHAT IF THERE'S ANOTHER PIECE?
More magic tricks!
How did you do that?
FLICK
NOM NOM
MM... MM...
Is it yummy?
Yummy.

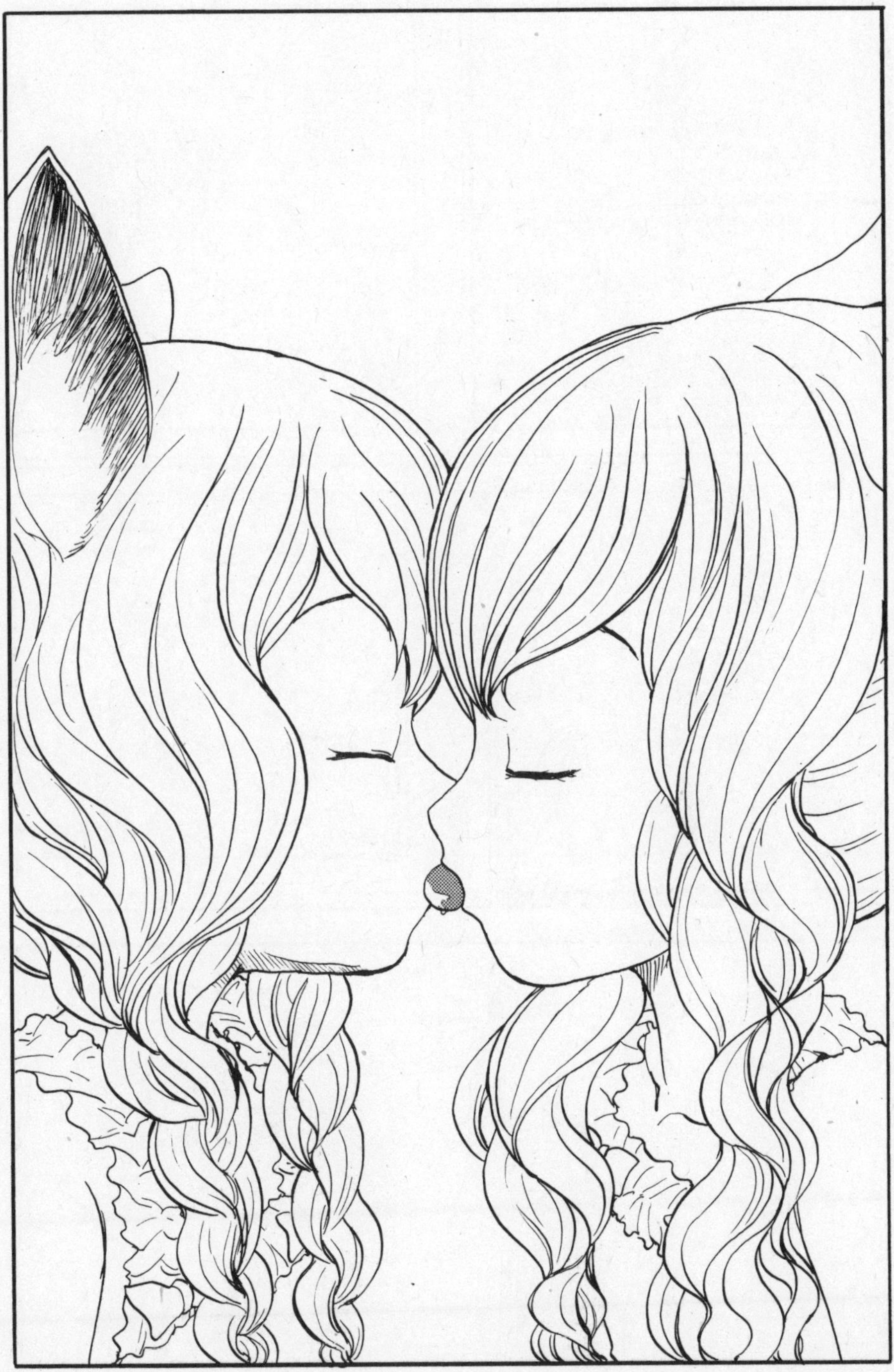

Is it yummy?
Yummy.
I'm drooling.
Yummy.
I'm...
more hungry now.
YOU GUYS ARE SO CLOSE TO EACH OTHER, YOU MAKE MY HEAD SPIN.
ALL RIGHT. IT'S EARLY, BUT I'LL FIX LUNCH. SIT TIGHT.
Hurry!
Sue wants kissy-kiss, too.

A Centaur's Life

HISTORY OF ARCHITECTURE IN JAPAN AND OTHER COUNTRIES: < 10 > NOMAD'S GER IN CENTRAL ASIA

THE GER WAS A PORTABLE DWELLING USED BY NOMADS. IT LOOKS SOMEWHAT SIMILAR TO THE MAMMOTH BONE HUT REVIEWED PREVIOUSLY, BUT WAS ACTUALLY A LIGHTWEIGHT WOODEN STRUCTURE THAT COULD BE FOLDED FOR STORAGE AND ASSEMBLED QUICKLY, WHICH MADE IT PORTABLE ENOUGH FOR MIGRATION. GERS ARE OFTEN DEPICTED AS BEING CARRIED PERSONALLY BY NOMADS IN THEIR MIGRATION, BUT IN REALITY, THEY WERE TRANSPORTED BY OX CARTS. IT'S OFTEN MISINTERPRETED AS A SIMPLE TENT, LIKE THOSE USED FOR MOUNTAIN CLIMBING, BUT IT WAS DESIGNED TO ALLOW NOMADS TO LIVE COMFORTABLY IN A STEPPE CLIMATE WITH DRAMATIC TEMPERATURE FLUCTUATIONS. THE INTERIOR WAS OFTEN LAVISHLY DECORATED.

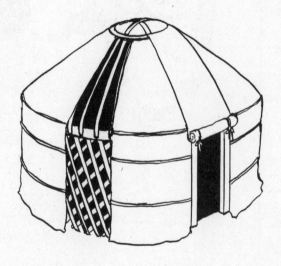

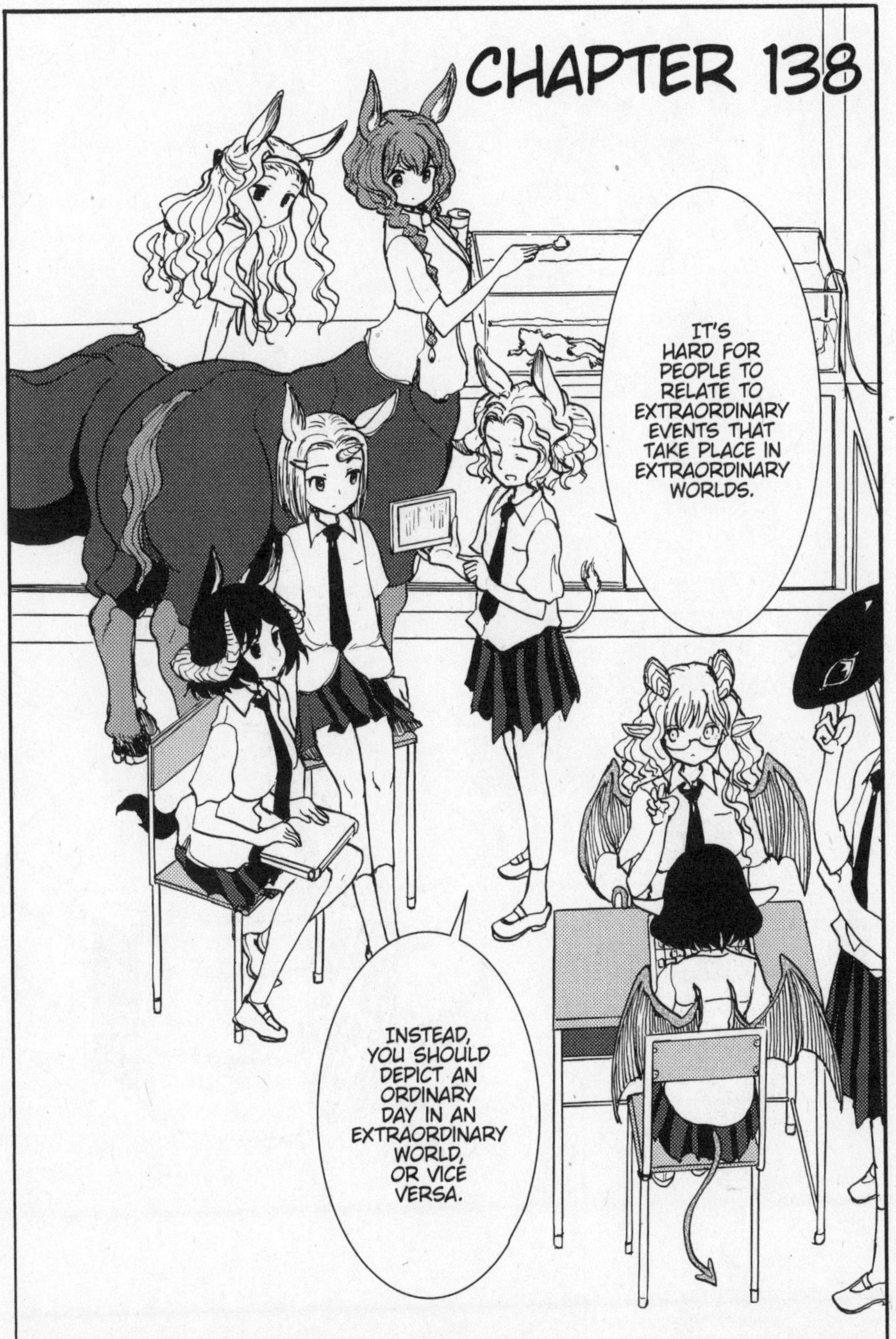
CHAPTER 138
IT'S HARD FOR PEOPLE TO RELATE TO EXTRAORDINARY EVENTS THAT TAKE PLACE IN EXTRAORDINARY WORLDS.
INSTEAD, YOU SHOULD DEPICT AN ORDINARY DAY IN AN EXTRAORDINARY WORLD, OR VICE VERSA.

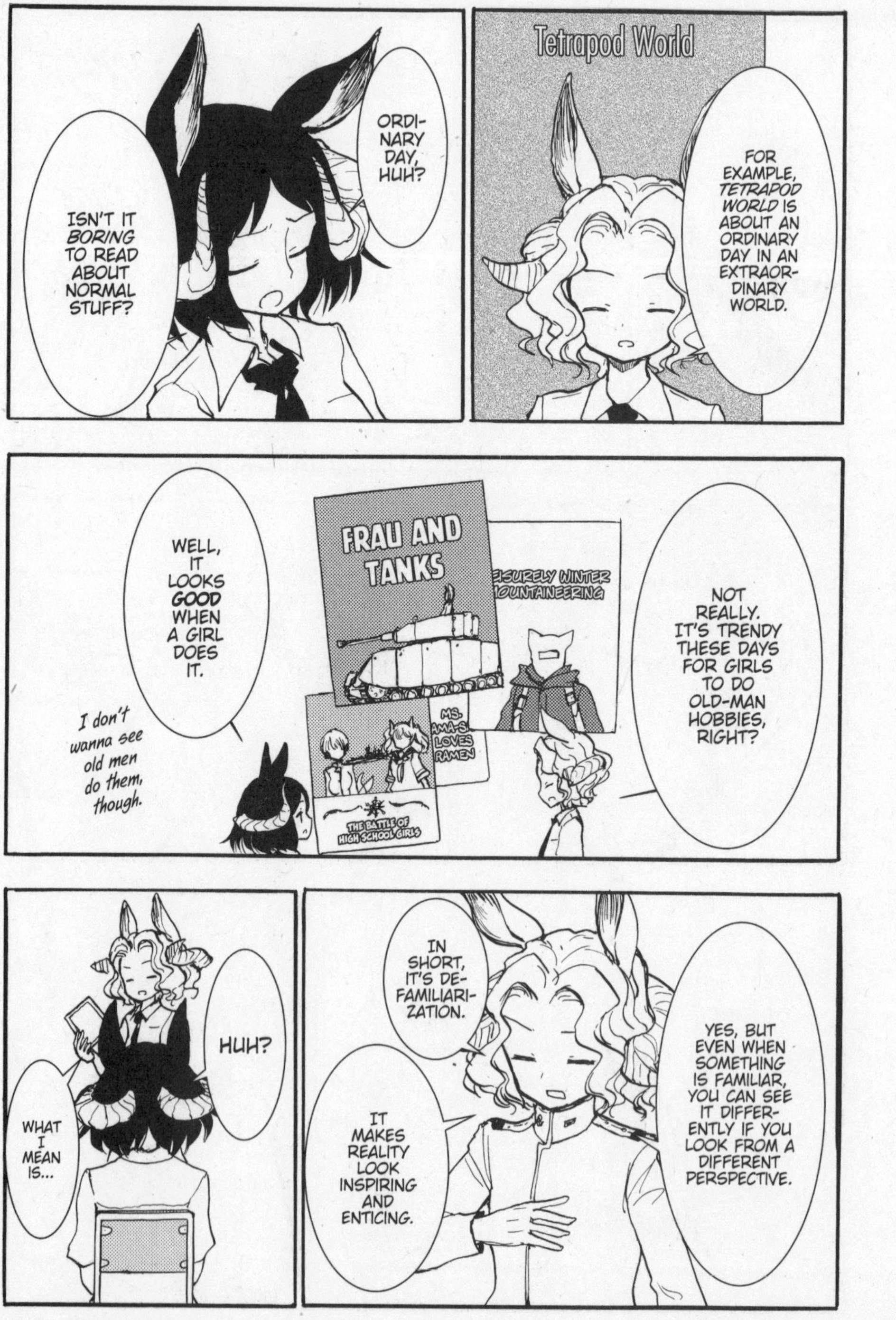
Tetrapod World
FOR EXAMPLE, *TETRAPOD WORLD* IS ABOUT AN ORDINARY DAY IN AN EXTRAORDINARY WORLD.
ORDINARY DAY, HUH?
ISN'T IT *BORING* TO READ ABOUT NORMAL STUFF?
NOT REALLY. IT'S TRENDY THESE DAYS FOR GIRLS TO DO OLD-MAN HOBBIES, RIGHT?
EISURELY WINTER OUNTAINEERING
FRAU AND TANKS
MS.
LOVES RAMEN
THE BATTLE OF HIGH SCHOOL GIRLS
WELL, IT LOOKS **GOOD** WHEN A GIRL DOES IT.
I don't wanna see old men do them, though.
YES, BUT EVEN WHEN SOMETHING IS FAMILIAR, YOU CAN SEE IT DIFFERENTLY IF YOU LOOK FROM A DIFFERENT PERSPECTIVE.
IN SHORT, IT'S DEFAMILIARIZATION.
IT MAKES REALITY LOOK INSPIRING AND ENTICING.
HUH?
WHAT I MEAN IS...

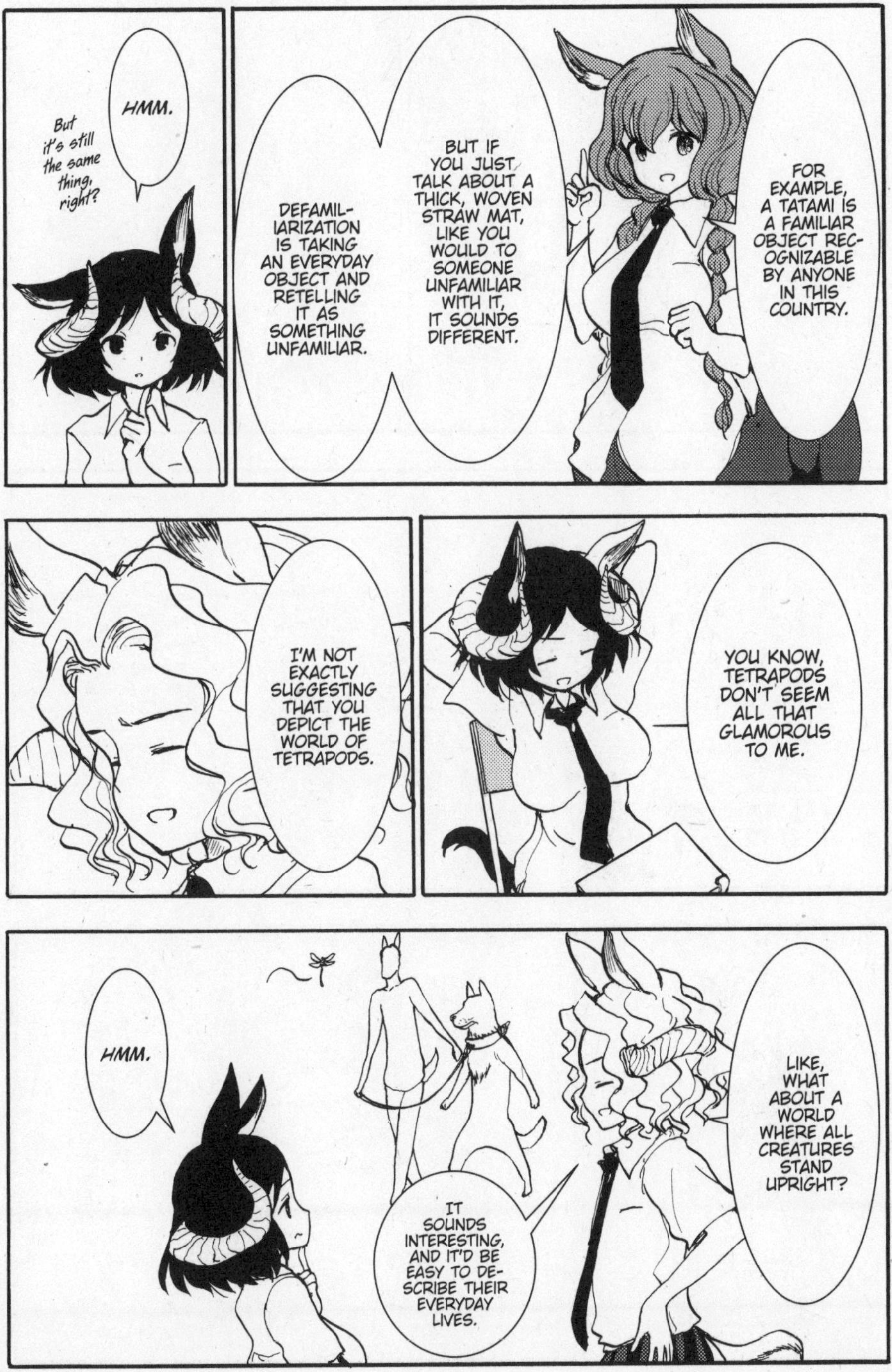
FOR EXAMPLE, A TATAMI IS A FAMILIAR OBJECT RECOGNIZABLE BY ANYONE IN THIS COUNTRY.
BUT IF YOU JUST TALK ABOUT A THICK, WOVEN STRAW MAT, LIKE YOU WOULD TO SOMEONE UNFAMILIAR WITH IT, IT SOUNDS DIFFERENT.
DEFAMILIARIZATION IS TAKING AN EVERYDAY OBJECT AND RETELLING IT AS SOMETHING UNFAMILIAR.
HMM.
But it's still the same thing, right?
YOU KNOW, TETRAPODS DON'T SEEM ALL THAT GLAMOROUS TO ME.
I'M NOT EXACTLY SUGGESTING THAT YOU DEPICT THE WORLD OF TETRAPODS.
LIKE, WHAT ABOUT A WORLD WHERE ALL CREATURES STAND UPRIGHT?
IT SOUNDS INTERESTING, AND IT'D BE EASY TO DESCRIBE THEIR EVERYDAY LIVES.
HMM.

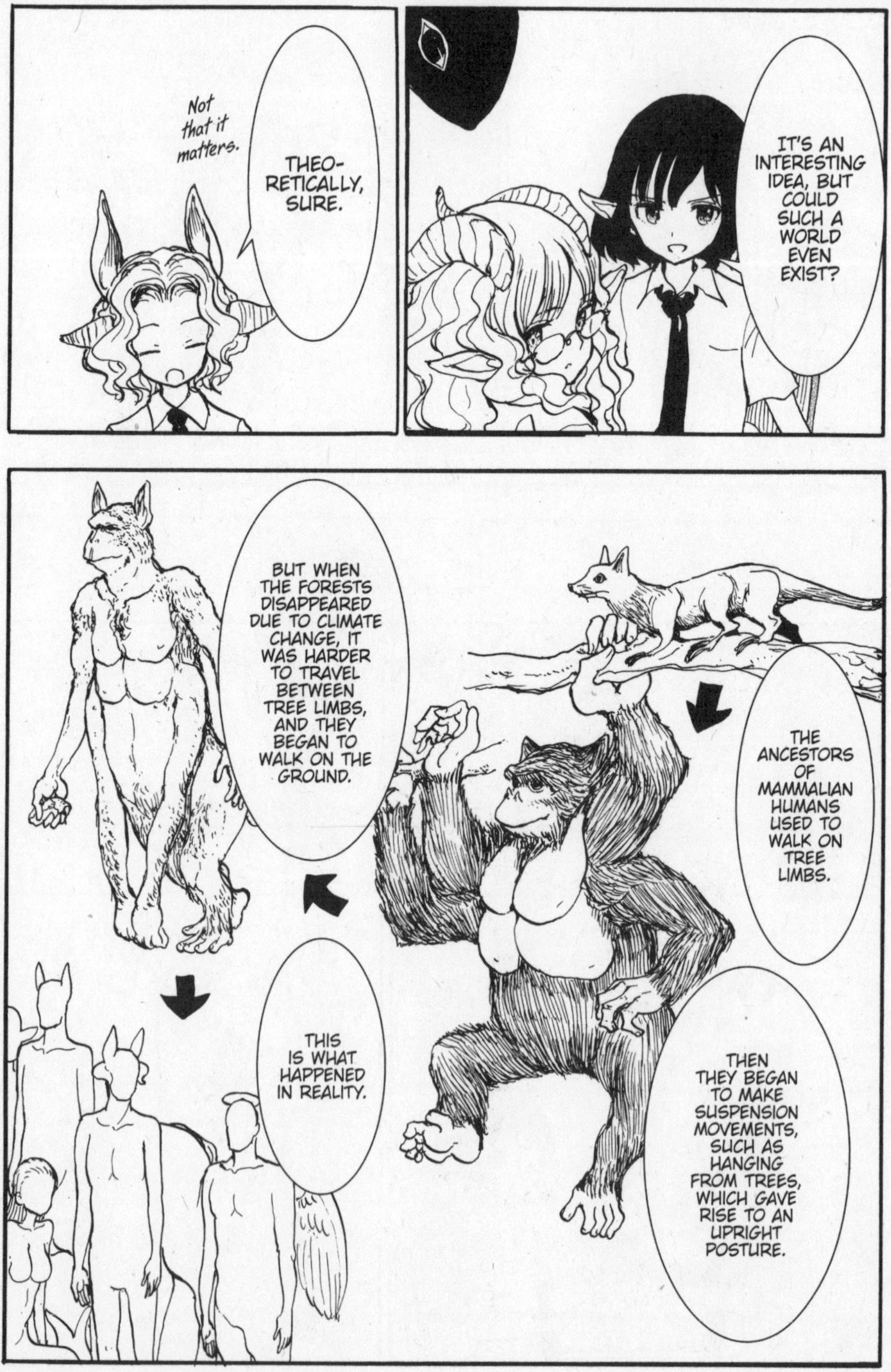
IT'S AN INTERESTING IDEA, BUT COULD SUCH A WORLD EVEN EXIST?
THEO-RETICALLY, SURE.
Not that it matters.
THE ANCESTORS OF MAMMALIAN HUMANS USED TO WALK ON TREE LIMBS.
THEN THEY BEGAN TO MAKE SUSPENSION MOVEMENTS, SUCH AS HANGING FROM TREES, WHICH GAVE RISE TO AN UPRIGHT POSTURE.
BUT WHEN THE FORESTS DISAPPEARED DUE TO CLIMATE CHANGE, IT WAS HARDER TO TRAVEL BETWEEN TREE LIMBS, AND THEY BEGAN TO WALK ON THE GROUND.
THIS IS WHAT HAPPENED IN REALITY.

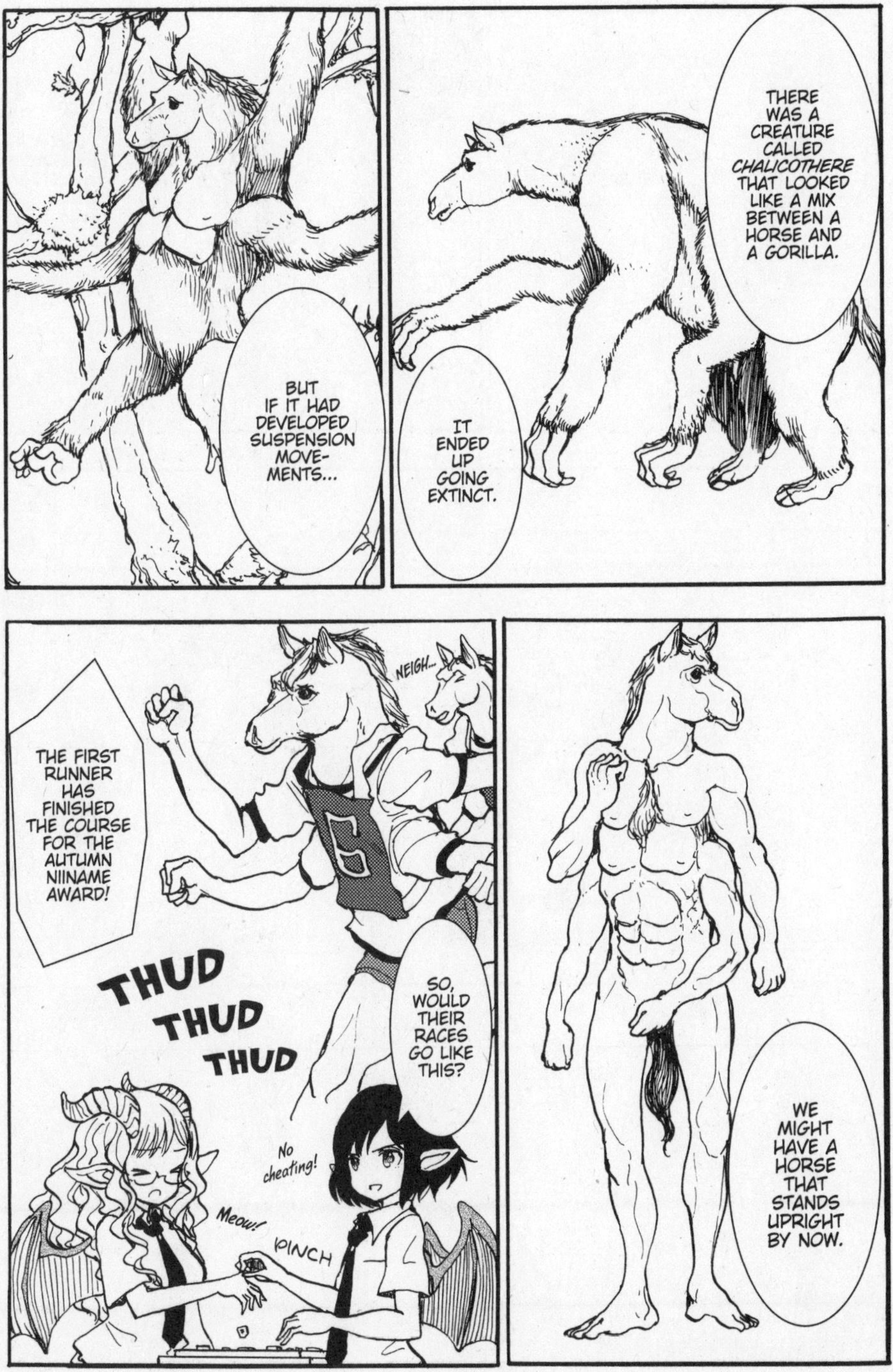
THERE WAS A CREATURE CALLED *CHALICOTHERE* THAT LOOKED LIKE A MIX BETWEEN A HORSE AND A GORILLA.
IT ENDED UP GOING EXTINCT.
BUT IF IT HAD DEVELOPED SUSPENSION MOVE-MENTS...
WE MIGHT HAVE A HORSE THAT STANDS UPRIGHT BY NOW.
NEIGH...
THE FIRST RUNNER HAS FINISHED THE COURSE FOR THE AUTUMN NIINAME AWARD!
SO, WOULD THEIR RACES GO LIKE THIS?
THUD
THUD
THUD
No cheating!
Meow!
PINCH

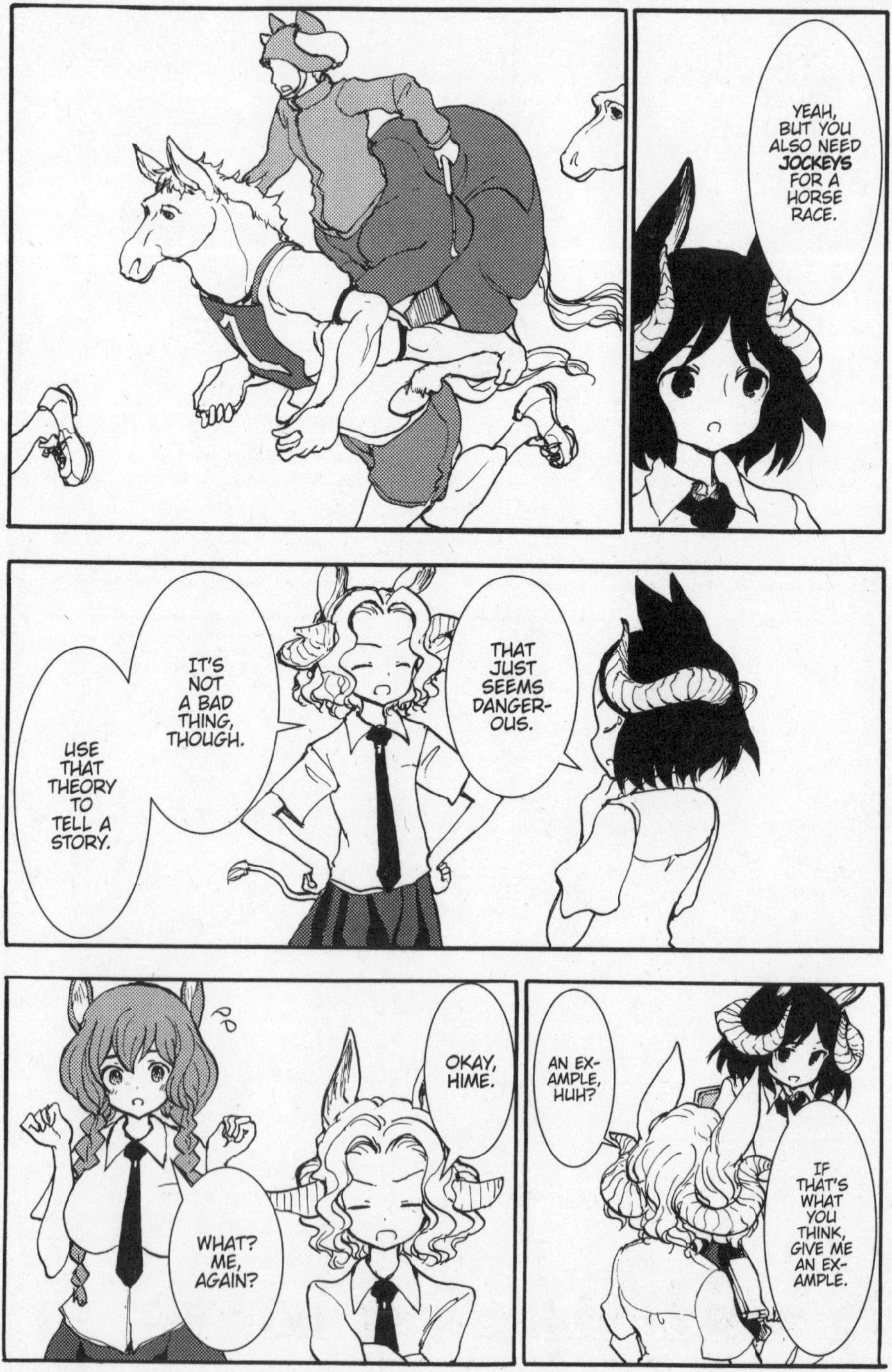
YEAH, BUT YOU ALSO NEED **JOCKEYS** FOR A HORSE RACE.
THAT JUST SEEMS DANGER-OUS.
IT'S NOT A BAD THING, THOUGH.
USE THAT THEORY TO TELL A STORY.
IF THAT'S WHAT YOU THINK, GIVE ME AN EX-AMPLE.
AN EX-AMPLE, HUH?
OKAY, HIME.
WHAT? ME, AGAIN?

A CentaUr's Life

HISTORY OF ARCHITECTURE IN JAPAN AND OTHER COUNTRIES: < 11 > WERETIGER'S ARBOREAL DWELLING

WERETIGERS ARE SAID TO HAVE GONE EXTINCT ABOUT TEN THOUSAND YEARS AGO, AND FEW OF THEIR DWELLINGS SURVIVED DUE TO THEM LIVING PRIMARILY IN TROPICAL FORESTS. OTHER MAMMALIAN HUMAN SPECIES INTERACTED WITH EACH OTHER THROUGH TRADE AND THE LIKE, DESPITE LIVING IN THEIR OWN SEPARATE GROUPS. WERETIGERS, ON THE CONTRARY, LIVED IN ISOLATION, WHICH CONTRIBUTED TO THE LACK OF WERETIGER ARTIFACTS. HOWEVER, A FEW ISOLATED ARTIFACTS FROM LAKESIDE WERETIGER DWELLINGS SOMEHOW SURVIVED THEIR FALL AND SUBSEQUENT BURIAL IN THE LAKEBED. FROM THESE, WE CAN SEE THAT WERETIGERS USED SHARP MICROLITHS, NETS MADE OUT OF ROPE, AND ELABORATELY-WOVEN BASKETS. ADDITIONALLY, THEIR ARBOREAL DWELLINGS HAD FLOORS MADE WITH ADVANCED TECHNOLOGY. THUS, IT SEEMS THAT THEIR SHARP CLAWS AND STRONG MUSCLES DID NOT IMPEDE THEIR DEVELOPMENT OF TOOLS OR TECHNOLOGY. DESPITE THE FEROCIOUS APPEARANCE OF WERETIGERS, FRUIT SEEDS AND NUT SHELLS FOUND IN BASKETS INDICATE THEY WERE OMNIVORES LIKE OTHER MAMMALIAN HUMANS, WHICH IS CONSISTENT WITH THE SHAPE OF THEIR TEETH. BASED ON ALL OF THIS, WE BELIEVE THAT WERETIGERS WERE SIMILAR TO OTHER SPECIES, AND THAT THEIR EXTINCTION WAS CAUSED BY THEIR ISOLATED LIFESTYLE.

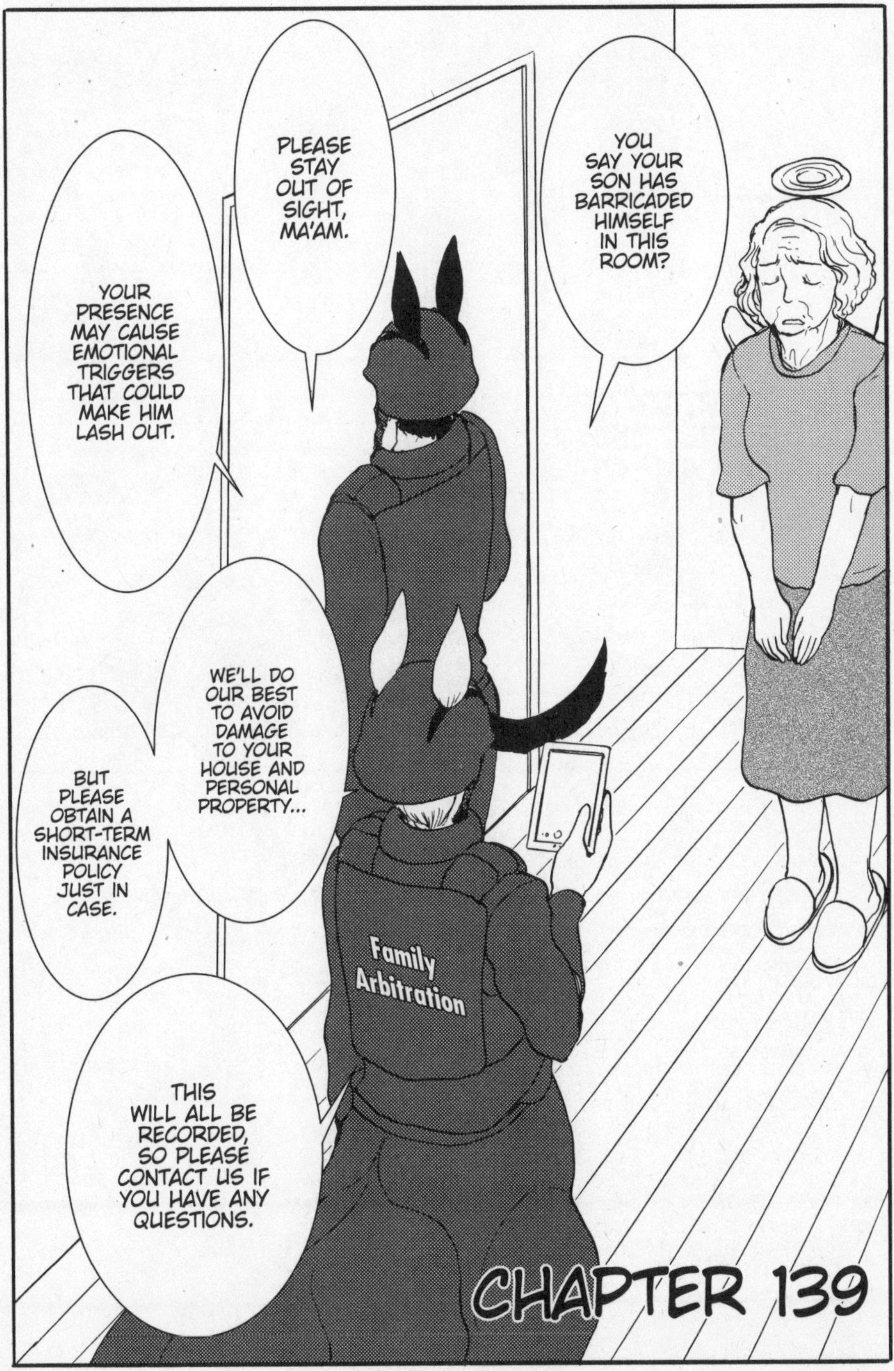
YOU SAY YOUR SON HAS BARRICADED HIMSELF IN THIS ROOM?
PLEASE STAY OUT OF SIGHT, MA'AM.
YOUR PRESENCE MAY CAUSE EMOTIONAL TRIGGERS THAT COULD MAKE HIM LASH OUT.
WE'LL DO OUR BEST TO AVOID DAMAGE TO YOUR HOUSE AND PERSONAL PROPERTY...
BUT PLEASE OBTAIN A SHORT-TERM INSURANCE POLICY JUST IN CASE.
Family Arbitration
THIS WILL ALL BE RECORDED, SO PLEASE CONTACT US IF YOU HAVE ANY QUESTIONS.
CHAPTER 139

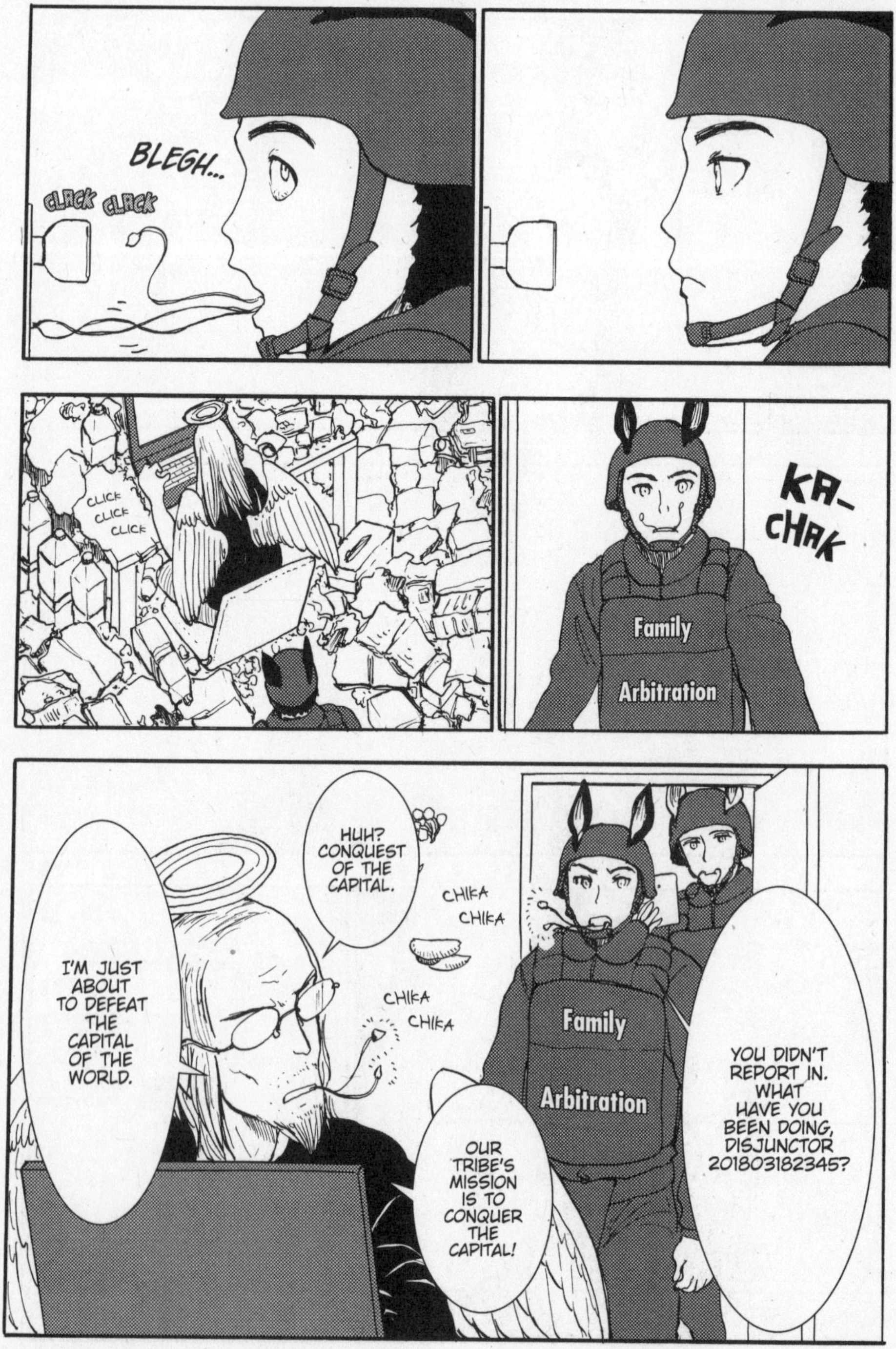
BLEGH...
CLACK CLACK
KA-CHAK
Family Arbitration
CLICK CLICK CLICK
YOU DIDN'T REPORT IN. WHAT HAVE YOU BEEN DOING, DISJUNCTOR 201803182345?
Family Arbitration
HUH? CONQUEST OF THE CAPITAL.
CHIKA CHIKA
CHIKA CHIKA
I'M JUST ABOUT TO DEFEAT THE CAPITAL OF THE WORLD.
OUR TRIBE'S MISSION IS TO CONQUER THE CAPITAL!

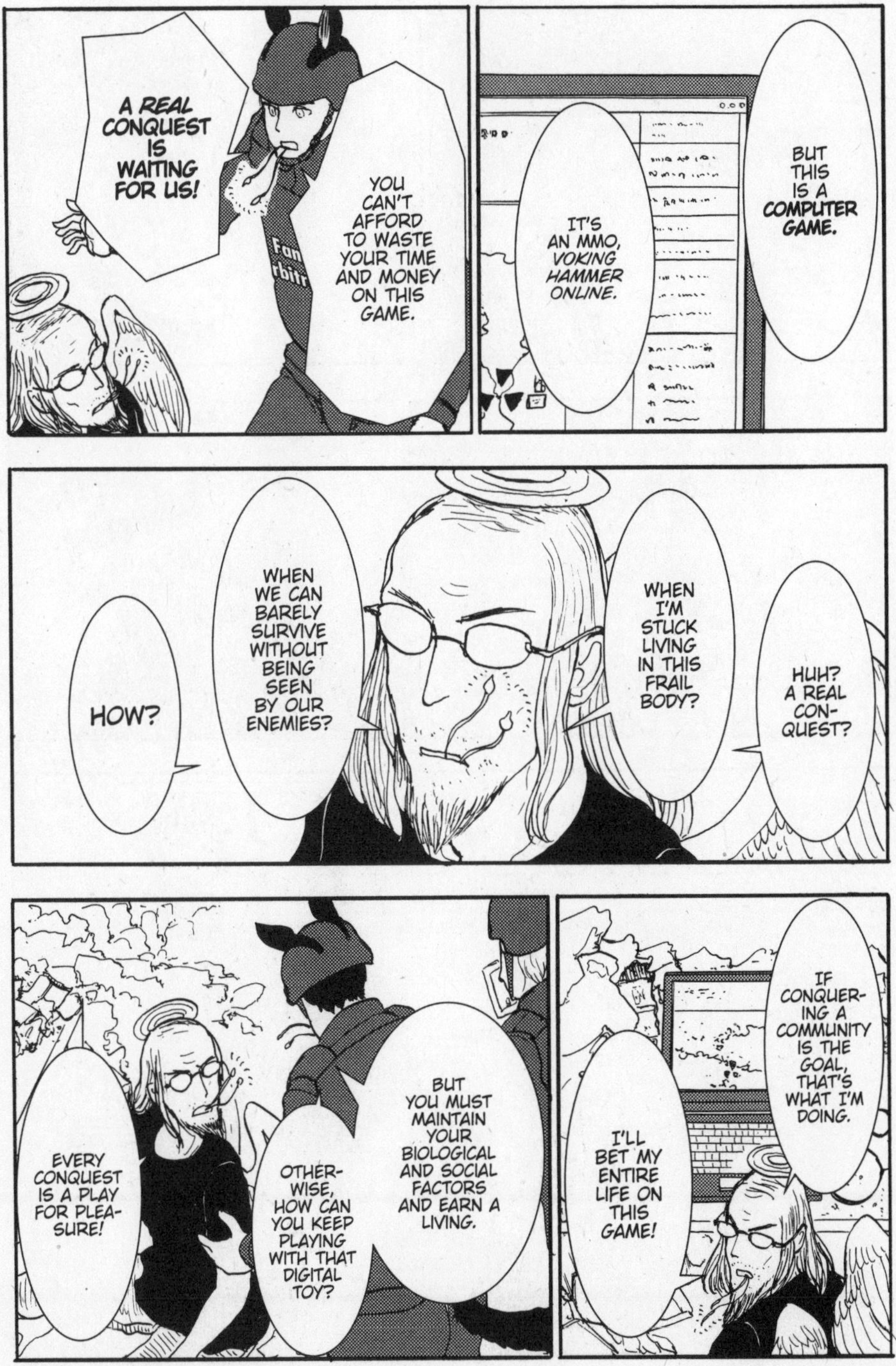
BUT THIS IS A COMPUTER GAME.
IT'S AN MMO, *VOKING HAMMER ONLINE.*
YOU CAN'T AFFORD TO WASTE YOUR TIME AND MONEY ON THIS GAME.
A *REAL* CONQUEST IS WAITING FOR US!
HUH? A REAL CON-QUEST?
WHEN I'M STUCK LIVING IN THIS FRAIL BODY?
WHEN WE CAN BARELY SURVIVE WITHOUT BEING SEEN BY OUR ENEMIES?
HOW?
IF CONQUER-ING A COMMUNITY IS THE GOAL, THAT'S WHAT I'M DOING.
I'LL BET MY ENTIRE LIFE ON THIS GAME!
BUT YOU MUST MAINTAIN YOUR BIOLOGICAL AND SOCIAL FACTORS AND EARN A LIVING.
OTHER-WISE, HOW CAN YOU KEEP PLAYING WITH THAT DIGITAL TOY?
EVERY CONQUEST IS A PLAY FOR PLEA-SURE!

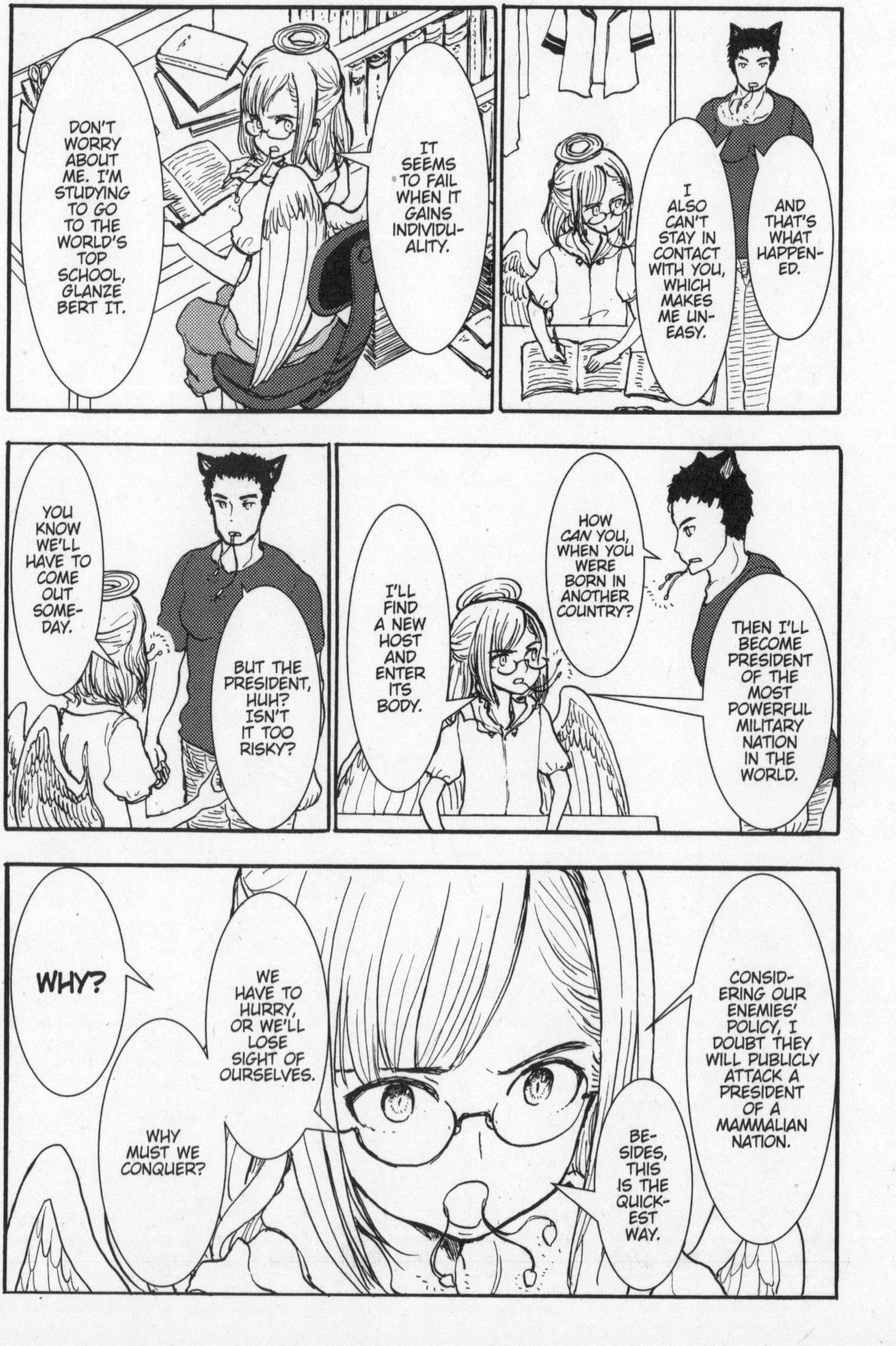
AND THAT'S WHAT HAPPEN-ED.
I ALSO CAN'T STAY IN CONTACT WITH YOU, WHICH MAKES ME UN-EASY.
IT SEEMS TO FAIL WHEN IT GAINS INDIVIDU-ALITY.
DON'T WORRY ABOUT ME. I'M STUDYING TO GO TO THE WORLD'S TOP SCHOOL, GLANZE BERT IT.
THEN I'LL BECOME PRESIDENT OF THE MOST POWERFUL MILITARY NATION IN THE WORLD.
HOW CAN YOU, WHEN YOU WERE BORN IN ANOTHER COUNTRY?
I'LL FIND A NEW HOST AND ENTER ITS BODY.
BUT THE PRESIDENT, HUH? ISN'T IT TOO RISKY?
YOU KNOW WE'LL HAVE TO COME OUT SOME-DAY.
CONSID-ERING OUR ENEMIES' POLICY, I DOUBT THEY WILL PUBLICLY ATTACK A PRESIDENT OF A MAMMALIAN NATION.
BE-SIDES, THIS IS THE QUICK-EST WAY.
WE HAVE TO HURRY, OR WE'LL LOSE SIGHT OF OURSELVES.
WHY?
WHY MUST WE CONQUER?

A CentaUr's Life

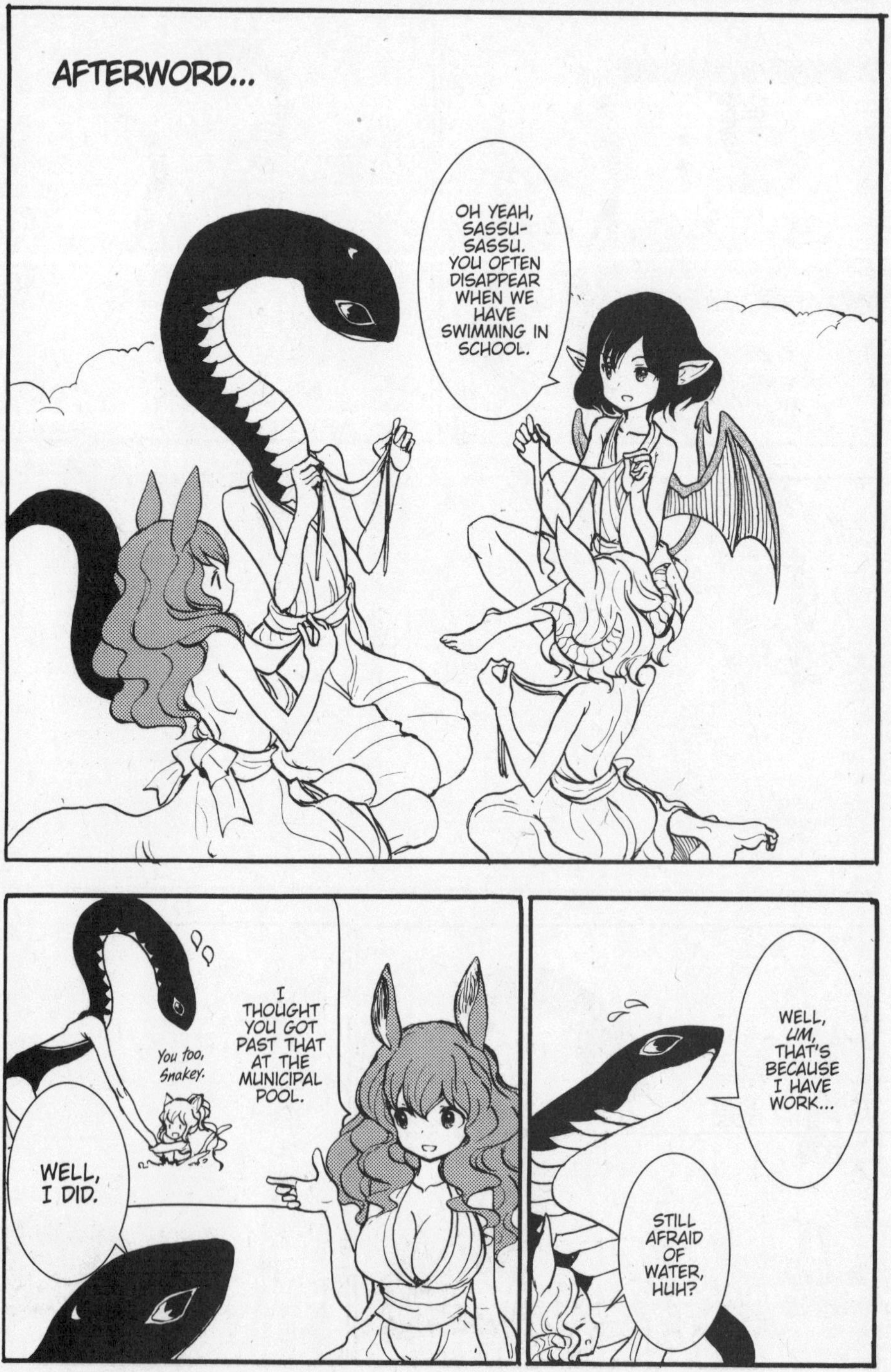
AFTERWORD...
OH YEAH, SASSU-SASSU. YOU OFTEN DISAPPEAR WHEN WE HAVE SWIMMING IN SCHOOL.
WELL, UM, THAT'S BECAUSE I HAVE WORK...
STILL AFRAID OF WATER, HUH?
I THOUGHT YOU GOT PAST THAT AT THE MUNICIPAL POOL.
You too, Snakey.
WELL, I DID.

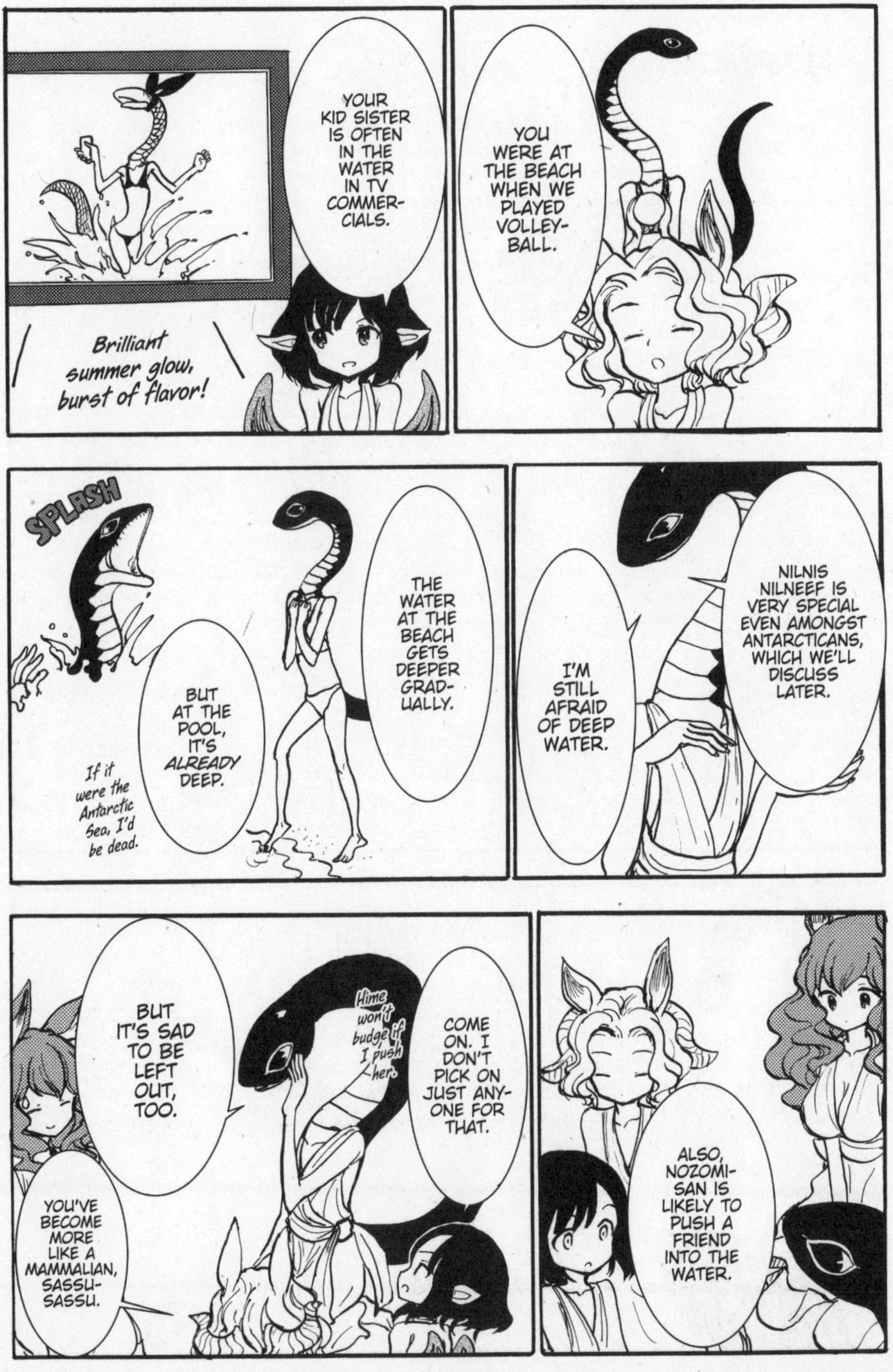
YOU WERE AT THE BEACH WHEN WE PLAYED VOLLEY-BALL.
YOUR KID SISTER IS OFTEN IN THE WATER IN TV COMMERCIALS.
Brilliant summer glow, burst of flavor!
NILNIS NILNEEF IS VERY SPECIAL EVEN AMONGST ANTARCTICANS, WHICH WE'LL DISCUSS LATER.
I'M STILL AFRAID OF DEEP WATER.
THE WATER AT THE BEACH GETS DEEPER GRAD-UALLY.
SPLASH
BUT AT THE POOL, IT'S ALREADY DEEP.
If it were the Antarctic Sea, I'd be dead.
ALSO, NOZOMI-SAN IS LIKELY TO PUSH A FRIEND INTO THE WATER.
COME ON. I DON'T PICK ON JUST ANY-ONE FOR THAT.
Hime won't budge if I push her.
BUT IT'S SAD TO BE LEFT OUT, TOO.
YOU'VE BECOME MORE LIKE A MAMMALIAN, SASSU-SASSU.

LEARN ABOUT OUR TOWN! KANATA CITY'S PAST, PRESENT, AND FUTURE.

RAVAGES OF WAR

For the Kanata District, war meant shortages and population loss. Unlike the military towns of Tsuchiura or Hitachi, which had military arsenals, the small farming community of Kanata was never attacked throughout the war. It is arguable, however, that the widespread shortages caused far more damage than the bombings that other areas endured. The Imperial Japanese Army was very successful in Operation Ichi-Go, the Battle of Imphal, and the attack on the Panama Canal, which allowed the spread of their military might to conflicts in other countries. As a result, their supplies--which were already tight--dwindled even further. This meant that agricultural communities like Kanata had nowhere near enough fertilizer, farming equipment, or labor.

Even after Japan launched an all-out war, it was obvious to anyone that production would fall rather than increase. The terrifying war came to an end with the explosive catastrophe of the new ultimate weapon, but shortages continued to ravage Japan. There was not even enough food to adequately support soldiers after their return from the front. Unlike its allies, Japan's government underwent only minor changes to its leadership, and remained mostly undisturbed. Ultimately, though Japan had launched a war of aggression to gain resources, it completely lost access to them while suffering more severe shortages and was left to make do with what it had. One method used to resolve these issues was land reform.

LAND REFORM

Replacing the landlord-tenant agricultural system with peasant proprietorship not only saved peasant farmers (a large majority of the population) from poverty, but also substantially increased labor efficiency and farm production. This was the goal of land reform, the framework of which existed before the war, and the meeting of vice ministers that took place during the war in Showa 2X. However, the situation in Japan was grim in terms of resources and manpower, and reform did not come about at those times. It was forcibly implemented immediately after the war due to a strong demand from the Supreme Commander for the Allied Powers.

Under land reform, large parcels of land were to be sold to the tenant farmers at low prices. Prior to the reform, the proposal had been to offer funds as loans to tenant farmers who were willing to purchase land and offer financial incentives if the sale was made as suggested. Landowners, however, generally resisted the forfeiture of their lands. In an effort to prevent them from avoiding forfeiture by making land transfers before the enactment of the law, a retroactive provision was added.

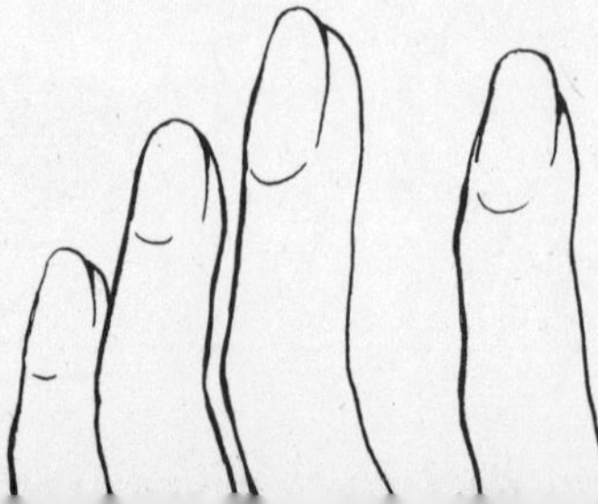

LEARN ABOUT OUR TOWN! KANATA CITY'S PAST, PRESENT, AND FUTURE.

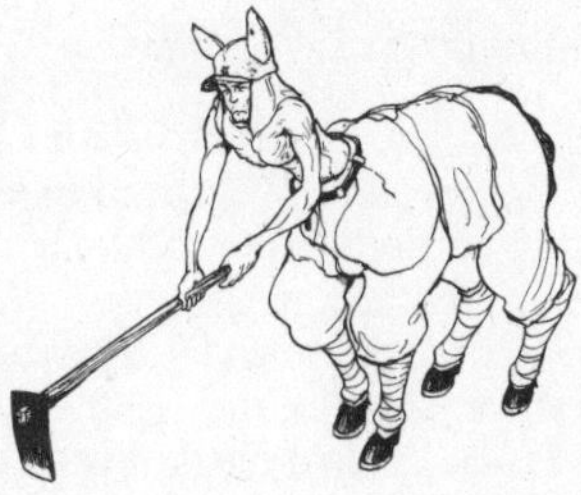

The urgency for reform pushed the government to go to great lengths to implement these new policies, which helped the nation weather the post-war food shortages. As previously mentioned, the pressure from the Supreme Commander for the Allied Powers played a major role in these laws being enacted without national consent. One of the Allies, the Saviet Union, was a key factor in committing the Allied Powers to land reform.

The Saviet Union carried out imprisonment or mass executions of their landlords under the guise of collectivization of farms, completely eliminating them as a class during its reconstruction. The majority of these landlords were actually small landowners who were considered a threat to the Communist party, or just another name to add to the execution list. Although these facts are true, this kind of liquidation of an entire class was a national policy strictly limited to the Saviet Union, which used its power to attempt to eradicate the landlord class.

Japan, as a democratic country, differed from the hierarchical Saviet Union, which was a federal republic with strong military capabilities. Japan did not follow the Saviet method of imprisonment or execution of landlords in its land reform, but rather established an agricultural land committee within each local government; organized awareness campaigns of the new law with cultivation surveys, films, and skits; and conducted the acquisition, mediation of sale, and settlement of lands.

As mentioned before, the population of Kanata was composed mainly of peasants, moreso than other prefectures. The holdings of Kanata landlords were generally smaller in size, which only served to make the landlords more protective of what they had. Despite the increased number of land disputes, most cases were reported to have been settled amicably due to the persuasion of committee members or agricultural administration staff. These settlements were made possible by the land reform and the landlords' understanding of the demands of the Supreme Commander for the Allied Powers.

Japan enacted these land reforms, but they did not result in an immediate increase in production or end the struggles faced by farming villages. Ultimately, the recovery of industry and the economy in Japan was due to increased demand caused by war in a neighboring country, which significantly improved the livelihood of farming villages.

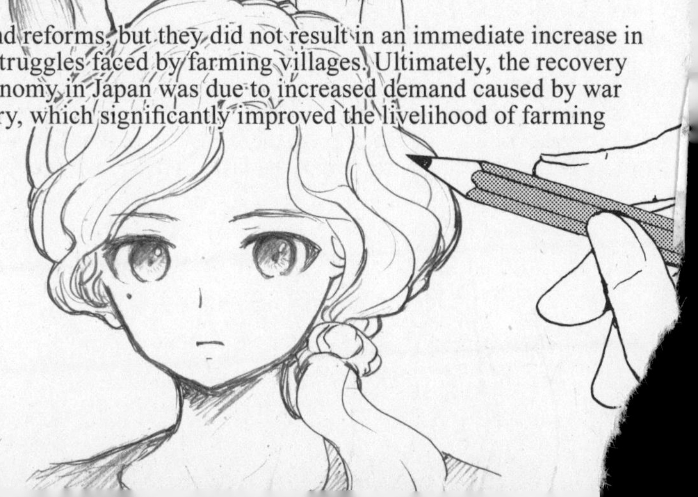

SEVEN SEAS ENTERTAINMENT PRESENTS

A Centaur's Life

story and art by KEI MURAYAMA

VOLUME 17

TRANSLATION
Elina Ishikawa

ADAPTATION
Holly Kolodziejczak

LETTERING AND RETOUCH
Jennifer Skarupa

LOGO DESIGN
Courtney Williams

COVER DESIGN
KC Fabellon

PROOFREADER
Janet Houck
Danielle King

EDITOR
Shanti Whitesides

PRODUCTION MANAGER
Lissa Pattillo

MANAGING EDITOR
Julie Davis

EDITOR-IN-CHIEF
Adam Arnold

PUBLISHER
Jason DeAngelis

Seven Seas press and purchase enquiries can be sent to Marketing Manager Lianne Sentar at press@gomanga.com. Information regarding the distribution and purchase of digital editions is available from Digital Manager CK Russell at digital@gomanga.com.

ISBN: 978-1-64275-689-0

Printed in Canada

First Printing: September 2019

10 9 8 7 6 5 4 3 2 1

READING DIRECTIONS

This book reads from ***right to left***, Japanese style. If this is your first time reading manga, you start reading from the top right panel on each page and take it from there. If you get lost, just follow the numbered diagram here. It may seem backwards at first, but you'll get the hang of it! Have fun!!

1
2
3
4
5
6
7
8
9

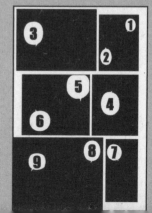